CW01183957

THE FIRST WORLD WAR
A MARXIST ANALYSIS OF THE
GREAT SLAUGHTER

Alan Woods

Wellred Books
London

The First World War: A Marxist Analysis of the Great Slaughter
Alan Woods

Wellred Books, June 2019

Copyright © Wellred Books
All rights reserved

UK distribution: Wellred Books, wellredbooks.net
PO Box 50525
London
E14 6WG
books@wellredbooks.net

USA distribution: Marxist Books, marxistbooks.com
WR Books
250 44th Street #208
Brooklyn
New York
NY 11232
wrbooks17@gmail.com

DK distribution: Forlaget Marx, forlagetmarx.dk
Degnestavnen 19, st. tv.
2400 København NV
forlag@forlagetmarx.dk

Layout by Jack Halinski-Fitzpatrick

ISBN: 978 1 913 026 08 0

I dedicate this book to my grandfather, George Woods, Private number 13793, the Welsh Battalion, who joint up on 1 September 1914 and served in France until he was demobilised on 24 March 1919. He taught me everything I needed to know.

CONTENTS

Introduction   1

1. Assassination in Sarajevo   7
2. On the Brink of the Abyss   25
3. The Strange Story of the Kaiser and the Tsar   43
4. Into the Abyss   59
5. The Great Slaughter Begins   69
6. Wilfred Owen and the Muse of War   81
7. Tsarist Russia and the War   95
8. Turkey Joins the War   105
9. Victims and Aggressors   117
10. The USA: War is Good for Business   127
11. Big Bandits and Small Bandits   143
12. Under Fire – The Real Face of War   155

13. 1916-17: The Turning of the Tide	169
14. The Middle East and the Sykes-Picot Treaty	183
15. How Revolution Ended the First World War	195
16. The Treaty of Versailles: The Peace to End All Peace	207
Epilogue: Revolutionary Optimism	227
Index	231

INTRODUCTION

The present book originally appeared as a series of articles on the First World War and the Versailles Treaty in the years 2009-2016. With some minor editing, they have now been gathered together in book form, which will hopefully make them available to a larger audience in a more convenient form. I believe that the message of the book retains its full validity and actuality today.

To deal in an introduction with the contents of the book would be both tedious and unnecessary. However, a few words about the method with which I have approached the subject matter is perhaps in order. As a Marxist, I have dealt with the First World War and the Versailles Treaty as I deal with any historical subject, strictly from the standpoint of historical materialism.

It is, of course, tempting to attribute great changes in history to the actions of individuals – whether good or evil. History is made by the actions of men and women. To state that is to state the obvious. But it is too superficial to interpret history purely in terms of the subjective intentions of this or that individual. Such a method reduces history to an endless series of anecdotes without rhyme or reason. It is sufficient to note that the ends that individuals had in mind at the commencement of the events they had set in motion very frequently differ to what actually occurs, and are often their diametrical opposite. That is certainly the case with the First World War, and even more so in the one that followed in 1939 to 1945.

If history is merely a string of accidents, it cannot be understood. In the words of Henry Ford, it would be "just one damn thing after another." But if the laws governing the universe, from the biggest galaxies to the smallest sub-atomic particles, can be explained and understood, if the evolution of every animal species can be explained by the laws of natural selection, why should the evolution of human society be excluded?

In saying this, it is not my intention to deny the role of individuals, or the complex interplay of political, economic, diplomatic and military-strategic factors that mutually interact to produce a kaleidoscope of events which, at first sight, is difficult to see as anything but incomprehensible chaos. To the untrained observer, the entire universe appears to be just such a chaos. But the scientist strives to penetrate behind this, and to discover the laws that govern nature. The entire history of science is precisely a constant endeavour to do just that.

Actually, anyone who takes the trouble to study history will immediately see that definite patterns emerge, certain processes are constantly repeated, and even certain types of characters emerge time and time again in definite circumstances. Marxists do not deny the role of individuals in shaping history. Indeed, in certain moments, that can be a decisive factor. But it is only one factor in a multifaceted interplay of elements, many of which are completely out of the control of individuals, and constitute powerful constraints to their ability to act at all.

THE ROLE OF THE INDIVIDUAL IN HISTORY

To anyone who wishes to arrive at a serious analysis of the causes of the First World War, and also its results in the Versailles treaty, I recommend a thorough study of Lenin's book, written in 1916, at the high point of this monstrous carnival of violence, *Imperialism: The highest stage of capitalism*. Lenin explains how the division of the world between the imperial powers arose in the second half of the nineteenth century and why German imperialism, arriving on the scene after the French and the British, needed to fight for a redivision of the world. Today, over a century since it first appeared, this remarkable book still represents the most profound, scientific and accurate analysis of the phenomenon of imperialism.

Instead of a trivial description of individual politicians and military figures, the book lays bare the real mainspring of war in the modern epoch, which is the contradiction between the interests of different capitalist states, which in the last analysis, are the interests of the big banks and monopolies. Whoever does not understand this fact will forever be incapable of understanding the nature of modern warfare. And it remains just as valid today as it was then.

I regret to say that one would look in vain for any rational explanation of the First World War in the flood of books, articles and television programmes that accompanied the centenary of that event. Of course, we are aware that the mass media are concerned primarily with entertainment, and to dwell upon the peculiarities of individual personalities is considerably more entertaining than a serious study of facts, figures and processes.

Let us take just one example of how the apparently inexplicable conduct of one prominent player in the great game that led to the outbreak of war in 1914 can be entirely misunderstood if it is viewed merely as the eccentricity of an individual person, divorced from the class interests that in fact determined his conduct. I refer here to Sir Edward Grey, the British Foreign Minister. It has become customary to attribute Sir Edward Grey's conduct on the eve of war as a manifestation of supreme incompetence, bumbling, blundering, or simple laziness.

These comments have been made so many times over decades, that they have become accepted as something given, obvious and incontrovertible. Here we have an explanation of the outbreak of war that is highly satisfying to those who wish to portray history as a mere sequence of inexplicable accidents. Great events are the results of either the stupidity or the genius of individuals. In this case, it is argued that Britain stumbled blindly into a war, led by an incompetent politician (or politicians) whose fervent wish for peace blinded him to the serious threat posed by the growing power of German militarism. Such an explanation also has the advantage of soothing the conscience of the

British public, who have been reassured for generations that the war was all the fault of the militaristic Germans.

For many years, Sir Edward has been portrayed as a typical example of an effete English aristocracy, whose supine passivity and indifference to events on the Balkans was the result of an overweening sense of superiority that led to a dangerous sense of invulnerability. It is certainly not my intention to gainsay the accusations directed against the British ruling class and its political representatives, but in this particular case, I believe that Sir Edward has been seriously misunderstood. Trotsky was far more perceptive when he stated that, right up to the outbreak of war, British imperialism was playing a complicated and cynical game of bluff, which was intended to fool the German Kaiser and lull him into a false sense of security, and thus lead him into a trap.

The repeated offers from London to act as a kind of honest broker between France and Germany were, in point of fact, designed to create an impression that Britain would not lift a finger if the Germans attacked France. The Kaiser was, in fact, deceived by this cynical stratagem, although right to the end, he was never quite sure what Britain's intentions actually were. But in the moment of truth, he was sufficiently sure that Britain would not get involved in the European land war to launch his assault on France, and at as a first step, to occupy Belgium.

The German plan was based on the assumption that a lightning advance would secure a rapid capitulation by the French, and the British would remain as onlookers. This was a serious miscalculation. It was always very clear to the British ruling class and its political and diplomatic representatives – including Sir Edward Grey – that in the event of war, Britain would have to intervene to defend France against Germany. This was dictated, not for any sentimental or moral reasons, but for the fundamental interests of British imperialism in Europe. I will not develop these points any further here, since they are dealt with in some detail in the course of this book.

The great Greek philosopher Heraclitus wrote: "War is father of all, and king of all. He renders some gods, others men; he makes some slaves, others free." To modern ears, these words may sound excessively brutal. Yet the slightest knowledge of human history shows that wars are a fact of life, and important issues between nations have always been solved by violent means. This is still true today.

After the fall of the Soviet Union, the Western media predicted a future of peace and prosperity for the whole world on the basis of the capitalist system and the market economy. The ink was scarcely dry on the statements, when bloody wars erupted in the Balkans, in the territory of the former Soviet Union and in Afghanistan, Africa and the Middle East. Today, the world is still torn by conflicts and wars, which ultimately have their roots in the unbearable contradictions produced by capitalism. In the words of Lenin, capitalism is horror without end.

When future generations look at the present epoch, they will experience the same sense of horror and revulsion with which we look on the cannibalism that was practised by our ancestors in bygone days. But although the indignant complaints of pacifists against war may be understandable, they are completely impotent to solve the problem that they so vehemently denounce. They can never eradicate war because they have never understood the causes of war, which, in the modern epoch, are rooted in the predatory nature of capitalism and imperialism.

The only way to abolish war is through the revolutionary abolition of capitalism. The only really just war is the class war. That is the real message of the present book, and hopefully it will provide some useful lessons to the present generation, who have the duty to carry this war to its final, victorious solution. A socialist world will be one in which unemployment, poverty, exploitation, oppression and war will be finally consigned to the dustbin history. Humanity will raise itself up to its full height in a world fit for men and women to live in.

London, 16 May, 2019

1. ASSASSINATION IN SARAJEVO THE FIRST SHOTS OF THE GREAT SLAUGHTER

A hundred years ago, on 28 June 1914, two pistol shots shattered the peace of a sunny afternoon in Sarajevo. Those shots reverberated around Europe and shattered the peace of the whole world.

It is commonly said that the First World War was caused by the assassination of the Austrian Crown Prince. However, this act falls rather under the category of a historical accident, which is to say, something that might or might not have occurred. If the assassin had missed his mark and Franz Ferdinand had survived, would the war not have occurred?

It is true that the immediate origins of the war flowed from the decisions taken by statesmen and generals following the assassination of the Archduke Franz Ferdinand by Gavrilo Princip. But the real causes of the war are to be found, not in the haphazard realm of historical accidents, but in the solid ground of historical necessity, which, as Hegel teaches us, can be expressed in accidents of all kinds.

In reality, Franz Ferdinand's assassination was not the cause, but only the catalyst of the outbreak of the Great Slaughter. It was the spark that ignited a powder keg that had been prepared for decades before 1914. It immediately exposed the fault lines that had been deepening over a long period. It brought to a head a diplomatic crisis that rapidly engulfed all Europe. It was a dialectical leap, the critical point where quantity becomes transformed into quality.

THE 'EASTERN QUESTION'

In order to understand the causes of the First World War it is necessary to analyse the processes that developed on a world scale during the decades before 1914: the economic evolution of German capitalism and its relation to the established capitalist states of Britain and France; the tangled web of inter-imperialist diplomacy in the same period; the struggle for colonies, markets and spheres of influence; the ambitions and expansionist tendencies of tsarist Russia; the wars in the Balkans and the contradictions arising from the decay of the Ottoman Empire and many other factors.

One poisonous ingredient in this explosive cocktail was the national question in the Balkans, which was intensified by the increasingly rapid decay of the old Ottoman Empire. Throughout the nineteenth century, the 'Eastern Question' was the dominant question for the great powers of Europe. Under the guise of 'pan-Slavism', tsarist Russia desired access to the warm waters of the Mediterranean for its navy. Its support for the Bulgarians and Serbs in their struggle against Turkish rule was merely a convenient cloak for a cynical and expansionist foreign policy.

For equally cynical reasons, Britain wished to deny Russia, which threatened British India in the East, access to the Mediterranean. In the nineteenth century it supported the integrity of the Ottoman Empire as a counterweight to Russia. But just in case the integrity of the Empire was no longer possible, the men in London took out an insurance policy by supporting a limited expansion of Greece. For its part, France wished to strengthen its position in the region, notably in the Levant (Lebanon, Syria and Palestine).

Austria-Hungary displayed the same signs of senile decrepitude as the Ottoman Empire. Terrified of any change in the international order that could destabilise the fragile balance between the multiple ethnic and linguistic groups that composed it, the Habsburg Monarchy, in the sclerotic person of Franz Josef, fervently desired the status quo. It understood very well that the collapse of the Ottoman Empire would undermine it fatally.

The men in Vienna feared that the appeal of Serbian nationalism would have a powerful effect on Serbs in Bosnia, which was under Austrian control. Meanwhile, the German Empire had its own, quite different plans. Under the policy known as 'Drang nach Osten' ('Thrust to the East'), it aimed to turn the Ottoman Empire into a German client state – a de facto colony. It was for this sincere and entirely philanthropic aim that Berlin supported its integrity.

THE BALKAN WARS

The Turkish rule, which had dominated the Balkans for centuries, was shaken by the national liberation movements of the Greeks, Serbs and Bulgarians in the nineteenth century. By the early twentieth century, Bulgaria, Greece, Montenegro and Serbia had achieved independence from the Ottoman Empire. However, the small and weak states that emerged from this immediately became the pawns of various foreign powers. In particular, tsarist Russia aimed to extend its tentacles into the Balkans by posing as the 'defender of the South Slavs against Turkish tyranny'. This grandiose claim conveniently overlooked the small detail of the monstrous tyranny exercised by the tsarist regime over all the peoples of its own Empire.

Before 1912, large numbers of Slav-speaking people remained under Ottoman rule, notably in Thrace and the area known as Macedonia, which included not only Skopje but also Salonika (Thessaloniki). There was a sharp conflict between Bulgaria and Greece for control of Ottoman Macedonia. Greeks, once the victims of national persecution under the Turks, became the oppressors of the Macedonian Slavs, who were compelled to experience the joys of forced 'Hellenisation'. In the same way, the Bulgarians carried out a policy of 'Bulgarisation' of Greeks. Bulgarians and Greeks sent armed irregulars into Ottoman territory to protect and assist their ethnic kindred. From 1904, there was constant warfare in Macedonia in which the Greek and Bulgarian guerrillas fought the Ottoman army in the rugged mountains of Macedonia.

In July 1908, the prolonged decay of the Ottoman state led to a coup d'état known as the Young Turk Revolution. Taking advantage of the upheavals in Constantinople, Bulgaria declared itself a fully independent kingdom. At the same time, Austria-Hungary seized the opportunity to annex Bosnia and Herzegovina, which it had occupied since 1878 but was in theory still an Ottoman province. This move, which frustrated Serbia's northward expansion, provoked fury in Belgrade, but Serbia was forced to accept the annexation with gritted teeth. Bosnia remained a ticking time bomb that was to explode and shake the world in June 1914.

In the meantime, the agents of St. Petersburg did not remain idle. In the spring of 1912, Russian diplomacy achieved a major success with the launching of the Balkan League – an alliance of Serbia, Bulgaria, Greece, and Montenegro. Its specific goal was to wrest Macedonia away from Turkey. In the First Balkan War (1912) the Balkan League won a crushing victory against the armies of the Ottoman Empire, the most important victory being scored by the Bulgarians, who defeated the main Ottoman forces and advanced to the outskirts of Constantinople (now Istanbul), laying siege to Adrianople (Edirne). In Macedonia, the Serbian army smashed the Turks at Kumanovo, captured Bitola and, together with the Montenegrins, entered Skopje. The Greeks, meanwhile, occupied Salonika (Thessaloniki) and advanced on Ioannina. In Albania, the Montenegrins besieged Shkodër, and the Serbs entered Durrës.

A peace conference opened in London but, in January 1913, the war was resumed. Again, the Balkan League defeated the Ottomans: Ioannina fell to the Greeks and Adrianople to the Bulgarians. On 30 May 1913, a peace treaty was signed in London, whereby the Ottoman Empire lost almost all of its remaining European territory, including all of Macedonia and Albania. Albanian independence was insisted upon by the European powers, and Macedonia was to be divided among the Balkan allies.

The Second Balkan War was a bloody struggle for the division of the spoils. Like dogs fighting over a bone, the voracious ruling classes of Serbia, Greece and Romania quarrelled with Bulgaria over the 'liberated' land of Macedonia. The formation of the Balkan League had not eliminated the deadly rivalries between its members, and victory only served to exacerbate them. In the original document of the League, Serbia had promised Bulgaria most of Macedonia. But the ruling cliques of Serbia and Greece had a secret plan to keep most of conquered territory. Serbia and Greece ganged up against Bulgaria in a war that broke out in June 1913.

Montenegro, Romania and the Ottoman Empire joined the fight against Bulgaria, which was in a very disadvantageous position. The Serbs and the Greeks had a considerable military advantage on the eve of the war because their armies confronted comparatively weak Ottoman forces in the First Balkan War and suffered relatively few casualties, while the Bulgarians took the brunt of the heaviest fighting in Thrace. Defeated and betrayed, Bulgaria lost most of the ground that it had conquered with so much blood.

Greece and Serbia divided up most of Macedonia between themselves, leaving Bulgaria with only an insignificant part of the region, while Romania seized southern Dobrudzha, and Bulgaria was forced to cede Salonika to Greece. The bitterness and resentment for this betrayal was to play a fatal role later when Bulgaria joined the Central Powers in a bloody attack on Serbia.

The Balkan Wars were, in essence, proxy wars mainly between tsarist Russia and Austria-Hungary. The Russians played the card of 'pan-Slavism' as a means of expanding their influence in the Balkans at the expense of both the Ottoman Empire and Austria-Hungary. Greatly enlarged by its conquests, the Serbian ruling class aimed at nothing less than the complete domination of the Balkans under the disguise of a union of the South Slavic peoples (Yugoslavia). This inevitably led to an open conflict with the Austro-Hungarian Empire, which saw itself threatened by Serbian and Russian ambitions.

These wars appear on the surface as wars of national liberation and self-determination of the peoples of the Balkans. In reality they were no such thing. Behind every one of the national bourgeois cliques stood a 'big brother' in the shape of one or another of the Great Powers of Europe. Just as today the American imperialists constantly pose as the defenders of one or other oppressed nationality or group (for instance, the Kurds and Shias of Iraq against Saddam Hussein), just as Hitler used the Sudetenland Germans as a pretext for invading Czechoslovakia, and utilised the bloody services of Ukrainian nationalism to enslave the Ukraine, so Russia, Germany, France, Britain and Austria-Hungary used the Balkan nations as small change in their intrigues and manoeuvres.

THE ASSASSINATION IN SARAJEVO

What occurred in Sarajevo in June 1914 even now appears to have an almost surreal character. On 4 June, reports appeared in the newspaper of a planned visit of the heir to the Austrian throne, Archduke Franz Ferdinand, and his wife to Sarajevo, the capital of Bosnia. The declared object was the Crown Prince's wish to create a favourable impression on his first visit to the Bosnian subjects of this recently acquired territory, to attend the army manoeuvres that were planned to take place in the mountains near Sarajevo.

The visit was an act of extreme stupidity, which could only have occurred to a dynasty in a state of dotage – to arrange a visit of the Crown Prince of an occupying power to Sarajevo on this, of all days. For 28 June was Serbia's national day, the anniversary of the battle of Kosovo in 1389, when the Serbian Kingdom had been vanquished by the Turks.

Who in their right mind could imagine that the Serbs of Bosnia would pay grateful homage to a member of the royal family that blocked the way to uniting all Serbs in Greater Serbia? To add insult to injury, the archducal visit to Sarajevo was preceded by military manoeuvres in the mountains south of the city – provocatively close to the frontier with Serbia. To even contemplate a public visit of members of the Austrian royal family in a place like Sarajevo – a hostile territory seething with intrigues, terrorist plots and dangers of all kinds – was an act akin to madness.

Many people foresaw a disaster. The Serbian minister in Vienna had suggested to the minister responsible for Bosnian affairs that some Serbs might regard the time and place of the visit as a deliberate insult. He

1. ASSASSINATION IN SARAJEVO

warned that some young Serb participating in the Austrian manoeuvres might seize the opportunity to fire at the archduke. Politicians and officials in Sarajevo urged that the visit be cancelled. The police warned that they could not guarantee the archduke's safety, particularly given the lengthy route that the royal couple were scheduled to take along the Miljacka river from the railway station to the city hall.

'Those whom the gods wish to destroy, they first make mad'. Following the old Greek saying to the letter, the Austrians disregarded all the warnings. On 26 June, the Crown Prince arrived in Sarajevo under the full glare of publicity and mingled complacently with the cheering crowds, unaware that his movements were being followed by a young Bosnian nationalist, the student Gavrilo Princip, intent on ending his life.

This was supposed to be a brilliant occasion that would glorify Austrian rule in Bosnia-Herzegovina. The archduke had been eagerly anticipating for months his triumphal entry into the city of Sarajevo, resplendent in his uniform as inspector-general of the Austro-Hungarian army, accompanied by his wife Sophie, Duchess of Hohenberg, in a full-length white dress with red sash, holding a parasol to shelter from the sun. Unfortunately, the parasol offered no protection against bullets.

Princip was a member of Mlada Bosna (Young Bosnia), a movement of young Slavs of different ethnic and religious persuasions dedicated to overthrowing Austro-Hungarian rule. Princip was inspired by a burning desire to take revenge on the Austrian oppressors in the cause of Serb national liberation. But he was something more than a Serb nationalist.

As a member of Young Bosnia, a Bosnian nationalist, not just a Serb, the son of a poor Bosnian Serb peasant, he was inclined to anarchist ideas and the 'propaganda of the deed'. He believed that it was possible to change society by assassinating leading members of the ruling class, an idea that he shared with the Russian terrorists of Narodnaya Volya (The People's Will). He gave his life for that idea.

The announcement that Franz Ferdinand and his wife Sophie were to make an official visit to Sarajevo presented Gavrilo and his comrades with a unique opportunity. While the archduke was busy attending welcoming ceremonies, a nineteen-year-old Danilo Ilić was meeting with six would-be assassins at a Sarajevo café to outline the plan: the assassins were to be placed at each of the three bridges crossing the river. Their best chance of success would come at these junctions, where a grenade could easily be lobbed into the car carrying the royal couple.

While handing out guns and grenades, Ilić gravely warned the others that the police may have discovered their plot. But there was no question of calling it off as such an opportunity as this was unlikely to occur again. Afterwards, several of the conspirators visited the grave of Bogdan Žerajić, a young Serb who had been martyred years earlier when he had attempted (unsuccessfully) to assassinate the emperor. It is said that his dying words were "I leave it to Serbdom to avenge me".

On Sunday, 28 June the atmosphere became even more surreal. Security arrangements seem almost to have been calculated to assist the assassins. In order to encourage as many spectators as possible to turn out to welcome the royal couple, the plans for the procession had been published in the local newspaper, the *Bosnische Post*. This most considerate measure enabled the group of young terrorists to station themselves at strategic points. More incredible still, the archduke gave orders that the royal car should be open and should proceed at a slow pace so that people could get a good view of its occupants and they could get a good view of the sights.

Nevertheless, the assassination almost failed when the first bomb thrown at the royal car bounced off the vehicle, injuring some of the guards. The Archduke calmly dismounted to speak to the wounded men, then continued his journey. His wife suffered a slight face wound. Her white dress was spattered with blood. An indignant Franz Josef berated the mayor: "I have come to visit you and they throw bombs at me." The mayor's reply is not recorded.

That ought to have been the end of the affair. The royal car was supposed to proceed at speed along the river back to the railway station, but fate took an unexpected turn. Later that day, in one of those strange accidents in which history is so rich, the driver of the car took a wrong turn and appeared unexpectedly, reversing down the narrow street outside the very cafe where Princip was standing. Scarcely believing his luck, he walked up to the carriage and fired two shots at point blank range at the royal couple. The first shot hit the archduke near the jugular vein; the second hit the duchess in the stomach. It was all over before either a doctor or a priest could be summoned.

An enraged crowd tried to lynch Princip, who was rescued by the police. He tried to swallow the cyanide capsule, but vomited it up. The Austrian judge who interviewed him almost immediately afterwards, wrote:

> The young assassin, exhausted by his beating, was unable to utter a word. He was undersized, emaciated, sallow, and sharp-featured. It was difficult to imagine that so frail looking an individual could have committed so serious a deed.

Gavrilo was tried by an Austrian court and naturally found guilty. He told the court:

> In trying to insinuate that someone else has instigated the assassination, one strays from the truth. The idea arose in our own minds, and we ourselves executed it. We have loved the people. I have nothing to say in my defence.

Being only nineteen years old, he was too young to be executed under Austro-Hungarian law. Instead, he was effectively buried alive. In Theresienstadt prison – now in the Czech Republic – he was condemned to solitary confinement and held in the harshest conditions, denied books or writing materials. Owing to the appalling prison conditions, he caught tuberculosis, which ate away his bones so badly that his right arm had to be amputated. In May 1918 he died, his body reduced to that of a skeleton. He had scratched on the wall of his cell: "Our ghosts will walk through Vienna, and roam the Palace, frightening the Lords."

REPERCUSSIONS OF THE ASSASSINATION

News of the assassination caused a wave of consternation and outrage. In Sarajevo and other Bosnian towns, pro-Austrian mobs attacked any Serb they could find, smashing Serb shops and businesses and entering people's homes and throwing furniture onto the streets. The anti-Serb pogrom resulted in many murders, and the state took bloody revenge by arresting hundreds of Serbs, whether or not they were associated with nationalism. Many were executed.

All this played into the hands of the War Party in Vienna who for some time were agitating for action against the Serbs. Now they had an ideal excuse. The heads of government met in an emergency session at which Berchtold, the Austrian foreign minister, and Conrad, the army chief of staff, discussed what action to take. The latter urged immediate military action against Serbia – something the Austrian General Staff had already been planning.

Austria placed responsibility for the assassination squarely at the door of the government of Belgrade. In fact, the Serbian military leadership, led by its intelligence chief Dragutin Dimitrijević, the founder of the Black Hand terrorist organisation, did train people in the black arts of terrorism, manipulating idealistic youngsters like Gavrilo Princip for their own sinister purposes. Terrorism is usually the weapon of the weak against the strong, and Serbia used it as an auxiliary arm for its diplomatic and military manoeuvres. This time, however, the terrorist weapon had succeeded too well. The assassination in Sarajevo gave Austria the perfect excuse to attack Serbia, and Belgrade was alarmed.

For reasons that seem incomprehensible, Serbia took no action to open an investigation into the events in Sarajevo. This might have provided the Belgrade government with grounds for a denial of any complicity in the assassination by groups in Serbia, which gave Austria a free hand to present its own version of events. Was it the result of divisions within the regime, or simple paralysis? Or did this stupefying inaction flow from fear that an investigation could have exposed facts that might prove embarrassing to the Serbian government? Either way, it invited a violent reaction from Vienna.

However, an Austrian offensive against Serbia was not yet inevitable. Such was the decayed and demoralised state of the Austro-Hungarian regime that the authorities in Vienna immediately began to vacillate. The Hungarian Prime Minister, Count Tisza, warned

1. ASSASSINATION IN SARAJEVO

Berchtold of the dangers involved in such a military adventure. The aged Emperor himself warned of the risk of Russia intervening on the side of Serbia and expressed doubts about German support. Before acting, it was first necessary to ascertain the position of Austria's ally Germany. The scene of the action thus moves rapidly from Vienna to Berlin.

Count Hoyos, an Austrian foreign ministry official, was sent to Berlin to sound out the Germans. The German military fervently backed early aggressive action by Austria, while Russia was still unprepared for war. By the summer of 1914, the leading circles in Germany seemed prepared to run the risk of a large-scale war in the name of its alliance with the crumbling Austro-Hungarian Empire. When the latter decided to take action against Serbia for the Sarajevo murder, Kaiser Wilhelm came down firmly on their side.

Wilhelm's bellicosity won the day. He urged the Austrians to teach the Serbs a lesson so that they would learn to fear them. His written note on the subject reads as follows: "Now or never ... matters must be cleared up with Serbia – and that soon." Since the monarch, together with his generals, decided all important questions, this amounted to a direct order. His ministers accepted his demands with silent resignation and a fatal chain of action and reaction was set in motion.

The Berlin government was offering unconditional support to the Austrians, despite the risk of war with Russia. It was a dangerous gamble. Wilhelm and his generals calculated that France, and particularly Britain, might refuse to support Russia. They even saw it as a way of breaking up the Entente. They believed it would unite the nation behind the government and thus halt the seemingly unstoppable rise of the social democracy. In addition, the generals wished to strike against Russia before it had finished rebuilding its military might by implementing a series of reforms after Russia's humiliating defeat by Japan in 1905.

On 5 July, the German Kaiser offered Austria what amounted to a 'blank cheque' – advising it not to delay in taking whatever action it considered necessary. On the strength of this, Conrad urged that the army be mobilised for war. However, the old fox Franz Josef, ever inclined to caution and fearing the breakup of his Empire, refused. An equally serious obstacle for the War Party in Vienna was the opposition of the Hungarian leader Tisza, whom it took two weeks to persuade.

In a letter to the Kaiser, the Austrian emperor stated that Austria's aim was to "isolate and diminish" Serbia (by giving away slices of its land to other Balkan states, so-called "territorial adjustments"), thus reducing Serb influence in the Balkans to insignificance. The Austrian government meanwhile had opened an investigation that claimed that the plot had been hatched in the Serb capital Belgrade and implicated a Serb employee of one of the government ministries as well as Serb army officers. Even if one accepts that these accusations might be true, there was no evidence that the Serb government itself was implicated in the assassination.

Bethmann-Hollweg, the German chancellor, advised Austria that it "may be sure that His Majesty (the Kaiser), in accordance with his treaty obligations and old friendship, will stand by Austria's side." There could therefore be no doubt whatsoever that the German government was endorsing the Kaiser's 'blank cheque' of 5 July. Austria's hands were completely free to do whatever the government in Vienna pleased. Greatly encouraged by these assurances, Berchtold hoped that the crisis could be contained by a localised war against Serbia alone.

These illusions appear to have been shared by the people in Berlin. An indication of just how far Wilhelm was removed from reality is the fact that, in such a difficult and dangerous moment, when Germany and the whole of Europe were staggering like drunken men towards an abyss, Kaiser Wilhelm left Germany for a Scandinavian holiday. His supreme self-confidence led him to believe that neither France nor Russia would take action over the Serbian question. On 7 July, the Serbian prime minister denied any foreknowledge of the plot. But it was already far too late for such denials. The machinery of war was already grinding into action.

THE AUSTRIAN ULTIMATUM

At a meeting of the Austrian Council of Ministers all but one urged military action. Fearful of Russian intervention, Tisza again advised caution. Austrian foreign minister Berchtold on the other hand demanded that any diplomatic action taken must "only end in war." He concluded that: "a war with Russia would be the most probable consequence of our entering Serbia." To clinch the matter, Count Hoyos, newly returned from Berlin, repeated the German promise of unconditional support to Austria.

Agreement was finally reached to present an ultimatum to Serbia, written in such a way that it would be rejected, thus preparing the ground for war. There was a slight complication when the Austrian Legal Counsellor reported on 13 July that the investigation of the Sarajevo crime revealed no complicity on the part of the Serbian government in the plot. Despite this annoying inconvenience, the ruling circles in Vienna pretended not to hear and stepped up their plans to attack Serbia.

Count Tisza confirmed to the German ambassador that the Austrian note to Serbia "is to be so phrased that its acceptance will be practically impossible." The men in Vienna were confident that the ultimatum would be rejected, but, just in case, they issued instructions to the Austrian ambassador in Belgrade that any reply from the Serbs must be turned down. Meanwhile, in secret, the Austrian mobilisation was already underway.

The ultimatum was dispatched to the Austrian ambassador in Belgrade on 20 July for presentation to the Serbian government three days later. The slight delay was occasioned by the presence of a French delegation in St. Petersburg, from whence the French president Poincaré issued a stern warning to the Austrian ambassador that "the Russian people are very warm friends of the Serbians, and France is Russia's ally." The French delegation in St. Petersburg solemnly affirmed their obligations under the Franco-Russian alliance.

But by now matters had gone far beyond the bounds of diplomatic manoeuvres and notes. At 6.00 pm on 23 July the Austrian ultimatum was handed to the Serbian government. The preamble referred to Serbia's permitting the anti-Austrian criminal activities of secret societies and press propaganda to go unchallenged, a "culpable tolerance" that had presented a "perpetual menace" to the peace of Austria. The demands of the ultimatum, specifically points five and six, amounted to nothing less than a complete surrender of Serbia's national sovereignty and submission to Austria. A French newspaper said that it required from Serbia an "acknowledgment of vassalage".

All this was nothing more than diplomatic camouflage for war. Berchtold noted: "Any conditional acceptance [of the ultimatum], or one accompanied by reservations, is to be regarded as a refusal". On being informed of the terms of the Austrian ultimatum, Sazonov, the Russian foreign minister, declared: "It's a European war". Playing for time, the Russian Council of Ministers asked Austria to prolong its time limit and not to engage in hostilities. St. Petersburg advised Serbia not to oppose an Austrian invasion. At the same time, the Council requested the tsar to authorise partial mobilisation, that is, one confined to the Austrian border.

Partial mobilisation was approved 'in principle' by the tsar, though it was not to be carried out until July. Such vacillations were vigorously opposed by the Russian General Staff, which, like the General Staffs of all the other powers, was in favour of a more aggressive policy. Army HQ had planned for a general mobilisation directed against both Austria and Germany. The French ambassador at St. Petersburg urged a "policy of firmness" on Sazonov.

Events were moving fast. The Serbian reply was rejected by Austria, which also rejected Russia's request to extend the forty-eight-hour time limit. Serbia ordered a general mobilisation and appealed to the tsar for help "in your generous Slav heart". But neither generosity nor Slav solidarity, nor yet Nicholas' heart had anything to do with the machinations in St. Petersburg, only naked self-interest and cynical great power calculations.

Once more, the Russian Ministerial Council met in the august presence of the tsar. The only item on the agenda: partial mobilisation as a means of exerting diplomatic pressure on Vienna and Berlin, or general mobilisation against both Germany and Austria that would mean war. Once again, the army chiefs pressed for all-out mobilisation; once again the Council opted for the less-dangerous alternative.

1. ASSASSINATION IN SARAJEVO

The hesitant, vacillating conduct in St. Petersburg was noted with satisfaction in Berlin. The Kaiser and his generals draw the obvious conclusion: Russia was not prepared to fight. That convinced them even more of the correctness of their hard-line stand in relation to the Serbs. On receiving a memorandum sent by the German ambassador to Russia containing Sazonov's view that Austria's "swallowing" of Serbia would mean Russia would go to war with Austria, the Kaiser noted: "All right! Let her…"

But Russia was now coming under intense pressure to act, not so much out of a philanthropic concern for the fate of her Serbian brothers, but to safeguard her prestige as a great power, and to attack Germany before Germany itself acted against Russia. In any case, few people were under any illusion that any decision for mobilisation, even partial, would be seen in Austria and Germany as anything less than "a sure step towards war".

This was now no longer just another Balkan War. The French commenced secret military preparations, such as the recall of troops from overseas. Only one of the great powers in Europe had yet to make clear where it stood. With less than a day before the expiration of the ultimatum, the British foreign minister, Sir Edward Grey, urged the German ambassador to attempt mediation by Germany, Britain, France and Italy, and extend the time-limit set by Austria. In a painful interview with Sir Edward in London, the French ambassador attempted to shake the British foreign minister out of his apparent complacency and accept that it would be too late for mediation once Austria moved against Serbia.

The complacency in London was only a mask for the cold calculations of self-interest that dictated Britain's foreign policy. While Sir Edward Grey was assuring the British parliament that Britain was not bound by the Russo-French agreement, in private conversations, the British political establishment agreed that it would be impossible for Britain to keep out of the coming war. Sir Eyre Crowe, a British foreign office official, noted:

> Our interests are tied up with those of France and Russia in this struggle, which is not for the possession of Serbia, but one between Germany aiming

at a political dictatorship in Europe and the powers who desire to retain individual freedom.

Needless to say, all this had nothing to do with 'individual freedom' or the self-determination of Serbia, Belgium, or any other country. To come into conflict with France and Russia was unthinkable because the British Empire needed their complicity to preserve British rule in India and their colonial possessions in Africa. Even more serious was the mortal threat to Britain if Germany got possession of the Channel ports.

The German ambassador assured Sir Edward Grey that his government had no prior knowledge of the Austrian ultimatum, which, of course, was a blatant lie. Grey answered that:

> [B]etween Serbia and Austria, I [feel] no title to intervention, but as soon as the question became one between Austria and Russia it was a question of the peace of Europe, in which we must all take a hand.

Everything was now in place. Individual actors in the historical drama stepped onto the stage, read their lines, played their part, big or small, and disappeared forever. The role of individuals, of course, cannot be eliminated from the complex interplay of historical factors. By their actions or omissions, the powerful currents of history can either be hastened or retarded. But, in the last analysis, it is these unseen but irresistible forces that determine the outcome, sweeping all before them.

For a few weeks, the name of Gavrilo Princip loomed large in the headlines of the world's press. But even if his revolver had failed to fire, even if his hand had shaken in the decisive moment, even if he had never been born, that terrible cataclysm later baptised as the Great War would have broken out anyway. On another pretext, with other names and other headlines, the unbearable contradictions between the imperialist states of Europe would have expressed themselves in the Great Slaughter.

It has been the common illusion of every period that history is made by the conscious decisions of kings, statesmen, politicians and generals.

1. ASSASSINATION IN SARAJEVO

Needless to say, such decisions have always played a part in determining events. Yet it frequently occurs that the end results are very different to the original intentions and even in flat contradiction to them.

Every one of the chief actors in the drama of 1914 miscalculated. Gavrilo Princip's courageous but misguided action did not lead to the liberation of the South Slavs, but only to the bloodbath of a World War. His mortal enemies in the House of Habsburg hoped to save the Empire by waging war on Serbia, only to bring about its complete destruction. Their ally Kaiser Wilhelm, who appeared to be the most powerful man in Europe, was swept away like a man of straw by the German Revolution.

In 1914, his cousin, Tsar Nicholas, had hoped to avoid a repeat of the 1905 Revolution by going to war, only to prepare the ground for an even-mightier proletarian revolution in November 1917. Thus, through all the complex cross-currents of events, the rise and fall of individual leaders, parties and governments, the laws of the dialectic assert themselves with iron inevitability. Long ago that great dialectical thinker Heraclitus said: "War is the father and king of all, and has produced some as gods and some as men, and has made some slaves and some free." These words are profoundly true, and we should remember that the class struggle is itself a kind of war.

The same Heraclitus discovered that wonderful dialectical law that says that, sooner or later, things change into their opposite. The Great Slaughter in the end gave birth to the greatest revolution in history. Out of all the savagery, slaughter, fire and destruction, deep beneath the surface of society, in the trenches and factories, in the fields and towns, in the peasants' huts and soldiers' barracks a new spirit was struggling to be born: a spirit of revolt against the existing order; the spirit that was determined to make such horrors a thing of the past, to raise humankind above the level of the animal struggle for existence and create a world fit for human beings to live in.

2. ON THE BRINK OF THE ABYSS

> "When the leaders speak of peace the common people know that war is coming."
> (Bertolt Brecht)

THE INDIVIDUAL IN HISTORY
Self-styled philosophers of the post-modernist kind deny the possibility of finding any rational explanations for human history. It is alleged that there are no general laws, no objective factors that lie behind the conduct of individuals and determine their psychology and behaviour. From this standpoint – the standpoint of extreme subjectivity – all history is determined by individuals acting according to their own free will. To attempt to find some inner logic in this turbulent and lawless sea would be as futile an exercise as to try to predict the precise momentum and position of an individual subatomic particle.

Despite a certain superficial attractiveness, this subjective approach to history is quite empty. It signifies a complete abandonment of any attempt to discover the laws whereby human society has evolved, since it denies the very existence of any such laws. Now this is a very extraordinary thing. Modern science teaches us that everything in the universe, from the smallest molecules and atoms to the biggest galaxies, are governed by laws, and it is precisely the discovery of such laws that is the main task and content of science.

We can confidently explain the origin and development of every species – including our own – by means of the laws of evolution through natural selection discovered by Charles Darwin, which has received a powerful boost from the most recent discoveries in the field of genetics. We can understand the development of the earth and the continents on the basis of plate tectonics and predict the movements of distant galaxies. Yet when it comes to our own social development, we are suddenly informed that we cannot find any rational explanation for it, since human beings are considered to be far too complex to be understood.

That human beings are complex both on an individual and collective level hardly needs to be stated. Yet it is patently untrue that human behaviour cannot be understood. Engels pointed out long ago that, whereas it is impossible to predict when an individual man or woman will die, it is perfectly possible to make such a prediction in the aggregate, a fact out of which insurance companies make healthy profits. In the same way, while it is not possible to determine with sufficient accuracy the position and momentum of a single subatomic particle, it is possible to make very precise predictions when dealing with a very large quantity of such particles.

To say that human history is a purely random affair flies in the face of the facts. Even the most superficial observer of history will immediately see the existence of definite patterns. Certain processes are constantly repeated: the rise and fall of certain socio-economic formations, societies and civilisations, economic crises, wars and revolutions. Just as in evolution, long periods of stasis are followed by sudden explosions that can impel development or lead to reversals and decline.

THE KAISER'S ARM
In all the mass of material – some good, much bad, and some frankly absurd – that has flooded onto the scene on the anniversary of what they used to call The Great War (which I prefer to call The Great Slaughter) the attempts to explain the causes of the War border on the comic.

2. ON THE BRINK OF THE ABYSS

Some historians, delving into the murky depths of the subconscious in their effort to find a suitably subjective (that is, mystical) explanation, think it was all due to the traumatic effects on Kaiser Wilhelm's mind caused by an accident of birth that broke his left arm.

We are asked to believe that the Kaiser's withered left arm, which he tried to hide from public view by the artful use of military cloaks and other dodges, so marked Wilhelm's psyche that it turned him into a warped and aggressive psychopath. Other historians point out that the poor man had a very difficult childhood. None of his royal cousins in England, Denmark or Russia wanted to play with the sullen, resentful boy. As a result, he became a bully, determined to take revenge on those who had humiliated him in his tender years, resulting in the outbreak of war. Here is just one example of this kind of 'history':

> He believed in force and the 'survival of the fittest' in domestic as well as foreign politics... William was not lacking in intelligence, but he did lack stability, disguising his deep insecurities by swagger and tough talk. He frequently fell into depressions and hysterics... William's personal instability was reflected in vacillations of policy. His actions, at home as well as abroad, lacked guidance, and therefore often bewildered or infuriated public opinion. He was not so much concerned with gaining specific objectives, as had been the case with Bismarck, as with asserting his will. This trait in the ruler of the leading Continental power was one of the main causes of the uneasiness prevailing in Europe at the turn-of-the-century. (Langer, W.L. [Ed.], *Western Civilization*, p. 528.)

It must be freely admitted that the individual character traits and personalities of the *dramatis personae* of history must play a role in shaping events, and even a determining one. But they can only do so to the extent that they correspond in some way to the demands of the situation. Doubtless the character of the German Kaiser was difficult and this was partly the result of the above-mentioned factors. But the resentfulness of the Kaiser, his aggressive and bullying tendencies and explosive temper cannot serve as the cause of millions of dead and the devastation of an entire continent. That must be looked for in powerful objective trends, without which Wilhelm's personality defects would have remained merely a source of irritation to his friends and immediate family.

Is it possible to relate the characters of individuals to the broader historical picture? It is quite extraordinary how similar social conditions produce similar kinds of individual. A comparison between the character of Charles I of England, Louis XVI of France and Tsar Nicholas II will provide much food for thought for both sociologists and psychologists, as would a comparative study of Cromwell, Robespierre and Lenin. A comparison of the English, French and Russian Revolutions will reveal some important differences, since the class character of these great historical events was different. But it will also reveal very striking similarities.

It would even be possible to draw three graphs that show that, in essence, all three Revolutions followed a very similar trajectory – both in their period of ascent and descent. And each stage of the Revolution called forth people whose characters corresponded more or less closely to the demands of the period. In making this point, I am very far from denying the importance of the role of the individual in history. On the contrary, in a given concatenation of circumstances, the actions of a relatively small group, or even a single individual, may be of decisive importance. Marx said: "Man makes his own history", but he added that the men and women who make history do not do so as entirely free agents. Rather, they are limited by the objective conditions that produced them and which impose strict limits upon their field of action.

In many ways the Kaiser's character and psychology were admirably suited to the interests of the German ruling clique at that time. Wilhelm was a reactionary and had a militarist Prussian mindset. He believed in nationalism, military dominance and the Divine Right of Kings. To compensate for his disability, he went out of his way to act the part of the Prussian militarist and to sound as powerful and aggressive as possible.

Wilhelm only seemed comfortable in the company of his army officers and reviewing army parades, dressing up in uniform and going out on manoeuvres. "In the Guards," he said, "I really found my family, my friends, my interests – everything of which I had up to that time had to do without." Dressed up in the fancy uniform of a Prussian officer, he began to strut about and speak in the brusque tone of command that brooked no contradiction. A nephew of Queen Victoria, Wilhelm's attitude to the vast British Empire was a contradictory mix of admiration and envy. He wanted Germany to have colonies and a powerful navy to match that of Britain's.

It has been alleged that Germany had been actively planning an aggressive war. Some historians believe that the decisive moment was not July 1914 but December 1912, when the Kaiser held a meeting at which, it is alleged, he decided to go to war in approximately eighteen months. The aggressive stance of Wilhelm and some of his generals adds some weight to this argument, although there was always an element of bluff in the swaggering conduct of the Kaiser, who vacillated continually over the war question, to the desperation of his ministers and, in particular, his generals, who displayed their impatience and frustration at his indecision.

Despite all his play-acting, Wilhelm never fought a real war until 1914 and even then, he irritated his generals by constantly changing his mind. The General Staff looked on the Kaiser with a mixture of disciplined deference towards the imperial office and contempt for the man who held it. In his memoirs, former German chancellor von Bülow says of the Kaiser:

> [H]e never led an army in the field… He was well aware that he was neurasthenic, without real capacity as a general, and still less able, in spite of his naval hobby, to have led a squadron or even captained a ship.

MATERIAL CAUSES OF WAR

With due respect to the amateur psychologists, one must look a bit further than the Kaiser's neuroses if we are to find the causes of one of the most momentous conflicts of modern times. There were many factors behind the conflicts between the great powers over the previous four decades, all of them closely concerning material interests. The most-powerful states of Europe were engaged in a scramble for colonies and markets. By the end of the nineteenth century, the world was already pretty well divided up between them. Great Britain, the country where capitalism developed earlier and was more deeply rooted than in any other country, had conquered the lion's share. France had established a colonial empire in North Africa and parts of Asia. What was later known as 'poor little Belgium' had brutally enslaved and looted the people of the Congo, and the Dutch possessed the riches of Java.

By contrast, Germany, which had only succeeded in uniting itself some fifty years earlier, had arrived too late and had only a few of the poorer African colonies in its grip. But it showed its military might by inflicting a humiliating defeat on France in the Franco-Prussian War of 1870-71, in compensation for which it had seized two French provinces with a partly German-speaking population: Alsace and Lorraine. This fact alone provided sufficient grounds for a future war between Germany and France.

Infatuated by the rise of its industrial and military power, Germany's industrialists, politicians, and the Kaiser himself, were increasingly inclined to an aggressive expansionist policy. They saw the creation of Mitteleuropa, a German-dominated customs union, as a first step to achieving German economic hegemony over Europe. French power would be broken, Belgium reduced to the position of a German vassal state, and a German colonial empire established in Africa and the East. Later, in 1917-18, having defeated Russia, Germany actually began to carve an empire out of the ruins of the tsarist Empire: in the Baltic States and Ukraine.

In 1898, Germany began to build up its navy; a move that could not fail to start the alarm bells ringing in London. Unlike other powers on the European mainland, Britain's condition as an island nation meant it did not have to maintain a huge standing army. Its shores being protected by the sea, it relied militarily on the strength of its navy. The world's most powerful maritime nation had a policy that its navy must always be stronger than the combined fleets of the next two most-powerful nations, for example, France and Germany.

2. ON THE BRINK OF THE ABYSS

London saw the build-up of the German fleet as a major threat to the security of Britain. The Entente Cordiale (Cordial Agreement) signalled a major shift in British policy towards Europe. Previously, the key element in British policy towards Europe was the maintenance of the balance of power, which aimed to prevent any one nation from achieving a dominance that would threaten its position. While carefully avoiding entanglements with continental powers, the British skilfully played one off against another. But the rise of German power compelled the British ruling class to conclude a series of agreements, albeit of a limited character, with her two main colonial rivals, France and Russia.

The contradiction between the rival imperialist powers was expressed by the formation of military blocs and alliances. When Kaiser Wilhelm II decided against renewing a treaty with Russia, it inevitably propelled Germany into an alliance with the declining Austro-Hungarian Empire with its geriatric monarch, antiquated manners and Balkan problems. This alliance was later joined by Italy, which was also anxious to acquire territory and colonies. In response to this move in 1894, France and Russia, which bordered Germany to the West and East, formed an alliance based on fear of Berlin's expansionist ambitions.

In the case of France, this fear was combined with bitter resentment after its national humiliation in the Franco-Prussian War of 1870-71. The French burned with a spirit of revenge and a desire to recover the lost territories and remove German troops from French soil. That was the immediate aim, but in addition the General Staff were determined to achieve the crushing of German power. They aimed to seize the Rhineland for France with the pretext of strengthening her defences. The voracious intentions of the French ruling class were subsequently revealed in the predatory Treaty of Versailles.

Nevertheless, at the beginning of 1914, the prospects for an all-European war seemed a remote possibility. All the leaders of the great powers spoke of peace, their abhorrence of war and violence. Even in late June of that year relations between Britain and Germany were sufficiently cordial for the Royal Navy to pay a courtesy visit to the German fleet in the port of Kiel. The London government was far more concerned with the Irish problem, which threatened to turn into civil war, than affairs in the Balkans.

In Russia, the government was preoccupied with an upsurge of workers' strikes and demonstrations, which was one reason why the German Kaiser thought it unlikely that Russia would go to war over the invasion of Serbia. All the governments solemnly swore allegiance to the sacred principles of international law. But this was all on the surface. As Solon of Athens accurately remarked, "the law is like a spider's web; the small are caught and the great tear it up."

Not everyone was surprised. The General Staffs of the main belligerents had long predicted the inevitability of such a conflict – some with eager anticipation, others with fear and trembling. But their fatalistic predictions were usually ignored by the politicians and diplomats, who knew only too well that it was in the interests of the military elite to exaggerate the danger of war as a convenient means of extracting large sums of money from the government.

Even as the politicians made speeches about peace, their governments were all busy building ever-more-formidable machines of war. The period leading up to 1914 witnessed a European arms race that dwarfed anything that had been seen before. Germany and Britain vied with each other to see who could build bigger and better battleships. The French were spending huge sums of money on frontier defences that proved useless in 1914 and equally useless in 1940. Even the smallest states in the Balkans were arming themselves to the teeth. The astonishing speed with which events unfolded after the assassination in Sarajevo revealed the falsity of the soothing mirage of serenity and peace. Within five weeks, Europe was at war.

"MEDIATION"

At the start of August there was a frenzy of diplomatic activity, principally caused by the anxiety of the British to avoid a European war. The rulers of Britain had no interest in a war, because it was already the wealthiest country with an Empire that spanned half the world. This explains Sir Edward Grey's fervent attachment to peace. He proposed to the German ambassador that, if Austria and Russia both mobilised, the other powers (Britain, Germany, France and Italy) should attempt to get them to negotiate before any crossing of each other's frontiers. But, as always in diplomacy, what is apparent does not necessarily coincide with what is real.

There was more than a small dose of hypocrisy in British protestations of pacifism. Germany's rapidly expanding military power, and especially the alarming growth of her naval strength, posed a serous threat to Britain. Something had to be done to rein in German ambitions. But the British ruling class was not anxious to get involved in a war on the European mainland. If there was going to be a war (and all the indicators pointed clearly in that direction), it would be preferable to get others to do the fighting, while Britain remained aloof from the conflict as far as that was possible. That, in essence, was the meaning of Sir Edward's strategy.

Grey, now increasingly alarmed, requested an urgent interview with the German ambassador. Indicating that Britain would not remain neutral in a war involving Germany and France, he warned the German ambassador of the urgent need for mediation to prevent a European war. He urged Germany to put pressure on Austria to accept the Serbian reply to the ultimatum, to try and restrain it "from prosecuting a... foolhardy policy" of crushing Serbia that would surely escalate into an Austro-Russian conflict. To underline the point, the London government authorised the release of the necessary funds for the immediate mobilisation of the fleet.

BRITAIN AND GERMANY

By 1914, Germany was the strongest continental power, economically, industrially, demographically and militarily. The most industrialised country in Europe, with a powerful army and navy, Germany was a young, vigorous and rising nation, ambitious to acquire the status of a world power. But its actual status, vis-à-vis the old established European powers, was not at all commensurate with its economic and military weight.

In a 1907 New Year's Day memorandum, Sir Eyre Crowe, the foremost expert on Germany at the British Foreign Office, formulated the question approximately thus: The world belongs to the strong. A vigorous nation cannot allow its growth to be hampered by blind adherence to the status quo. It was therefore foolish to suppose that Germany would not to want to expand. The ruling circles in London were therefore under no illusions that war with Germany could be avoided.

While German capitalism was on the rise, Britain was entering into a phase of relative decline. Glutted by the plunder of Empire, Britain was extraordinarily wealthy, but its industries were increasingly outclassed by Germany and other competitors. Its vast global Empire was difficult to defend, its huge navy overstretched. Its share of world trade was in decline, although the value of her exports was boosted by her dominance of 'invisible' trades and huge overseas investment. More than any other nation, Britain was dependent on international trade.

In principle, the British bourgeoisie was interested in preserving peace – which is only another way of saying preserve the status quo. However, it was in the interest of British imperialism to prevent any particular power from gaining hegemony. For centuries, Britain had fought to maintain the balance of power in Europe, to ensure that no state achieved domination in the European mainland. The Kaiser's Germany was becoming a threat to that scheme.

If France had been defeated, Britain would have been faced with the nightmare of a continent dominated by a single, aggressive state. In the given conditions, therefore, Britain would have to back France against Germany to prevent the latter achieving dominance. This was the cornerstone of the policy of Sir Edward Grey.

To cover these cynical calculations, the British government naturally put forward 'democratic' war aims, offering the idea of some sort of self-determination for the nationalities within the Austro-Hungarian and Turkish Empires, attempting to appeal to the German people over the heads of the Imperial government. But this was just a smokescreen. The real attitude towards self-determination was shown by the comments of the *Manchester Guardian*, which wrote that, if only it were possible, the best thing to do with Serbia would be to tow it out to sea and sink it.

2. ON THE BRINK OF THE ABYSS

It is interesting to compare the character of Wilhelm to that of Sir Edward Grey. The contrast between the unflappable, phlegmatic, almost somniferous Grey and the pushy, arrogant, impulsive Kaiser is striking. Grey has been criticised by many historians for his apparent apathy and lack of initiative. Throughout all this atmosphere of diplomatic frenzy and hysteria, the British government and its foreign minister appear curiously aloof. After the assassination in Sarajevo, the foreign minister showed no outward signs of alarm and only slight interest: yet another muddle in the Balkans that need not concern us, and that will soon blow over, and so on.

In the weeks leading up to the declaration of war, Grey manoeuvred constantly between France, Germany, Russia and Austria, putting forward various schemes for mediation in the conflict between Austro-Hungary and Serbia, and fobbing off the insistent demands of the French with evasive answers. Almost until the eleventh hour the British Foreign Secretary appeared to show little concern about the urgency of the situation, adopting a wait-and-see attitude, apparently more interested in what was for dinner in his club than the spicy dishes that were being brewed in the Balkans.

This seemingly organic indecision, which infuriated allies, enemies and colleagues alike, may or may not have been an integral part of his personality (there are some people for whom vacillation is second nature), but it was a faithful reflection of the interests of British imperialism. In fact, the temperamental differences between Wilhelm and Grey reflected the differences between Britain, an old established Empire, and Germany, the upstart with a mighty industrial base and a powerful army and navy, which was blocked and frustrated on all sides by its rivals.

What was involved was a fight between two robbers for a more equitable share-out of the loot. One robber was already in possession of half the world and had no wish to be disturbed in the enjoyment of its plunder. The other robber was gnawed by envy at his neighbour's wealth and thirsted to lay his hands on it. It was not in the interests of British imperialism to be dragged into a land war in Europe but rather to let others do the fighting. For Germany, on the contrary, a war with Russia and its French ally was not only desirable but absolutely necessary. If it were possible to keep Britain out of it, that would be obviously desirable. But if it meant war with Britain, so be it.

Behind the facade of indifference, British imperialism was engaged in a complicated manoeuvre, as Trotsky points out:

> English diplomacy did not lift its visor of secrecy up to the very outbreak of war. The government of the City obviously feared to reveal its intention of entering the war on the side of the Entente lest the Berlin government take fright and be compelled to eschew war. In London they wanted war. That is why they conducted themselves in such a way as to raise hopes in Berlin and Vienna that England would remain neutral, while Paris and Petrograd firmly counted on England's intervention.
>
> Prepared by the entire course of development over a number of decades, the war was unleashed through the direct and conscious provocation of Great Britain. The British government thereby calculated on extending just enough aid to Russia and France, while they became exhausted, to exhaust England's mortal enemy, Germany. But the might of German militarism proved far too formidable and demanded of England, not token, but actual intervention in the war. The role of a gleeful third partner to which Great Britain, following her ancient tradition, aspired fell to the lot of the United States. (Trotsky, L., *The First Five Years of the Communist International*, Vol. 1, p. 60.)

There were naturally divisions in the British establishment. When all is said and done, war is a damned risky affair, and bad for business. But behind the smiling mask of pacifism and the kindly offers of mediation, there was also an element of cold and cynical calculation. To put it bluntly, London would not be too upset if Germany started a war, as long as that war did not involve a heavy expenditure of blood and gold for Britain. If the Germans and French wanted to fight each other, let them get on with it. That was no affair of ours. We could let them fight each other to a standstill, then step in at the last minute and dictate the terms of a peace, which, naturally, would be to Britain's advantage. In fact, it might not be a bad idea to push the others into a war, and to do so before the German fleet had completely overtaken the Royal Navy.

Seen from this point of view, the vacillations of Sir Edward may be open to a different interpretation. By giving Berlin the impression that Britain would not participate in a European war, he was, in effect, giving Germany the green light to launch an attack on France. The British were well aware of the existence of the Schlieffen Plan, with all its implications. The Chief of the Imperial German General Staff, Count Alfred von Schlieffen, had drawn up the plan in 1905. It was supposed to be Germany's answer to its central strategic problem: how to fight a war successfully on two fronts, against France in the west and Russia in the east.

The Schlieffen Plan envisaged a massive attack through the Low Countries into northern France, which was supposed to bring about a French surrender within six weeks. Troops could then be sent east by rail to defend East Prussia against the 'Russian steamroller', which was expected to be slow to get moving. Schlieffen's plan was correctly interpreted by Britain as a virtual "intention to violate Belgian neutrality". A German occupation of the Low Countries and the Channel ports represented a serious threat to Britain's naval domination. The Germans were convinced by the constant vacillations from London that Britain would not be prepared to enter the war to defend France. That was a serious error on their part, for which they paid a very high price.

Entering into this complicated diplomatic game of hide-and-seek, the German Chancellor attempted to soothe nerves in London by promising that, in a general war, Germany would not annex any French territory in Europe if Great Britain remained neutral in the impending conflict.

But he refused to give any assurance about respecting the neutrality of Belgium (which was a main concern of Great Britain), indicating that she would have to bow to "military necessity", and, as we know, necessity knows no law. This, and all other questions, would be decided not by diplomacy and treaties but by the General Staff, in accordance with the Schlieffen (war) Plan.

Despite von Schlieffen's optimistic assumptions, the German General Staff was under no illusion about the catastrophic implications of war. Chief of Staff General von Moltke, a nephew of the great Prussian general who led Germany to victory over France in 1870, warned that an Austrian offensive against Serbia would mean war with Russia, and Germany would be drawn in with fatal consequences. It would mean a European war "which will annihilate the civilisation of almost the whole of Europe for decades to come". This was not far from the truth. But how this war was to be avoided, the general did not venture to explain. In fact, although von Moltke and his fellow generals feared war, they concluded that it was inevitable and, therefore, Germany's best chance was to strike first and strike hard.

In the end, the Schlieffen Plan was executed by his successor, Helmuth von Moltke in August 1914, with some modifications. But it did not turn out as expected by its author. The Netherlands was not invaded; more troops than planned were kept in Alsace-Lorraine to defend it against a French offensive. The British came into the war, and 250,000 troops were diverted to East Prussia to help fend off an unexpectedly speedy Russian advance. But we are anticipating. At this stage in the proceedings, the war was being fought, not with bullets and bayonets, but with diplomatic papers.

The worries about the future were not confined to London, St. Petersburg and Berlin. The diplomats hoped that the coming war could be confined to a small war on the Balkans, as had happened in the past. Bethmann-Hollweg, the German chancellor suggested to the Austrians that they should consider acceptance of the British proposals for four-power mediation: "We must urgently and emphatically commend to the consideration of the Vienna Cabinet [i.e., the Austrian government] the acceptance of mediation," he wrote.

German plans were seriously dented by the nagging worry that Britain would, after all, support Russia and France in a war. Bethmann-Hollweg therefore advised the Austrians that, in view of the opposition of Britain and likely lack of support from Italy, she should undertake only 'minimal' measures against Serbia (the occupation of Belgrade, perhaps) and thus avoid a wider war among the powers.

The idea of mediation was quite attractive to Berlin because it would give Germany an important say in future arrangements in Europe. But the Austrians had other ideas and rejected Bethmann-Hollweg's proposal. The puppets were tugging at the strings and upsetting the plans of the puppet master! The German chancellor did not conceal his irritation: "We are ready… to fulfil our obligations as an ally, but must refuse to allow ourselves to be drawn by [Austria] into a world conflagration frivolously and in disregard of our advice."

Matters had taken a serious turn – serious enough for the Kaiser to interrupt his Scandinavian cruise and return to Berlin. Of particular concern was the position of Great Britain, which Wilhelm and his English wife were hoping would keep out of the conflict. But the Kaiser had been informed of alarming developments during his absence. Britain had decided to concentrate its fleet in the home ports (that is to say, that it must be ready for action). This was sufficient to cause a panic on the German stock exchange.

At this point, Wilhelm's nerves underwent a rapid transformation. The same man who was prodding the Austrians to take decisive action against the Serbs and crush them once and for all, now began to have second thoughts, no doubt encouraged by the thought that Germany would have to take on the most powerful navy in the world. Having read the Serb reply to the Austrian ultimatum, the Kaiser interpreted it as Serbia's capitulation to Austria's "wholly uncompromising attitude."

The Kaiser proposed that Austria should "halt in Belgrade," that is, to occupy the Serb capital as a preliminary to negotiations between Austria and Serbia. However, it seems more than likely that this was just an attempt to fool international public opinion and in particular to keep Britain out of the war. While publicly talking about mediation, Bethmann-Hollweg called on Austria to take early action in the absence of full compliance from Serbia. And behind the scenes, the Austrian ambassador in Germany quietly informed Vienna that the German government would not support the idea of Grey's mediation conference:

> Here it is universally taken for granted that an eventual negative reply by Serbia will be followed by a declaration of war from [Austria]… Any delay in commencement of military operations is regarded here [i.e., by the German government] (as presenting) a great danger of the interference of other Powers. They urgently advise us to go ahead and confront the

world with a fait accompli… The German government tenders the most binding assurances [to Austria] that it in no way associates itself with the (English) proposals (for mediation); is even decidedly against their being considered, and only passes them on in order to conform to the English request. [According to the Austrian chief-of-staff, sixteen days would be required before operations could begin, but, under German pressure, it was decided to declare war on 28 July.]

'THE WOLF AND THE LAMB'

In the end, the urgent appeals from London for a mediated settlement of the Balkan question were rejected by Berlin. The Kaiser noted: "It is futile, I will not join in." It is doubtful whether he ever intended to. The Austrian emperor finally signed the order for mobilisation. The one thing that might have avoided an escalation was for the Serbs to capitulate entirely to the Austrian demands. But, feeling confident of Russian support, Belgrade refused to surrender. Even if they had done so, it would not have prevented war, but merely led to new Austrian claims, such as payment for the costs of mobilisation. Such situations are frequently found whenever a more powerful state is looking for a pretext to attack a chosen victim.

The workings of diplomacy, which always aim to place the blame for war on the other side, were well described by old Aesop in his fable 'The Wolf and the Lamb':

> A Wolf, meeting with a Lamb astray from the fold, resolved not to lay violent hands on him, but to find some plea to justify to the Lamb the Wolf's right to eat him. He thus addressed him: "Sirrah, last year you grossly insulted me." "Indeed," bleated the Lamb in a mournful tone of voice, "I was not born then." "Very well," said the Wolf: "Then you are grazing in my pasture." "No, good sir," replied the Lamb, "I have not yet tasted grass." And the Wolf retorted: "You drink from my well." "No," exclaimed the Lamb, "I never yet drank water, for as yet my mother's milk is both food and drink to me." Upon which the Wolf seized him and ate him up, saying, "Well! I won't go without my supper, even though you refute every one of my accusations."

2. ON THE BRINK OF THE ABYSS

The moral is: The tyrant will always find a pretext for his tyranny. And so it was here. Buoyed by the assurances from Berlin, on 28 July at 6.00 pm, Austria declared war on Serbia. The very next day, Austrian artillery divisions commenced the bombardment of Belgrade across the Danube River. The war had been brought forward from the planned date of 12 August, apparently under pressure from Berlin.

This seems to confirm the suspicion that Bethmann-Hollweg was playing a double game – pretending to co-operate with Russia and Great Britain for mediation while urging on Austria to commence hostilities. In this respect it may not be an accident that the Kaiser's proposal was not forwarded to Vienna until the following day, *after* war had been declared. In any case, all these diplomatic comings and goings are irrelevant, because Austria was going to declare war on Serbia in any event. As always, the purpose of diplomacy is to make the other side responsible for one's own aggression, which must always seem to be of a defensive character.

Bethmann-Hollweg gave the game away when he sent the following directive to the German ambassador in Vienna:

> It is imperative that the responsibility for the eventual extension of the war among those nations not originally immediately concerned, should, under all circumstances, fall on Russia… you will have to avoid very carefully giving rise to the impression that we wish to hold Austria back. The case is solely one of finding a way to realize Austria's desired aim, that of cutting the vital cord of the Greater Serbian propaganda, without at the same time bringing on a world war, and, if the latter cannot be avoided in the end, of improving the conditions under which we shall have to wage it…

The Austro-Hungarian forces taught the Serbs a wonderful lesson in the values of civilisation. These heroes massacred, plundered and raped to their hearts' content, burning villages, hanging peasants and cutting the throats of men, women and children without distinction. But the same heroism was not displayed when they came face to face with the Serbian army. The Austrians thought that the invasion of Serbia would be a simple affair. But they were mistaken. They were thoroughly thrashed and driven back across the frontier as a disorganised rabble. But by now the echoes of the war were reverberating in St. Petersburg and Berlin.

3. THE STRANGE STORY OF THE KAISER AND THE TSAR

The Austrian attack on Serbia did not lead immediately to war with Russia. In St. Petersburg the generals were impatient to take action. However, Russian foreign minister Sazonov seems not to have shared the blind confidence of his generals. He feared the effects of war on the unstable political situation in Russia and was not convinced that the Russian army could win in a conflict with the formidable German military machine.

Instead, he favoured a partial mobilisation aimed at putting pressure on Austria to make her abandon the idea of war with Serbia. But the result was exactly the opposite. The threat posed by a Russian mobilisation only pushed Germany further towards Austria and to encourage the latter to hasten its aggressive plans.

In Berlin all eyes were now directed to the East. Reports were reaching the German government from Russia indicating outrage at Austria's bad faith in ignoring the extremely compliant Serbian reply to the Austrian note and declaring war on Serbia. But Russia had already performed a humiliating retreat over the Austrian annexation of Bosnia during the crisis of 1908-9. Why should one believe that she would fight now? The Germans and their Austrian satellites were prepared to gamble. But it was a very risky move.

To abandon the Serbs once more would have been a mortal blow to Russia's prestige. And prestige can play a very important part in world affairs. This assertion may strike one as strange. What is the value of prestige? It may be said to resemble the word honour, of which Falstaff says: "*What is honour? A word. What is in that word honour? What is that honour? Air.*" Yet on closer inspection there is more content to it than it would seem. In everyday life one finds people who try to gain personal prestige by dressing in the latest fashion and wearing expensive watches and jewellery. Many would regard this as cheap ostentation, mere appearance. Yet such appearances can have a material base. It may increase one's chances of obtaining credit or even a wealthy spouse. Prestige can carry a price tag, just like honour. How many young boys have been murdered for their designer trainers? Prestige can also kill you.

A nation's prestige can be measured in many ways: financial, industrial, cultural and so on and so forth. But ultimately, particularly in the case of what we call the great powers, prestige is measured by the size of your army, navy and air force. The US Marines have an interesting motto: "Speak softly and carry a big stick." Soft words may sometimes be effective, but they are infinitely more effective if the listener's attention is drawn to the presence of the big stick. Diplomacy tends to be most effective when it is backed up by the threat of military action. A great power that did not carry a very big stick would soon cease to be a great power. This may be a sad reflection on the current state of humankind, but it is undoubtedly true. Devout believers may object to this, but all history shows that Napoleon had a point when he said: "God is on the side of the big battalions".

Having been humiliated by Austria during the Bosnian crisis of 1908, Russia's ruling class could not tolerate a new and even more shameful humiliation by leaving Serbia in the lurch. Such a surrender would have completely undermined Russia's status as a great imperial and military power in Europe. It would have laid her open to further and even-more-insolent demands from both Austria and Germany. The Russian General Staff would never have tolerated it.

Before Austria had commenced hostilities, the German ambassador in St. Petersburg requested an interview with Sazonov. In the course of this amiable conversation, the purpose of which was clearly for the

Germans to get a clear idea of Russia's intentions, Sazonov admitted to the ambassador that "certain military preparations had already been taken to avoid surprises" but that mobilisation would not be ordered until Austria had crossed the Serb frontier.

Berlin was duly informed that Russia was preparing to mobilise its army. In vain the German government was advised that "no aggressive intention exists on the part of Russia towards Germany." Few people in Berlin were fooled by such tranquillising statements. The partial mobilisation of the Russian army (i.e., against Austria only) ordered in the wake of the Austrian declaration of war on Serbia only confirmed Berlin's suspicions.

DIVISIONS IN ST. PETERSBURG

The Russian ruling clique was divided, vacillating between Germany and the Entente. The ambitions of tsarist Russia in Asia provoked a lengthy conflict with the British Empire, leading to clashes over Turkey, Afghanistan and Persia and ultimately posing a threat to British rule in India. But Russian policy in Europe depended on an alliance with France, and the Entente Cordiale between Britain and France meant that, in order to preserve its alliance with France, Russia would have to move closer to Britain, despite their continued rivalry in Asia. British imperialism and tsarist Russia both wanted to halt the rise of German power in Europe. To that extent their interests coincided.

The inevitable outbreak of hostilities was preceded by the usual diplomatic manoeuvres. One of the most singular, not to say bizarre episodes of this period was the exchange of telegrams between the Kaiser and his cousin the Russian tsar, who he called "Nicky", urging him to "do what you can to stop your ally from going too far." The correspondence between the German Kaiser and the Russian tsar reads like a throwback to the days of the eighteenth and nineteenth centuries, when diplomacy could be conducted by the crowned heads of state, most of whom were related to each other by blood or marriage or both.

The tsar's German wife, Alex of Hesse, known as Alexandra Feodorovna, was a granddaughter of the British Queen Victoria. She was hated by most Russians, in the same way as Marie Antoinette ('the Austrian woman') was hated by the people of France before the Revolution. The pro-German clique at the court of St. Petersburg attempted to push Russia towards Germany and had even used the tsar to agree to a secret treaty with his cousin the German Kaiser. On 23 July, 1905, while Russia was in the grip of Revolution, the two monarchs met secretly on board the Kaiser's yacht, the *Hohenzollern*, to sign a defence treaty that read as follows:

> Their Imperial Majesties, the Emperor of All the Russias on the one side, and the German Emperor on the other, in order to ensure the peace of Europe, have placed themselves in accord on the following points of the herein treaty relative to a defensive alliance:
>
> Art. I. If any European state attacks one of the two empires, the allied party engages to aid the other contracting party with all his military and naval forces.
>
> Art. II. The high contracting parties engage not to conclude with any common enemy a separate peace.
>
> Art. III. The present treaty will become effective from the moment of the conclusion of the peace between Russia and Japan and may be denounced with a year's previous notification.
>
> Art. IV. When this treaty has become effective, Russia will undertake the necessary steps to inform France of it and to propose to the latter to adhere to it as an ally.
>
> [Signed] Nicholas. William.
>
> [Countersigned] Von Tschirschky. Count Bekendorf. Naval Minister, Birilev.

Unfortunately, the document was not worth the paper it was printed on. The dominant wing of the Russian ruling class understood very well that an alliance with Germany would mean the total subjugation of Russia. And nobody understood this better than Sergei Yulyevich Witte, the foremost representative of the liberal wing of the Russian

3. THE STRANGE STORY OF THE KAISER AND THE TSAR

aristocracy, who was then in a commanding position in the Russian government.

The Russian Revolution of 1905-6 obliged Witte to make concessions. Feeling the ground shake under his feet, and with a heavy heart, Nicholas made Witte a Count and gave him unprecedented powers as the Chairman of the Council of Ministers. Witte recommended reform from the top in order to prevent Revolution from below: sensible advice for which the tsar never forgave him. Nicholas accepted these recommendations reluctantly and issued the 17 October Manifesto, which supposedly turned Russia into a constitutional monarchy. That, of course, was just a smokescreen to allow Nicholas to manoeuvre to preserve his autocratic power. Having saved the throne, six months later Witte was rewarded by ignominious dismissal from the Imperial service.

However, all this was the music of the future. At the time of the pretended deal between Nicholas and Wilhelm, Witte was still in a strong enough position to override the tsar's foreign policy. As a firm supporter of the Entente, Witte insisted that the treaty could only come into effect if it was approved by France – that is, never. His authority shaken by the revolutionary storm, the tsar bit his lip and backed down. The tsar's deal with the Kaiser collapsed.

The cowardice of the tsar threw the Kaiser into one of his frequent rages. Wilhelm, appalled, vented his fury on his Imperial cousin: "We joined hands and signed before God, who heard our vows! What is signed is signed! And God is our witness!" Wilhelm did not yet know what it was to deal with insubordinate ministers in the middle of a Revolution. That pleasure awaited him in the autumn of 1918. As for the fact that the Almighty had been present on the Kaiser's yacht when the deal was signed and conferred His blessings upon it, that carried little weight with the Russian bourgeoisie where its material interests were concerned.

THE CORRESPONDENCE OF WILLIE AND NICKY
In the summer of 1914, the Kaiser tried his hand at diplomacy once more. This time his goals were more modest: to induce Russia to halt

the mobilisation and negotiate with Austria. But what was there to negotiate? The only way to avoid war would be for Russia to accept the rape of Serbia, to look the other way and do nothing while her principal ally on the Balkans was crushed under an Austrian soldier's jackboot.

The leading elements in the German General Staff wished to declare war on Russia immediately, before the Russians had a chance to carry out a projected reform of their armed forces that would pose a serious threat to Germany's eastern borders. But even at his stage, Wilhelm still imagined that he could talk his imperial cousin in Petersburg into halting the mobilisation of the Russian army. This is revealed in an astonishing exchange of telegrams.

Both the tsar and the Kaiser had to constantly look over their shoulders to interpret what their respective generals were thinking, for by now it was the General Staff that decided everything. The Russian generals believed, mistakenly, that Germany had begun her own mobilisation. The tsar therefore had to obey the military and issued the order for a general mobilisation to come into effect the following day, thus making a general war almost inevitable.

The tsar admitted that Russian secret military preparations had begun on 24 July. Cousin Willy expressed his displeasure. Cousin Nicky tried to justify the move:

Tsar to Kaiser
29 July 1914, 1.00 am
Peter's Court Palais, 29 July 1914
Sa Majesté l'Empereur
Neues Palais

Am glad you are back. In this serious moment, I appeal to you to help me. An ignoble war has been declared on a weak country [Serbia]. The indignation in Russia shared fully by me is enormous. I foresee that very soon I shall be overwhelmed by the pressure forced upon me and be forced to take extreme measures which will lead to war. To try and avoid such a calamity as a European war I beg you in the name of our old friendship to do what you can to stop your allies from going too far.

3. THE STRANGE STORY OF THE KAISER AND THE TSAR

Kaiser to Tsar
29 July 1914, 1.45 am (this and the previous telegraph crossed)
28 July 1914

It is with the gravest concern that I hear of the impression which the action of Austria against Serbia is creating in your country.

The unscrupulous agitation that has been going on in Serbia for years has resulted in the outrageous crime, to which Archduke Francis Ferdinand fell a victim. The spirit that led Serbians to murder their own king and his wife still dominates the country.

You will doubtless agree with me that we both, you and me, have a common interest as well as all Sovereigns to insist that all the persons morally responsible for the dastardly murder should receive their deserved punishment. In this case politics plays no part at all.

On the other hand, I fully understand how difficult it is for you and your Government to face the drift of your public opinion. Therefore, with regard to the hearty and tender friendship which binds us both from long ago with firm ties, I am exerting my utmost influence to induce the Austrians to deal straightly to arrive to a satisfactory understanding with you. I confidently hope that you will help me in my efforts to smooth over difficulties that may still arise.

Your very sincere and devoted friend and cousin,

Willy

Wilhelm here attempts to use psychology to influence his cousin by playing on the theme of the assassination of Franz Ferdinand. The Russian tsar was painfully aware of the risk posed to monarchs by revolutionary anarchists and terrorists, who had already succeeded in sending his grandfather Alexander II to an early grave. Did the Habsburg Monarchy not have a sacred duty to protect itself against the forces of anarchy and inflict upon the Serbs a well-deserved chastisement? And was it really worth risking an all-out European war to defend the wretched Serbs who, after all, had only themselves to blame for supporting terrorists?

> Kaiser to Tsar
> 29 July 1914, 6.30 pm
> Berlin, 29 July 1914
>
> I received your telegram and share your wish that peace should be maintained.
>
> But, as I told you in my first telegram, I cannot consider Austria's action against Serbia an 'ignoble' war. Austria knows by experience that Serbian promises on paper are wholly unreliable. I understand its action must be judged as trending to get full guarantee that the Serbian promises shall become real facts. This, my reasoning, is borne out by the statement of the Austrian cabinet that Austria does not want to make any territorial conquests at the expense of Serbia.
>
> I therefore suggest that it would be quite possible for Russia to remain a spectator of the Austro-Serbian conflict without involving Europe in the most horrible war she ever witnessed. I think a direct understanding between your Government and Vienna possible and desirable, and as I already telegraphed to you, my Government is continuing its exercises to promote it.
>
> Of course, military measures on the part of Russia would be looked upon by Austria as a calamity we both wish to avoid and jeopardise my position as mediator, which I readily accepted on your appeal to my friendship and my help.
>
> Willy

Diplomacy always functions at two different levels. On the official level, every attempt is made to sooth public opinion and deceive the other side concerning one's real intentions. On another level, preparations are being made for war. While the Kaiser whispers

3. THE STRANGE STORY OF THE KAISER AND THE TSAR

soothing words of peace in the ears of his beloved cousin in order to prevent a general mobilisation of the Russian armed forces, his generals are furiously speeding up plans for war with Russia and its ally, France. The Germans are actually stepping up their encouragement to Austria and become ever more insolent. The tsar, who is well informed about German duplicity, writes to his cousin in indignant tones:

> Tsar to Kaiser
> 29 July 1914, 8.20 pm
> Peter's Court Palace, 29 July 1914
>
> Thanks for your telegram conciliatory and friendly. Whereas official message presented today by your ambassador to my minister was conveyed in a very different tone. Beg you to explain this divergence! It would be right to give over the Austro-Serbian problem to the Hague conference. Trust in your wisdom and friendship.
>
> Your loving Nicky

Despite its tone of hurt innocence, the tsar's reply is conciliatory. Like a drowning man clinging to a rotten plank, he proposes that the disputed questions be referred for arbitration at the International Court at The Hague. This proposal is regarded (correctly) as "nonsense" by the Kaiser. On 30 July, the Russian proposal is rejected. Austria will not cease her military operations as long as Russia is mobilised, while Russia will not cease hers while Austria is at war with Serbia. Compared to this, the Gordian knot was a very simple matter! The tsar writes again in even more anxious tones:

> Tsar to Kaiser
> 30 July 1914, 1.20 am
> Peter's Court Palais, 30 July 1914
>
> Thank you heartily for your quick answer. Am sending Tatishchev this evening with instructions.

The military measures which have now come into force were decided five days ago for reasons of defence on account of Austria's preparations.

I hope from all my heart that these measures won't in any way interfere with your part as mediator which I greatly value. We need your strong pressure on Austria to come to an understanding with us.

Nicky

A perfunctory reply came back on 30 July 1914, 1.20 am:

Kaiser to Tsar
Berlin, 30 July 1914

Best thanks for telegram. It is quite out of the question that my ambassador's language could have been in contradiction with the tenor of my telegram. Count Pourtalès was instructed to draw the attention of your government to the danger & grave consequences involved by a mobilisation; I said the same in my telegram to you. Austria has only mobilised against Serbia & only a part of her army. If, as it is now the case, according to the communication by you & your Government, Russia mobilises against Austria, my role as mediator you kindly entrusted me with, & which I accepted at you[r] express prayer, will be endangered if not ruined. The whole weight of the decision lies solely on you[r] shoulders now, who have to bear the responsibility for Peace or War.

Willy

If the Russian army was mobilised, there would be very little point in asking Wilhelm to mediate anything. The only mediation possible would be that of bombs, shells and bayonets. The language of the Kaiser could not be clearer. Russia must immediately demobilise, or accept sole responsibility for the war that must inevitably ensue. Evidently the sacred bonds of family and friendship have their limits, a point that is made painfully clear in the following telegram:

3. THE STRANGE STORY OF THE KAISER AND THE TSAR

Kaiser to Tsar
31 July 1914
Berlin, 31 July 1914

On your appeal to my friendship and your call for assistance began to mediate between you and the Austro-Hungarian Government. While this action was proceeding your troops were mobilised against Austro-Hungary, my ally. Thereby, as I have already pointed out to you, my mediation has been made almost illusory.

I have nevertheless continued my action.

I now receive authentic news of serious preparations for war on my Eastern frontier. Responsibility for the safety of my empire forces preventive measures of defence upon me. In my endeavours to maintain the peace of the world I have gone to the utmost limit possible. The responsibility for the disaster, which is now threatening the whole civilised world, will not be laid at my door. In this moment it still lies in your power to avert it. Nobody is threatening the honour or power of Russia, who can well afford to await the result of my mediation. My friendship for you and your empire, transmitted to me by my grandfather on his deathbed has always been sacred to me and I have honestly often backed up Russia when she was in serious trouble, especially in her last war.

The peace of Europe may still be maintained by you, if Russia will agree to stop the milit[ary] measures, which must threaten Germany and Austro-Hungary.

Willy

Here the friendly forms of address are dispensed with altogether. In place of "Your very sincere and devoted friend and cousin" we have the dry language of an official communiqué, which, however, stands far closer to reality than the previous hypocritical protestations of love and friendship. The smiling mask has slipped to reveal the cruel and rapacious face of power politics. In reply, the Russian tsar displays a pathetic weakness that only serves to make his cousin even more implacable, for weakness always invites aggression:

Tsar to Kaiser
31 July 1914 (this and the previous telegram crossed)
Petersburg, Palace, 31 July 1914

Sa Majesté l'Empereur, Neues Palais

I thank you heartily for your mediation which begins to give one hope that all may yet end peacefully.

It is *technically* impossible to stop our military preparations which were obligatory owing to Austria's mobilisation. We are far from wishing war. As long as the negotiations with Austria on Serbia's account are taking place my troops shall not make any provocative action. I give you my solemn word for this. I put all my trust in God's mercy and hope in your successful mediation in Vienna for the welfare of our countries and for the peace of Europe.

Your affectionate,

Nicky

The appeals to the tender mercies of the Almighty have, of course, no effect. Far more important than Divine Intervention are the remarks about the *technical* impossibility of halting "military preparations which were obligatory owing to Austria's mobilisation". The difficulty was not at all of a technical but rather of a political character. The tsar simply could not go against his generals who had acted on military grounds. Translated into plain language, the tsar is saying: 'I cannot halt a mobilisation that was decided by my generals as a response to the activities of your Austrian friends.' To which the Kaiser might well have replied: 'Don't talk to me about your generals: I have generals of my own.'

Tsar to Kaiser
1 August 1914
Peter's Court Palace, 1 August 1914
Sa Majesté l'Empereur
Berlin

I received your telegram. Understand you are obliged to mobilise but wish to have the same guarantee from you as I gave you, that these measures do not mean war and that we shall continue negotiating for the benefit of our countries and universal peace deal to all our hearts. Our long-proved friendship must succeed, with God's help, in avoiding bloodshed. Anxiously, full of confidence await your answer.

Nicky

Once again, the tsar appeals to the Almighty and once more the Kaiser answers in the driest and most imperious tones:

Kaiser to Tsar
1 August, 1914
Berlin, 1 August 1914

Thanks for your telegram. I yesterday pointed out to your government the way by which alone war may be avoided.

Although I requested an answer for noon today, no telegram from my ambassador conveying an answer from your Government has reached me as yet. I therefore have been obliged to mobilise my army.

Immediate, affirmative, clear and unmistakable answer from your government is the only way to avoid endless misery. Until I have received this answer alas, I am unable to discuss the subject of your telegram. As a matter of fact, I must request you to immediately [sic] order your troops on no account to commit the slightest act of trespassing over our frontiers.

Willy

Wilhelm's excursion in the realm of diplomacy yielded no results. The Kaiser, sensing bad faith on the part of the Russians, broke off his attempts at mediation, which, in any case, were probably no more than a ploy to have Russia later branded as an aggressor. Following the insistent demands of the German High Command, Wilhelm demanded the impossible of his imperial cousin in St. Petersburg: immediate withdrawal of the Russian mobilisation order, a demand that would have signified a humiliating surrender that would have seriously undermined Russia's status as a great power.

The German government summarised its views on the crisis in a circular to its foreign ambassadors:

> The final object of the Pan-Slavic [i.e., Greater Serbia] agitations carried on against Austria-Hungary is… the destruction of the Danube Monarchy [i.e., the Austro-Hungarian empire], the breaking-up or weakening of the Triple Alliance (of Germany, Austria-Hungary and Italy), and, as a result, the complete isolation of the German empire. Accordingly, our own self-interest summons us to the side of Austria-Hungary.

ITALY BREAKS RANKS

Europe was now clearly divided into two armed camps: The Central Powers (Germany, Austro-Hungary and Italy with Romania as a subsidiary ally) and the Entente (France and Russia with the subsidiary support of Serbia and Montenegro). Britain, as usual, adopted an ambiguous position in an attempt to keep out of the war, a position it maintained right up to the eleventh hour.

While Germany was stiffening Austria's resolve and secretly urging her on to war, the French army chief was promising the Russian military attaché in Paris France's "full and active readiness faithfully to execute her responsibilities as an ally." It seems that both Germany and Austria believed that their combined strength would induce the other powers to back off. This was a grave miscalculation, and one that was further exposed when Italy suddenly broke away from the Central Powers.

The attitude of Italy, which until now had been an ally of both Germany and Austria, underwent a sudden change when she declined to act together with Austria whose "ultimatum was so aggressive and inept as to be unacceptable to Italian and European public opinion". The Italian diplomats – those worthy descendants of Machiavelli – were pursuing their trade with commendable vigour. It was one thing to attach oneself to an Alliance in time of peace, when it did not imply any kind of sacrifice or loss. It was quite another to continue in such an alliance in time of war, when very serious sacrifices were required.

Like Germany, Italy only achieved national independence in the last part of the nineteenth century. But the Italian bourgeoisie was not lacking in imperial ambition. It cast an envious glance at the empires of Britain and France and seemed to have harboured grandiose dreams of recreating the Roman Empire. For the time being, however, it satisfied itself with diplomatic manoeuvres and more modest schemes to seize bits of the Balkans and dominate the Adriatic Sea.

The weak Italian bourgeoisie was obliged to express its grandiose imperial ambitions in a series of diplomatic intrigues and manoeuvres, now sidling up to one Great Power, now to another, bartering its support in exchange for the promise of territorial expansion like an impecunious pimp importuning a wealthy client for custom. What the impotent Italian bourgeoisie lacked in power it made up for with cunning. Like the good, practical, hard-headed men of business that all real diplomats are at heart, the Italians promptly upped the price of their membership of the Central Powers, in accordance with the new market conditions.

Not receiving a satisfactory reply from their old allies, they naturally went to look for new customers who would offer them a more satisfactory price for their most valuable friendship. Being met in Paris and London with broad smiles, open arms and the most mouth-watering promises of rewards to come, they immediately broke off all relations with the tight-fisted and overbearing Austrians and Germans and rapidly drifted towards the camp of the Entente. The content of these conversations was revealed one year later, when Italy signed the secret Treaty of London. In this treaty Britain offered Italy large sections of territory in the Adriatic Sea region – parts of the Austrian Tyrol, Dalmatia and Istria.

The nationalists, with their dreams of a Greater Italy, were horrified at the government's decision to stay out of the war in 1914. But Mussolini, who at that time was a member of the Italian Socialist Party, came out against the war. In July 1914, when he reflected the general anti-war mood of the ranks of the party, he had written: "Down with the war. Down with arms and up with humanity." However, by October 1914, he had changed his mind and referred to the war as "a great drama": "Do you want to be spectators in this great drama? Or do you want to be its fighters?" Mussolini was consequently expelled from the Socialist Party and began moving in the direction of fascism.

Mussolini and the Italian chauvinists did not have long to wait to participate in the 'great drama'. On 26 April 1915, faithfully carrying out the orders of their masters in London and Paris, Italy entered the war. However, as so often happens in deals between Mafiosi, the Italian robbers never got all the rewards they had been promised. At Versailles the big robbers cheated the small ones. And as always, the ordinary people paid the price for the avarice of the ruling class.

By the end of the war in 1918, 600,000 Italians were dead, 950,000 were wounded and 250,000 were crippled for life. The war cost more than the government had spent in the previous fifty years. Italy had only been in the war for three years, but the country was ruined. With soaring inflation and mass unemployment, Italy was in the grip of mass strikes and factory occupations. In Italy too, war was only a preparatory school for revolution – and counter-revolution.

4. INTO THE ABYSS

Some thirty years ago the Danish physicist Per Bak wondered how the exquisite order seen in nature arises out of the disordered mix of particles. He found the answer in what we now know as phase transitions, the process by which a material transforms from one phase of matter to another, such as the transition from water to steam or from steam to plasma. The precise moment of transition – when the system is halfway between one phase and the other – is called the critical point, or, more colloquially, the 'tipping point'.

In studying avalanches, Per Bak used the analogy of sand running from the top of an hourglass to the bottom. The sand accumulates grain by grain until the growing pile reaches a point where it is so unstable that the addition of a single grain may cause it to collapse in an avalanche, which may be big or small. When a major avalanche occurs, the base widens, and the sand starts to pile up again, until the next critical point is reached. But there is no way to tell whether the next grain to drop will cause an avalanche or just how big an avalanche will be.

In point of fact, this idea was discovered long ago and found its most comprehensive exposition in Hegel's *Logic*. Modern science has proven beyond doubt that the law of the transformation of quantity into quality has a ubiquitous character and is present in a vast number of cases throughout the universe. There are tipping points not only in avalanches and nuclear reactions but also in heart attacks, forest fires, the rise and fall of animal populations, the movement of traffic in cities and many other spheres.

Despite all the stubborn attempts of the subjectivists to exclude human society from this general law, history furnishes a vast number of instances that prove that quantity turns into quality repeatedly. The same dialectical law can be observed in such phenomena as stock exchange crises, revolutions and wars. What happened in 1914 is a very good example of this.

The tensions between the major European powers, which were ultimately rooted in the struggle for markets, colonies and spheres of interest, were increasing steadily in the decades before 1914. They found their expression in a series of 'incidents', each of which contained the potential for the outbreak of war. If they did not reach this logical conclusion, that was because the objective conditions were not yet sufficiently mature. These incidents are similar to the small landslides that precede a major avalanche in the above example.

The First World War could have broken out on several occasions before 1914. In 1905-6, an international crisis erupted when Germany clashed with France over the latter's attempts to get control over Morocco. In 1904, France had concluded a secret treaty with Spain for the partitioning of Morocco, having also agreed not to oppose Britain's moves to grab Egypt. This deal between two robbers, however, enraged another would-be robber, Germany. Under the hypocritical guise of supporting an 'open-door' policy in the area (which meant leaving the door open for the German robbers), Berlin was preparing to establish its own control in the region.

In a typically theatrical display of imperial power, Kaiser Wilhelm II visited Tangier. From the comfort of the imperial yacht on 31 March, 1905, he declared his support for the independence and integrity of Morocco. This was the cause of the First Moroccan Crisis. It provoked an international panic, which was resolved the following year by the Algeciras Conference. A gentleman's agreement was reached between the different robbers whereby Germany's economic rights were recognised, while the French and Spanish robbers were allowed to 'police' Morocco. Naturally, nobody ever asked the people of Morocco whether they either needed or desired such policemen on their streets, but they got them anyway.

THE VIEW FROM LONDON

In the middle of the First Moroccan Crisis Sir Edward Grey was appointed British Foreign Secretary and remained in office until the outbreak of war. The Entente Cordiale between Britain and France was still recent and it was clear that, by stepping on the toes of French imperialism in North Africa, Germany was trying to test the new partnership or even destroy it. Berlin's aim was to isolate France, expose Russia's weakness, and British perfidy. Britain would have to decide whether or not to stand by the French. In the end it was compelled to do so.

The most important thing for British imperialism was to ensure its rule in Egypt. As part of the deal, London would support France in Morocco. If Britain had remained neutral in this conflict, the Entente Cordiale would have been as dead as a dodo and France and Russia might even have moved closer to Germany against Britain. Grey warned that:

> [T]he French will never forgive us… Russia would not think it worthwhile to make a friendly arrangement with us about Asia… we should be left without a friend and without the power of making a friend and Germany would take some pleasure… in exploiting the whole situation to our disadvantage. (Williams, B., *Great Britain and Russia: 1905-1907*, in Hinsley, F.H., *British Foreign Policy Under Sir Edward Grey*, pp. 133-4.)

Nevertheless, Britain was still reluctant to get involved in any war on the European continent, and Grey did everything in his power to avoid any diplomatic commitment that could lead to such an entanglement. London entered into an agreement with Russia, while assuring Germany that there was no intention to encircle it. Although that was indeed the intention, he was anxious not to arouse German suspicion, which might provoke Germany into a war to destroy a hostile and threatening encirclement.

There were new tensions in the Balkans in 1907 when Austria-Hungary annexed Bosnia and Bulgaria declared its independence, which led to a diplomatic clash between Austria and Russia. But, still reeling from a humiliating defeat in the war with Japan and the 1905-6 Revolution, Russia backed down.

THE AGADIR INCIDENT

On 8 February, 1908, a new deal was signed between the French and German robbers, in which they solemnly ratified Morocco's independence, while at the same time recognising France's 'special political interests' and Germany's 'economic interests' in North Africa. But robbers are never satisfied and are always casting envious glances at the loot in the other man's bag. Not long after the deal was struck, the Second Moroccan Crisis (the Agadir Incident) exploded. This time, instead of the Kaiser's yacht, the Germans dispatched the gunboat, Panther.

In April 1911, contravening the agreement of the Algeciras Conference, France despatched troops to Fez to suppress an uprising by the 'natives', who were apparently somewhat dissatisfied with the services of their foreign policemen. In response, the Germans sent the Panther to Agadir on 1 July. It was not that Berlin objected to the French killing Arabs. On the contrary, they backed it. But this action, taken allegedly to protect German interests, was in reality intended to intimidate the French. The robbers in Berlin demanded compensation from the bandits in Paris for keeping their nose out of Morocco.

Once again, the international scene was racked by tension. The threat of war was in the air. The British even started to make preparations for war. But conditions for an all-out war had not yet ripened sufficiently and, once again, a diplomatic solution was found. The robbers argued over a division of the colonial spoils. Behind the scenes the real aim of this deal was to split the Entente.

The gentlemen in London were annoyed that France had disturbed the status quo. This was decidedly 'not cricket'. The British were inclined to the view that Germany was entitled to compensation – as long as someone else paid the bill. On the other hand, British interests demanded that the Entente be preserved and French toes not be trodden upon. A tricky situation indeed!

Germany wanted to humiliate France by demanding the whole of the French Congo in return for German non-intervention in Morocco. Such a demand, as Eyre Crowe, the foremost expert on Germany at the British Foreign Office, remarked, was "not such as a country having an independent foreign policy can possibly accept". Since Britain held the balance in Europe, it was able to twist arms in Berlin, as well as in Paris, to get what it wanted: the preservation of the European equilibrium and the avoidance of war, which was a distinct possibility at that time. In the end, France was given the right, not just to police the ungrateful Moroccans, but to exercise a protectorate over them. In return, the Germans were thrown a few scraps of territory from the French Congo.

Morocco's old colonial masters in Spain naturally complained at this grossly unfair decision, but a disapproving growl from the British lion was enough to silence them. The French were very happy, the Germans less so and the Spanish less still. But the British were satisfied and war had been averted. As for the Moroccans and Congolese, nobody thought their views on the subject worth recording.

THE NAVAL QUESTION

The Agadir Incident had carried Europe to the brink of war. But of far more fundamental importance to the interests of British imperialism was the alarming growth of German naval power. A basic principle of London's foreign policy was that Britain must have naval superiority. But attempts to get Germany to limit its programme of naval expansion only aroused resentment and hostility in Berlin, which offered only to slow the pace of naval expansion, and then only on condition that Britain would remain neutral in a European war. The British refused to give any such undertaking, which would have alienated France and Russia and left her powerless and isolated.

The attempts of British diplomacy (the Haldane Mission) to placate Germany only created an impression of weakness, and weakness invited aggression. Admiral von Tirpitz replied angrily that he would not accept the suggestion of a reduction of his fleet by even a single ship. To persist in negotiations when there was nothing to discuss was an act of stupidity that merely served to convince the generals and politicians in Berlin that Britain would not fight in a European war, an idea that persisted right up to the summer of 1914 and played a fatal role in Germany's calculations.

They went on to haggle over colonial and territorial exchanges like merchants in the market place. Germany agreed to give Britain a controlling interest in the southern section of the Baghdad Railway in return for Zanzibar and Pemba and a slice of Angola. But these were minor matters of an entirely secondary importance. By accepting the German offer of a reduction in the tempo of naval construction instead of reducing the size of the German navy, Haldane gave von Tirpitz and the Kaiser what they wanted and got almost nothing in return.

Emboldened by their success, the Germans again demanded British neutrality in a European war. Sir Edward Grey prevaricated. Instead of rejecting this insolent demand out of hand, he suggested an ambiguous formula to the effect that: "England shall neither make nor join in any unprovoked attack upon Germany".

Here we have a truly classical example of the meaningless language of the diplomatic Pharisees. What is the meaning of the word unprovoked? The very notion of a promise not to make an unprovoked attack is absurd, since every country will decide to go to war whenever it suits their interests to do so, and provocations are the easiest things in the world to manufacture.

In underlining that word 'unprovoked', Grey was resorting to diplomatic trickery, angling to cast British imperialism as arbiter in a future conflict between France and Germany and not a combatant. But once again this showed weakness and confirmed the belief in Berlin that, in the event of war, Britain would not want to fight. Far from saving Britain from war, it brought war a lot closer.

THE TIPPING POINT

Events then reached the tipping point at which there could be no turning back. When news of the Russian mobilisation reached Berlin at midday on 31 July, Germany had the excuse it needed to proclaim a state of 'threatening danger of war'. The 'Cossack menace' gave the Kaiser and his generals the green light to justify before the German people and world opinion a move against Russia and her ally France. Here again the question of who fires the first shot is of no importance. German imperialism was acting in accordance with war plans that had been drawn up a long time before.

In response, France ordered military preparations for the protection of her frontier with Germany, though no troops were to move closer than about six miles from the German border. All this time the French president was straining every muscle and nerve to get Britain to declare her intention to support France in the face of the threat from Germany. But the British, to the furious indignation of the French, remained stubbornly non-committal, at least in public, intending to keep their hands free until the last minute and avoid any firm commitment.

In a desperate attempt to secure such a commitment, the French government assured London that "France, like Russia, will not fire the first shot". But "who fired the first shot" can never determine who was really responsible for a war, or even who was the aggressor and who was the victim. It is always possible to manufacture an incident, to provoke someone into firing the first shot and thus to convince public opinion that the aggressor is really the victim and the victim is really the aggressor.

From the standpoint of British imperialism, the most crucial question was Belgium. The insistence on Belgian neutrality was, however, not dictated by sentimentality or any attachment to the sacred principle of self-determination. Britain was concerned about Belgium only to the extent that it was determined to stop any power dominating the continent and, more specifically, if the Belgian ports fell into the hands of an enemy power, that would present a serious threat to British naval supremacy and open the possibility of an invasion of Britain itself. These were the real reasons why the British ruling class had no real option but to enter the War.

The British issued a memorandum to France and Germany requesting assurances that Belgian neutrality would be respected. France gave an immediate unqualified assurance. Germany ignored the request. Threatened to the East by the Russian mobilisation, the German General Staff needed to deliver a crushing blow to the West, defeat France and knock her out of the war before the mighty Russian army had a chance to cross Germany's eastern frontier.

Since the French had taken the precaution of strengthening their frontier defences against a German attack, the only logical road to take was through neutral Belgium. In London, yet another tense conversation took place between Grey and the French ambassador, Paul Cambon, in which the latter asked whether England would help France if she were attacked by Germany. Even at this late hour Grey's reply was evasive: "…as far as things had gone at present… we could not undertake any definite engagement." France and Germany were kept guessing as regards Britain's intentions.

Now it was Germany's turn to ask France to declare its intentions, and to do so within eighteen hours. France replied cryptically that she would "act in accordance with her interests". In practice, there is nothing the French could have done to avert the danger of war. It was later revealed that, if France had opted for neutrality, Germany would have demanded the turning over to Germany of her vital frontier fortresses of Toul and Verdun, to be held as a pledge of French neutrality until the end of the war with Russia. It was the tale of the wolf and the lamb all over again, except that in this case it was the tale of two rival wolves snapping and snarling at each other, one older and fatter, the other leaner and hungrier.

Already, on 26 July, a document had been drafted in Berlin containing a demand for "benevolent Belgian neutrality", that is to say, Belgium must give German troops free access to its territory. On 3 August, Belgium refused the German demands and Germany declared war on France. The following day, 4 August, German troops crossed the Belgian frontier and blasted the Belgian defensive fortifications with heavy artillery. The British reaction was immediate. London issued an ultimatum to Germany. Its rejection meant war with Germany. Two days later, Austria declared war on Russia.

The German army advanced, scoring relatively easy victories that gave Germany control over most of Belgium and some parts of northern France, with its rich agriculture and important industries. Everywhere, the German army looted, burned and pillaged, earning the hatred of the population. In Belgium, they shot anyone suspected of being a sniper or of opposing the German army in any way. They took hostages and inflicted brutal massacres of the civilian population.

The German atrocities in Belgium provided the British with a rich supply of gruesome stories about the 'Hun brutality', some true, some invented, all suitably embellished by expert propagandists. These stories were used to demonise the enemy, who are presented as inhuman monsters, and thus aid recruitment. But the propaganda about 'poor little Belgium' was entirely hypocritical. The British imperialists went to war because they saw German domination of Europe as a threat to Britain's position in the world and German ambitions as a threat to the British Empire.

In his memoirs, Sir Edward Grey mentioned the remark he made on 3 August, 1914. It sounded like an obituary for the old world:

> A friend came to see me on one of the evenings of the last week – he thinks it was on Monday, August 3rd. We were standing at a window of my room in the Foreign Office. It was getting dusk, and the lamps were being lit in the space below on which we were looking. My friend recalls that I remarked on this with the words: "The lamps are going out all over Europe. We shall not see them lit again in our life-time".

It was the start of the Great Slaughter.

5. THE GREAT SLAUGHTER BEGINS

How do you commemorate a war that swept away four empires, killed 18 million people and left tens of millions of others with their lives shattered? A very good question, and now we have the answer. As the world marks the centenary of the Great Slaughter, our television screens are full of programmes dedicated to the systematic trivialisation of that catastrophe.

We have learned professors expressing their opinions as to whether the War was really necessary, and who was really to blame, and so on and so forth. In the end, we are none the wiser, but we have hopefully spent a pleasurable hour or so in front of the television screen.

WAR AS ENTERTAINMENT

In this orgy of saccharine nostalgia, the old songs such as 'Pack Up Your Troubles in Your Old Kit Bag, and Smile, Smile, Smile' are repeated ad nauseam to show what a jolly affair it all was. School children have even been encouraged to build replica trenches out of papier-mâché, thankfully without the mud, blood, rats and human excrement that would have been found in the genuine article. Whatever will they think of next? Will they encourage kids to produce chlorine and mustard gas in the school laboratory?

To be absolutely fair, the occasional mention is made to the 'terrible waste of war'. But such depressing digressions do not last long enough to deprive us of the immensely enjoyable spectacle provided by memories of the Great War. The other night we were treated to a programme about the Woolwich Arsenal factory, where women workers, producing arms and explosives for the front, were brutally exploited, exposed to overwork, appalling conditions and poisons that ruined their health and, in some cases, drove them to suicide.

That was a good idea in principle, but for some reason, known only to the producers, it was all seen through the eyes of a wealthy lady who, bored by her life of pampered inactivity, took herself off to the factory to see how the other side (not the Germans, but the working class) lived. Indignant at the treatment of 'those poor wretches', she actually joined a trade union and was promptly sacked, whereupon she returned to her luxurious home in Mayfair (or wherever it was) where, presumably, she lived happily ever after. In short, what we have here is nothing more or less than War as entertainment for the masses.

WHY DID THEY FIGHT?

Some people have expressed wonder that so many could have been won over so quickly to the cause of war. Why did so many ordinary working-class people flock to the flag? In reality, there is no great mystery about it. It was a relatively easy matter for the governments to stir up an orgy of patriotic flag waving. One sees the same thing at the start of almost every war. The vast propaganda machine swung into action. The story was different, as were the names of the enemy, but every government used identical methods to demonise the other side and whip up pro-war sentiment among the masses. The Austrian government played up the assassination in Sarajevo to intensify anti-Serb moods. The German government played on fears of an invasion by hordes of barbarous Cossacks. The British and French governments played on the theme of German atrocities in Belgium. None of them, it seems, were aggressors but all were the innocent victims of unprovoked aggression by the other side.

The press (nowadays the mass media, which are considerably more powerful than they were in 1914), the preachers in the pulpits, the politicians, schoolteachers, university lecturers and other 'formative

5. THE GREAT SLAUGHTER BEGINS

influences on public opinion', were immediately mobilised to churn out masses of material aimed at demonising the enemy and creating a mood of war fever. By degrees people began to see war not just as inevitable but even desirable.

In those days the Church was far more influential in people's lives than today. In every one of the belligerent nations the priests and pastors lined up to bless the War. Catholics and Protestants, Orthodox and Lutherans, all assured the faithful that God was on their side, although how one and the same God could be on the side of so many antagonistic states it is difficult to explain. The clouds of incense helped to dull the senses of the hundreds of thousands of men marching to their doom to the sound of trumpets and drums. And since God was on their side, who could argue with that?

The leaders of all the political parties naturally fell over themselves in their efforts to wave the flag and shout patriotic slogans louder than the others. Their patriotic speeches were reproduced in the pages of the newspapers the very next day. But the most advanced workers did not necessarily believe what they read in the papers, which they knew were owned and controlled by their enemies, the bankers and capitalists. If the trade union and labour leaders had opposed the War, if there had been just one dissenting voice, that could have made a difference. But the labour leaders were more anxious to prove their devotion to the ruling class of 'their' nation, and hastened to enter governments of wartime coalition with the bourgeoisie.

But there was another reason why so many went voluntarily to war. For many workers, joining the army was seen as an adventure, a means of escaping from a hard, dreary and monotonous existence. The people of Britain in particular had forgotten what war was like. The wars against Napoleon were a distant memory. The recent Boer War in South Africa was little more than a skirmish from the British point of view (though not from the point of view of the Afrikaner farmers and their families) and, in any case, it ended in victory. Nobody could imagine the horrors that were being prepared when twentieth century science and technology would be combined with the cannibalism that humankind has inherited from the Palaeolithic.

In my house there is a big old bible complete with coloured pictures of men with flowing robes and long beards, its huge pages closed with metal clasps. This was the family bible, which contains the details of the births and deaths of family members, starting with my grandparents.

There is also a whole page entitled Roll of Honour, being a record of the members of this family who served in the Great War. It is resplendent in colour, bordered with the draped flags and banners of our allies: France, Belgium, Italy, the USA and, ironically, the twin headed eagle of tsarist Russia. It shows that George Woods, just eighteen years of age, volunteered for the army on the 1 September, 1914 – which was just about as soon as he could – and he served in the artillery in France throughout the war, being finally demobilised on 21 January, 1919.

In 1914, my grandfather was a young worker in a tinplate factory in Swansea, South Wales. His was a life of hard and relentless graft and just enough wages to survive on. On his arm there was a tattoo of red and blue of a lady with a helmet on her head carrying a large shield. I was fascinated by this tattoo, which I later learned was a picture of Britannia, the ultimate symbol of the greatness of imperial Britain. I guess he must have had it done shortly after joining the army, possibly in France. When I was a child, I would ask him about the War, hoping to hear stirring stories about battles and glory. But to my great disappointment he would never talk to me about it, except to say: "It was just workers fighting each other for the cause of the rich people."

That tattoo tells me that, in 1914, like many other young men who went to fight in France, he had been a convinced patriot, and that big old bible tells me that he had also once been a religious man. But the War changed all that. My grandfather was one of the lucky ones. He was gassed, which affected his lungs, but, unlike many of his comrades, he survived. The experience of the War and the bitter class struggles that followed it changed him forever. He became an active trade unionist, an ardent supporter of the Russian Revolution and joined the Communist Party. He kept his fervent socialist beliefs until the end of his life.

5. THE GREAT SLAUGHTER BEGINS

FEAR OF REVOLUTION

The betrayal of the leaders of the Second International in voting for the war credits provided an immense service to the ruling classes on both sides. It demoralised and disoriented the workers and delivered them, bound hand and foot to the imperialists. 'Our leaders are supporting the government, so the war must be a just one,' they would conclude. This was a not an unimportant factor that would explain why millions of workers on both sides eagerly joined the army in the early stages of the War. Everywhere, the left wing and the internationalists found themselves isolated and helpless in the face of the unstoppable wave of patriotism.

For some governments, fear of revolution was precisely what inclined them to go to war. That was certainly the case with Russia. During the two years before the outbreak of war, Russia was in the throes of a new revolution. The workers had finally recovered from the defeat of the 1905 Revolution and had launched a wave of strikes and mass demonstrations. The influence of the Bolsheviks over the working class was growing exponentially. This revolutionary upsurge culminated in the great general strike of July 1914, which paralysed more than four-fifths of St Petersburg's industrial, manufacturing and commercial plants. One right-wing newspaper described the situation as revolutionary, saying "We live on a volcano". In July 1914, when the French President Poincaré was in Petersburg to discuss the international situation with the tsar, he was shocked to see barricades in the streets and red flags everywhere.

The outbreak of war in early August 1914 cut across all this. The class struggle was drowned in a torrent of flag-waving patriotism. When conscription orders were distributed, more than ninety-five per cent of conscripts reported willingly for duty, most of them backward and illiterate peasants under the influence of the priest and easy prey to patriotic propaganda. In the ranks of the tsarist army the workers were in a small minority. The voice of the revolutionaries was silenced by the din of patriotic slogans and hymns. The Bolshevik Party was smashed, its leaders arrested.

Yet the war itself posed dangers that the most far-sighted representatives of the ruling class understood only too well. Sir Edward

Grey's words about the lights going out all over Europe are well known. But not so well known are other words that express very clearly the fears of a section of the ruling class of the ultimate consequences of a world war. In his autobiographical work he quotes his warning: "It is the greatest step towards Socialism that could possibly have been made. We shall have Labour governments in every country after this." (Grey, E., *Twenty-five Years*, vol. 2, p. 234.)

Sir Edward's prediction was shown to be correct. The War, despite all its horrors, eventually turned into a vast school for revolution, sweeping aside kings and empires and raising the working class to the level where power was within its grasp in one country after another.

BATTLE OF THE MARNE

In the beginning, everybody was convinced that the war would be a short one. All the belligerent powers based their plans on this supposition. The British did not even believe that there would be any need to put soldiers on the ground; Britain's contribution, they thought, would be confined to the navy. In reality, the mighty British navy barely participated in the fighting. It quickly became clear that the German Army threatened to defeat the French and Belgian armies, and the British were forced to come to their aid. The War in Europe, as in the past, would be fought by the 'poor bloody infantry'.

But in the beginning, this was not understood. 'We will be home by Christmas' was the common delusion of the soldiers of all the armies. And it goes without saying that they would all return victorious. They were to experience a terrible lesson in the trenches and killing fields of the Marne and the Somme, in Tannenberg and Gallipoli. But that was still in the future.

The first battles of the War were unlike the later bloody battles of attrition fought out in the trenches. On the contrary, the start of the War was an extremely mobile affair in which, for the last time (at least on the western front), cavalry played a prominent role. The First Battle of the Marne took place just thirty miles northeast of Paris in the Marne River Valley of France from 6-12 September, 1914. Following the Schlieffen Plan worked out before the War, the Germans were hoping to win a quick victory in the West before the Russians could attack from the East.

So confident were the men in Berlin of success that they believed the French would be knocked out of the war within three weeks. This was wildly optimistic, but at first, they seemed poised to do just that. The Germans advanced rapidly towards Paris, while the French Army crumbled before the violence of the onslaught. By the first week of September, the French government had fled from Paris. The German First and Second Armies (led by Generals Alexander von Kluck and Karl von Bülow respectively) were following parallel paths southward, with the First Army a little to the west and the Second Army slightly to the east.

Kluck and Bülow had been ordered to approach Paris as a unit, supporting one another. But, instead of heading directly to Paris, Kluck decided to pursue the exhausted, retreating French Fifth Army. Intoxicated by his early successes, Kluck pressed onwards. His telegrams to Berlin were triumphant and over-confident, as if it were all just a pleasant stroll in the countryside. But, in opening up a gap between the German First and Second Armies, he exposed the First Army's right flank to a French counter-attack.

On 3 September, Kluck's First Army crossed the Marne River and entered the Marne River Valley. In 1914, the French army was heavily outnumbered. But they were fighting with their backs to Paris and, when they staged a surprise attack in the First Battle of the Marne, the position was dramatically reversed. Troops on both sides were exhausted from the long and fast march south, but the French, closer to Paris, had the advantage of shorter supply lines, while those of the advancing Germans were stretched to breaking point.

The Battle of the Marne was the first of a series of bloody slaughters. It seemed impossible that a broken and demoralised army could turn and fight, but that was what happened. The French fought with desperate bravery. It was during this battle that Foch is said to have sent the celebrated telegram to Joffre: "Mon centre cède, ma droite recule, situation excellente, j'attaque." [My centre is giving way, my right is retreating, situation excellent, I am attacking.]

The German advance was brought to a shuddering halt, but at a terrible cost in lives. Casualties for the French forces (killed and wounded) were roughly estimated at 250,000 men; German casualties were about the same. The far smaller British force lost 12,733.

The Germans fell back to the Aisne valley, where they prepared to stand and fight. In the Battle of the Aisne, the Allied forces were unable to break through the German line, and the fighting quickly degenerated into a stalemate, with neither side willing to give ground. Bleeding profusely from the wounds inflicted by the Battle of the Marne, the German army was forced to abandon its idea of a quick victory and dig trenches for defensive purposes.

With the repulse of the German army at the Marne, the nature of the War underwent a profound transformation. At first, the digging of trenches was only meant to be a temporary measure, but it marked a fundamental change in the military tactics. The days of open warfare were over. Both sides were now stuck in the mud and blood of the trenches. Men remained trapped in these underground lairs until the end of the war. And the war that was supposed to be over by Christmas was to last for four long years.

However, the revolutionary change in tactics did not immediately lead to a corresponding change in the mentality of the generals. The French Commander-in-Chief, Joffre, even in comparison with the many brutal and incompetent generals of the First World War, stands out as a brilliant example of lack of military talent and humanity in equal measure. Behind his large beneficent face, with its permanent expression of absolute imperturbability, there lay a mind so rigid that it might have belonged to a mummified Pharaoh. Here, mule-like obstinacy and imbecile inflexibility acted as substitutes for that genuine tenacity and audacity that are the necessary qualities of a great commander.

Firmly convinced of his absolute superiority to the human race, and his fellow officers in particular, Joffre saw himself as the God-given saviour of France. Foch said of him that, despite his lack of originality, he never hesitated to make a decision and "he did not know what France would do without him." Needless to say, le pere Joffre, as he was known, never changed his mind once it was made up, or allowed anything to interfere with his sleep.

Displaying the most complete indifference to the loss of life among his own troops, Joffre was constantly putting pressure on them to go onto the offensive. The French army was ordered into a series of senseless piecemeal attacks, the only result of which was heavy casualties. The attacking units were mown down by merciless rifle and machine gun fire long before they even reached the enemy trenches. Many casualties were left to die agonising deaths lying in no man's land or dangling like scarecrows on the enemy barbed wire. But Commander-in-Chief Joffre slept soundly.

CHRISTMAS IN THE TRENCHES, 1914

The German defeat at the Marne put an end to Berlin's dreams of a quick victory. It also put an end to Moltke's military career. He was summarily dismissed. But if anything, the disappointment on the side of the Allies was still greater. The Germans, despite their defeat, were left in control of around one tenth of the territory of France. Moreover, the occupied territory included some of her richest agricultural lands, eighty per cent of her coal, almost the whole of her iron resources and much of her industries. The Allies had won a battle but not the War, which had now produced a deadlock.

The first trenches were merely improvised affairs, often just shell-holes in which terrified soldiers would take refuge from the devastating hail of machine-gun bullets. But soon they acquired a more stable and complex character, especially on the German side, where the soldiers enjoyed far better conditions than their French and British counterparts. Their trenches were deeper, better protected and provided with kitchens and other amenities.

All wars consist of short bursts of violent activity separated by long periods of boredom. The static nature of trench warfare and its sheer tedium led to a growing curiosity about what was happening on the other side. The close proximity of the enemy meant that they could be heard although rarely seen. The smells from their breakfast cooking reached the men on the other side, who were facing the same conditions of wet and cold as they. There were occasional shouted conversations between trenches, and in some cases, an exchange of goods. In this way a mutual respect began to develop that prepared the way for fraternisation.

In the early months of immobile trench warfare, there was a kind of mood of 'live and let live', whereby soldiers in close proximity to each other would cease fighting and engage in small-scale fraternisation. In some sectors, there would be unofficial truces to allow soldiers to leave the trenches and recover wounded or dead comrades. Sometimes they would arrive at a tacit agreement not to shoot while men rested, exercised, or worked in full view of the enemy.

On 1 January 1915, the *Norfolk Chronicle* and *Norwich Gazette* published the following letter that provides an eye-witness account of this:

> Amusing trench incident. 'Tommy' and 'Fritz' exchange presents. One of the oddities of the war in the Western battlefields at all events (says the *Daily Chronicle*) is the close proximity of the opposing forces in the trenches, thus giving opportunities for conversation. But the record must surely be made by an incident described in a letter from Private H. Scrutton, Essex Regiment, to relatives at Wood Green, Norwich. He writes:
>
> "As I told you before, our trenches are only 30 or 40 yards away from the Germans. This led to an exciting incident the other day. Our fellows have been in the habit of shouting across to the enemy and we used to get answers from them. We were told to get into conversation with them and this is what happened: From our trenches: 'Good morning, Fritz.' (No answer). 'Good morning, Fritz.' (Still no answer). 'GOOD MORNING, FRITZ.' From German trenches: 'Good morning.' From our trench: 'How are you?' 'All right.' 'Come over here, Fritz.' 'No. If I come, I get shot.' 'No, you won't. Come on.' 'No fear.' 'Come and get some fags, Fritz.' 'No. You come half way and I meet you.' 'All right.' One of our fellows thereupon stuffed his pocket with fags and got over the trench. The German got over his trench, and right enough they met half way and shook hands, Fritz taking the fags and giving cheese in exchange. It was good to see the

5. THE GREAT SLAUGHTER BEGINS

Germans standing on top of their trenches and the English also, with caps waving in the air, all cheering. About 18 of our men went half way and met about the same number of Germans. This lasted about half an hour when each side returned to their trenches to shoot at each other again. What I have written is the truth but don't think we got chums as two of our fellows were killed the same night, and I don't know how many of them."

The dangers inherent in this were not lost on the generals. They were particularly concerned about the approach of the Christmas season. On 5 December, 1914, II Corps HQ [General Sir Horace Smith-Dorrien] issued an instruction to commanders of all Divisions:

> It is during this period that the greatest danger to the morale of troops exists. Experience of this and of every other war proves undoubtedly that troops in trenches in close proximity to the enemy slide very easily, if permitted to do so, into a 'live and let live' theory of life... officers and men sink into a military lethargy from which it is difficult to arouse them when the moment for great sacrifices again arises... the attitude of our troops can be readily understood and to a certain extent commands sympathy... such an attitude is however most dangerous for it discourages initiative in commanders and destroys the offensive spirit in all ranks... the Corps Commander therefore directs Divisional Commanders to impress on subordinate commanders the absolute necessity of encouraging offensive spirit... friendly intercourse with the enemy, unofficial armistices, however tempting and amusing they may be, are absolutely prohibited.

But such prohibitions were powerless to stop the tendency towards fraternisation. The snatches of carol singing that drifted over the trenches in the week leading up to Christmas encouraged German and British soldiers to exchange seasonal greetings and songs between their trenches. Finally, they began to venture out of the relative safety of their dugouts and establish direct contact with the other side, exchanging gifts and souvenirs.

Instinctively, the workers in uniform realised that the men in the other trenches were workers like themselves, engaged in a senseless slaughter to protect the interests of kings, lords and capitalists. Many soldiers from both sides spontaneously walked into no man's land (the area between the German and British) trenches, where they exchanged food and cigarettes and even held joint burial ceremonies, sometimes with meetings ending in carol-singing.

The Germans began by placing candles on their trenches and on Christmas trees, then continued the celebration by singing carols, to which the British replied with their own songs. On Christmas Eve, 1914, both sides declared an unofficial truce and a football match was played in no man's land. In some places the truce lasted a week. It is calculated that as many as 100,000 men took part.

A most touching story, and it happens to be true. But it is not one with a happy ending. The officer caste on both sides was enraged by this spontaneous move to fraternise with 'the enemy'. The following Christmas, sentries on both sides had orders to shoot any soldier who tried to spread the Christmas message of 'peace on earth and good will to all men'. Any soldier who put his head above the parapet would receive a small Christmas present in the shape of a bullet in the brain.

The aim of the ruling class is always to divide the working class along national, racial, linguistic and other lines. This is even more necessary in war than in peacetime. The generals were horrified by the instinctive fraternisation of the workers in uniform. The posting of snipers along the front line was designed precisely to prevent any further fraternisation and to foment hatred against 'the enemy' at all times. This barbarity was finally ended by the Russian Revolution, which immediately broke down the iron barriers that divided soldier from soldier, man from man, brother from brother and sister from sister, establishing the basis for the unity of the international proletariat that is the prior condition for the emancipation of the working class and of all humanity.

6. WILFRED OWEN AND THE MUSE OF WAR

> "The people of England needn't hope. They must agitate."
> (Wilfred Owen, letter to his mother)

It has been said that, when the cannons are heard, the muses are silent. In a general sense, that is true. The thunder of war drowns out the voice of the poet and the artist. The grim poetry of artillery shells, hand grenades and machine guns is far stronger than the weak voice of human beings, protesting against the monstrous cannibalism that periodically disrupts the old equilibrium and threatens to destroy the conditions of civilised existence. However, to every rule there is an exception.

The First World War – that grotesque carnival of death and destruction that pushed Europe to the brink of barbarism – produced some of the most remarkable anti-war literature that has ever been written. From the German side we have the famous novel by Erich Maria Remarque, *All Quiet on the Western Front* (*Im Westen nichts Neues*), which was twice made into a notable film. From the French side we have *Under Fire* (*Le Feu*), the masterpiece of Henri Barbusse, who became a Communist. These immortal works of literature provide us with a graphic picture of the terrible reality of trench warfare from the standpoint of the ordinary soldier.

At the same time, Britain produced a whole generation of what became known as the war poets. Of these, the most outstanding was Wilfred Owen, who died tragically in November 1918 only a few days before the War ended. In his poems, the so-called Great War for Civilisation is depicted in all its cruel savagery. His work provides an effective antidote to the avalanche of patriotic propaganda that found its reflection in the literary field in the kind of sentimental patriotic verse written by earlier war poets such as Rupert Brooke.

Wilfred Edward Salter Owen was born on 18 March, 1893, in Oswestry, on the border between Wales and England. He began writing poetry as a teenager, inspired by the great English lyric poets of the nineteenth century, especially Keats and Shelley (the latter was also greatly admired by Marx). Paradoxically, Owen's character was utterly unsuited to the role of a soldier. As a person he was sensitive, shy, inoffensive, bookish and introverted. He was also deeply religious and even became lay assistant to the vicar of Dunsden, near Reading, shortly before the war, teaching Bible classes and leading prayer meetings.

But great historical events produce remarkable changes in the psychology of both the masses and of individuals. It was the First World War that transformed Wilfred Owen, both as a person and as a poet. When the War broke out, he was working in France as a private tutor, in a place close to the Pyrenees. The bursts of shellfire and the stuttering of machine guns did not disturb the tranquil repose of those distant parts. To Owen, the war seemed something remote that did not have any relevance to him. But, as he scanned the columns of *The Daily Mail*, which his mother sent him from England, he began to have an uneasy conscience. He returned to England in October 1915 and, in common with so many young men of his generation, he volunteered for the army.

As an educated person from the respectable lower-middle classes, Owen was commissioned as an officer in the Manchester Regiment. He trained in England for over a year, enjoying the admiring stares of people as he walked along the street in his smart soldier's uniform. The reality of war was still a closed book to this innocent young mind. In his earliest verses, written in 1914, we hear the voice of a naïve young man, yet to experience the horrors of war, whose brain is still intoxicated by the fumes of patriotism. On 30 December, 1916, having completed his military training, Wilfred Owen sailed for France.

He arrived there full of boyish high spirits and patriotic fervour. But these illusions were very soon knocked out of his head by the cruel reality of a bloody war of attrition. Initially, he was shocked by the uncouthness of the men under his command. But, very soon, he grew to respect and love them as brothers condemned to face the terrors of death together. One of his most powerful and moving poems is called 'Inspection'. It is written in the first person singular, which adds to its power. As an officer, Owen had to inspect his men. In the course of one such inspection, he sees a stain in a soldier's uniform and reprimands him for appearing on parade with dirty clothes. Only later does he find out that the stain was the man's blood, and the theme of blood and sacrifice is brought to an intense climax at the end of the poem.

There are echoes of Owen's religious upbringing: the blood of the sacrificial lamb that takes away the sins of the world. But here the lambs that are led to the slaughter are millions of young men, sacrificed on the altar of a cruel and pitiless God:

INSPECTION

> "You! What d'you mean by this?" I rapped.
> "You dare come on parade like this?"
> "Please, sir, it's—" "Old yer mouth," the sergeant snapped.
> "I takes 'is name, sir?" – "Please, and then dismiss."
> Some days 'confined to camp' he got,
> For being 'dirty on parade'.
> He told me, afterwards, the damned spot
> Was blood, his own. "Well, blood is dirt," I said.
> "Blood's dirt," he laughed, looking away,
> Far off to where his wound had bled
> And almost merged for ever into clay.
> "The world is washing out its stains," he said.
> "It doesn't like our cheeks so red:

Young blood's its great objection.
But when we're duly white-washed, being dead,
The race will bear Field-Marshal God's inspection."

Soon he was wading along trenches knee deep in filthy water, surrounded by the stench of rotting corpses. Within a week he had been transported to the front line in a cattle wagon and was sleeping seventy or eighty yards from a heavy gun, which fired every minute or so. He witnessed the horrors of gas attacks. His company slept out in deep snow, plagued by bitter frost. By now he was beginning to understand the meaning of war. He wrote home: "The people of England needn't hope. They must agitate."

By 9 January, 1917, he had joined the Second Manchesters on the Somme – at Bertrancourt, near Amiens. Here he took command of Number Three Platoon, 'A' Company. He wrote to his mother:

> I can see no excuse for deceiving you about these last four days. I have suffered seventh hell. – I have not been at the front. – I have been in front of it. – I held an advanced post, that is, a 'dug-out' in the middle of No Man's Land. We had a march of three miles over shelled road, then nearly three along a flooded trench. After that we came to where the trenches had been blown flat out and had to go over the top. It was of course dark, too dark, and the ground was not mud, not sloppy mud, but an octopus of sucking clay, three, four, and five feet deep, relieved only by craters full of water…

On 16 January, 1917, Owen wrote again:

> In the platoon on my left the sentries over the dug-out were blown to nothing. One of these poor fellows was my first servant whom I rejected. If I had kept him, he would have lived, for servants don't do Sentry Duty. I kept my own sentries half-way down the stairs during the more terrific bombardment. In spite of this, one lad was blown down and, I'm afraid, blinded.

Owen's experience found its expression in the poem 'The Sentry', which was finally completed in France in September, 1918, a few weeks before his death. The content of the poem is as follows: Owen and his men have found an old German ('Boche') dug-out, but they have been spotted by the Germans and subjected to constant bombardment. The men stand waist-high in mud from which it is impossible to escape and the place stinks. The dug-out is directly hit by an exploding shell (a 'whizz-bang'), which blows the sentry off his feet. He falls down the steps into the mud. The soldiers expect to find a corpse but the sentry is still alive. He cries out that he is blind, but Owen tries to reassure him that if he can see just a faint light from the candle he holds to his eyes then he will, in time, recover his sight. The sentry tells him that he can see nothing. The man's blinded eyes still haunt him in his dreams:

THE SENTRY

> We'd found an old Boche dug-out, and he knew,
> And gave us hell, for shell on frantic shell
> Hammered on top, but never quite burst through.
> Rain, guttering down in waterfalls of slime
> Kept slush waist high, that rising hour by hour,
> Choked up the steps too thick with clay to climb.
> What murk of air remained stank old, and sour
> With fumes of whizz-bangs, and the smell of men
> Who'd lived there years, and left their curse in the den,
> If not their corpses…
> There we herded from the blast
> Of whizz-bangs, but one found our door at last.
> Buffeting eyes and breath, snuffing the candles.
> And thud! flump! thud! down the steep steps came thumping
> And splashing in the flood, deluging muck –
> The sentry's body; then his rifle, handles
> Of old Boche bombs, and mud in ruck on ruck.
> We dredged him up, for killed, until he whined
> "O sir, my eyes – I'm blind – I'm blind, I'm blind!"
> Coaxing, I held a flame against his lids
> And said if he could see the least blurred light

He was not blind; in time he'd get all right.
"I can't," he sobbed. Eyeballs, huge-bulged like squids
Watch my dreams still; but I forgot him there
In posting next for duty, and sending a scout
To beg a stretcher somewhere, and floundering about
To other posts under the shrieking air.
Those other wretches, how they bled and spewed,
And one who would have drowned himself for good, –
I try not to remember these things now.
Let dread hark back for one word only: how
Half-listening to that sentry's moans and jumps,
And the wild chattering of his broken teeth,
Renewed most horribly whenever crumps
Pummelled the roof and slogged the air beneath –
Through the dense din, I say, we heard him shout
"I see your lights!" But ours had long died out.

The unimaginable horrors of the First World War were sufficient to shatter the nervous system of even the strongest men. One soldier recalled:

> We went up into the front line near Arras, through sodden and devastated countryside. As we were moving up to our sector along the communication trenches, a shell burst ahead of me and one of my platoon dropped. He was the first man I ever saw killed. Both his legs were blown off and the whole of his body and face was peppered with shrapnel. The sight turned my stomach. I was sick and terrified but even more frightened of showing it.

This was an everyday experience.

Subjected to continuous bombardment day and night for weeks on end, exhausted, cold and wet, men's minds were broken as well as bodies. Owen had suffered concussion when he fell into a shell hole. Then he was blown high into the air by a trench mortar, and spent several days lying in a field. As a result, he was evacuated to Britain suffering from what became known as shell shock. Between 1914 and

1918, the British Army identified 80,000 men with what would now be defined as the symptoms of post-traumatic stress disorder.

Those who suffered from severe shell shock could not stand the thought of being on the front line any longer. Some of them deserted. Once caught, they received a court martial and, if sentenced to death, shot by a twelve-man firing squad. In World War One, 306 British and Commonwealth soldiers were executed for crimes such as desertion and cowardice.

The most devastating symptoms of shell shock included uncontrollable shaking, terrifying nightmares and severe convulsions. But at the time, most shell shock victims were treated harshly and with little sympathy as their symptoms were not understood and they were seen as a sign of weakness. Those whose condition was so severe that they had to be sent back to Britain (known in soldier's slang as 'Blighty') were often regarded with contempt as cowards and malingerers, faking mental illness to avoid fighting.

In his moving poem 'The Dead Beat', Owen describes the case of a shell-shocked soldier who lies prostrate on the ground and refuses to get up even when kicked and threatened with an officer's revolver. The man is taken away by stretcher-bearers, who have no doubt he is faking illness in order to get home to 'Blighty'. The whisky-sodden army doctor maintains the same opinion of the 'scum', even when the man has died of his supposedly fake disease.

THE DEAD-BEAT

> He dropped, – more sullenly than wearily,
> Lay stupid like a cod, heavy like meat,
> And none of us could kick him to his feet;
> Just blinked at my revolver, blearily;
> – Didn't appear to know a war was on,
> Or see the blasted trench at which he stared.
> "I'll do 'em in," he whined, "If this hand's spared,
> I'll murder them, I will."
> A low voice said,

"It's Blighty, p'raps, he sees; his pluck's all gone,
Dreaming of all the valiant, that AREN'T dead:
Bold uncles, smiling ministerially;
Maybe his brave young wife, getting her fun
In some new home, improved materially.
It's not these stiffs have crazed him; nor the Hun."
We sent him down at last, out of the way.
Unwounded; – stout lad, too, before that strafe.
Malingering? Stretcher-bearers winked, "Not half!"
Next day I heard the Doc.'s well-whiskied laugh:
"That scum you sent last night soon died. Hooray!"

OWEN AND SASSOON

While convalescing at the Craiglockhart War Hospital near Edinburgh Owen's doctor, Arthur Brock, encouraged him to translate his experiences, specifically the experiences he relived in his dreams, into poetry as a kind of therapy. It was here that he met the poet Siegfried Sassoon, who had a profound effect on him. Sassoon was born into a wealthy Jewish merchant family. An officer in the Royal Welsh Fusiliers, he displayed such bravery in the front line that he was known as Mad Jack for his near-suicidal exploits. His brother was killed in November 1915 at Gallipoli. The aristocratic Sassoon had been twice decorated for bravery, but developed anti-war views which got him into serious trouble with the authorities.

In June 1917 he wrote a letter that was published in *The Times* in which he argued that the war was being deliberately and unnecessarily prolonged by the government. In the prevailing climate of chauvinism, such subversive declarations from a decorated war hero inevitably caused a furore. It was only the intervention of his friends that saved him from a court-martial. Anyone who raised his voice against the Great War for Civilisation was considered to be either a traitor or a madman. The poet, Robert Graves, managed to convince the authorities that Sassoon was suffering from shell-shock. He was sent to Craiglockhart for treatment for his 'mental illness'.

Sassoon was already a well-known poet, and contact with him transformed both the style and content of Owen's verse. In place of the dreamy romanticism of his early work, he was inspired by Sassoon's harsh realism, taking as his subject matter his personal experience of war. Owen worshipped Sassoon. He wrote to his mother that he was "not worthy to light [Sassoon's] pipe". In reality, he became a greater poet than Sassoon ever was. However, it was Sassoon who is to be thanked for promoting Owen's poetry, both before and after Owen's death.

The horrors of trench warfare were by now deeply engraved on Owen's consciousness. The opening verses of 'Anthem for Doomed Youth' convey Owen's burning anger and deep sense of injustice at the loss of so many young lives. He is not writing from the comfort of his study but from his own bitter experience. Here is the voice of one who has seen the horrors of which he writes:

ANTHEM FOR DOOMED YOUTH

> What passing-bells for these who die as cattle?
> Only the monstrous anger of the guns.
> Only the stuttering rifles' rapid rattle
> Can patter out their hasty orisons.
> No mockeries now for them, no prayers nor bells;
> Nor any voice of mourning save the choirs, –
> The shrill demented choirs of wailing shells;
> And bugles calling for them from sad shires.

Sassoon was posted to Palestine and then returned to France, where he was again wounded and sent back to England, where he spent the remainder of the war. Owen himself could have stayed on home-duty indefinitely. But he decided otherwise. In July 1918 he returned to active service in France. Probably he saw it as his duty to follow the example of Sassoon so that the public should be told of the horrific realities of the war. Sassoon was flatly opposed to the idea of Owen returning to the trenches, even threatening to "stab [him] in the leg" if he tried it.

On 26 August, Owen was declared fit for front line action and instructed to embark for France. He did not inform his friend of his departure until he was already on the other side of the Channel. He wrote to Sassoon, "Everything is clear now; and I am in hasty retreat towards the Front." On returning to the front, Owen served with distinction. On 1 October 1918 he led units of the Second Manchesters storming a number of enemy strong points near the village of Joncourt. In recognition of his bravery in action he was awarded the Military Cross. The official citation reads as follows:

> 2nd Lt, Wilfred Edward Salter Owen, 5th Bn. Manch. R., T.F., attd. 2nd Bn.
>
> For conspicuous gallantry and devotion to duty in the attack on the Fonsomme Line on October 1st/2nd, 1918. On the company commander becoming a casualty, he assumed command and showed fine leadership and resisted a heavy counter-attack. He personally manipulated a captured enemy machine gun from an isolated position and inflicted considerable losses on the enemy. Throughout he behaved most gallantly.

In his last letter to his mother, Owen tries to reassure her and calm her fears:

> It is a great life. I am more oblivious than alas! yourself, dear Mother, of the ghastly glimmering of the guns outside, and the hollow crashing of the shells… Of this I am certain: you could not be visited by a band of friends half so fine as surround me here.
>
> Ever, Wilfred x

Shortly after writing these lines, on 4 November 1918, Wilfred Owen led his men – his band of friends – into action for the last time. At 5.45 in the morning, under a hail of machine gun fire, the Royal Engineers attempted to construct a bridge out of wire-linked floats so that Owen's brigade and the Fifteenth and Sixteenth Lancashire Fusiliers could cross and destroy or capture the enemy. Group after group of soldiers advanced into the deadly shower of lead.

Wilfred Owen was standing at the water's edge of the Sambre Canal at Ors, encouraging his men when he was cut down. He was twenty-five years old. In a tragic irony, his mother received the letter informing her of his death on 11 November, the very day when the church bells were ringing out all over the land to celebrate the end of the Great War for Civilisation.

Owen's early death robbed humanity of a great poet. His literary reputation rests on a single slim volume of verses, edited by his friend Sassoon, which first saw the light of day in 1920. Despite its scant size, this volume contains some of the most moving English poetry of the First World War, including 'Insensibility', 'Dulce et Decorum Est', 'Futility' and 'Anthem for Doomed Youth'. These powerful works represent a cry of protest against the senseless sacrifice of millions of young men in the mud, blood and poison gas of the trenches, the mindless cruelty of cynical generals who, without blinking an eye, sent these men to their deaths as sheep to the slaughter, an entire generation sacrificed on the bloody altar of imperialism.

The paradox that Owen saw so clearly is that there is no poetry in war. He wrote:

> Above all I am not concerned with Poetry.
> My subject is War, and the pity of War.
> The Poetry is in the pity.

Owen saw his role as making others see what he could see. Having been in the trenches he could no longer take refuge in patriotic falsehoods or paint beautiful pictures of an ugly and brutal reality. Unlike those who tried to fool the public by presenting a sanitised and inspiring picture of the imperialist slaughter, Owen fearlessly told the truth.

Today, as a mournful reminder of the appalling loss of life in the First World War, one can still see in towns and villages all over Britain, stone monuments with the names of dead soldiers, below which one reads the inscription: Dulce et decorum est pro patria mori. This means 'It is sweet and fitting to die for your country'. These Latin words, taken from an ode by the Roman poet Horace, now seem to us to be a cruel mockery of the dead. But, at the start of the War, these words were frequently quoted (by people, conveniently, far from the front line) as a justification for the imperialist slaughter. In what is probably his best-known poem, 'Dulce et decorum est', Owen uses a horrifically graphic account of a poison gas attack to mercilessly destroy these illusions:

DULCE ET DECORUM EST

>Bent double, like old beggars under sacks,
>Knock-kneed, coughing like hags, we cursed through sludge,
>Till on the haunting flares we turned our backs
>And towards our distant rest began to trudge.
>Men marched asleep. Many had lost their boots
>But limped on, blood-shod. All went lame; all blind;
>Drunk with fatigue; deaf even to the hoots
>Of tired, outstripped Five-Nines that dropped behind.
>Gas! Gas! Quick, boys! – An ecstasy of fumbling,
>Fitting the clumsy helmets just in time;
>But someone still was yelling out and stumbling
>And flound'ring like a man in fire or lime…
>Dim, through the misty panes and thick green light,
>As under a green sea, I saw him drowning.
>In all my dreams, before my helpless sight,
>He plunges at me, guttering, choking, drowning.
>If in some smothering dreams you too could pace
>Behind the wagon that we flung him in,
>And watch the white eyes writhing in his face,
>His hanging face, like a devil's sick of sin;
>If you could hear, at every jolt, the blood
>Come gargling from the froth-corrupted lungs,
>Obscene as cancer, bitter as the cud
>Of vile, incurable sores on innocent tongues, –
>My friend, you would not tell with such high zest
>To children ardent for some desperate glory,
>The old Lie: Dulce et decorum est
>Pro patria mori.

Owen's poetry is not a manifestation of an anaemic pacifism, but a faithful reflection of the lives, deaths and sufferings of the soldiers in the trenches. It gives voice to the feelings of rage and indignation that later exploded in mutinies in the French and British armies and in the Russian and German revolutions of 1917 and 1918. The name of Wilfred Owen will always be cherished by everyone who fights against tyranny and injustice, for a better world in which the horrors of war will be nothing more than a nightmare vaguely remembered from a barbarous past.

7. TSARIST RUSSIA AND THE WAR

In the bloody struggle for world domination Russia entered as a second-rate partner of the Entente. The apparent strength of the Russian Empire concealed its internal contradictions and fundamental weaknesses. Russian tsarism combined elements of a semi-feudal, semi-colonial country, heavily dependent upon foreign capital, with the aggressive characteristics of imperialism. Indeed, despite the economic backwardness of Russia, which never exported a single kopek of capital, Lenin included it as one of the five main imperialist countries.

However, Russia's war aims were of a regional and provincial character, reflecting its relative weakness. Tsarism did not aspire to dominate Europe, but to seize the Turkish Straits and lay hands on Constantinople. This would then turn the Black Sea into a Russian lake and allow its navy free passage into the Mediterranean. It wished to expand its military-bureaucratic domination into Polish Galicia, to dominate the Balkans at the expense of Austria, and to strengthen its stranglehold over the Caucasus by the incorporation Armenia at the expense of Turkey.

Britain and France were quite happy to promise these things, which they had no intention of delivering. But, in return for such promises, there was a price to be paid. Threatened by the seemingly unstoppable German advance, the French imperialists were urgently demanding that the Russian army should attack in the East in order to relieve pressure on France and divert German forces from their goal: Paris.

French imperialism was pressing Russia to begin hostilities as a means of diverting German forces to the East. Since tsarist Russia was heavily in debt to French finance capital, there was no question of refusing to comply with the request from Paris, which was really more like a direct order. The men in Paris were now calling in their debts. Russia paid with the blood of her people for her right to be a member of the rich man's club of imperialism.

UNDERLYING WEAKNESS

On paper, Russia was an awesome military force, and the mood of Russia's ruling circles was one of optimism. In March 1914, an article appeared in the Russian press that was generally thought to be the work of the War Minister, Sukhomlinov. It said:

> The army is not only large but excellently equipped. Russia has always fought on foreign soil and has always been victorious. Russia is no longer on the defensive. Russia is ready.

The cruel irony of these words was fully revealed before the end of the year.

The Russian army was accustomed to fighting more backward peoples in the Caucasus and Central Asia. It was hopelessly inadequate to face the formidable forces of modern, industrial Germany. The inherent weakness of the Russian army had been cruelly exposed by the war with Japan in 1904-5, which led directly to the Revolution of 1905-6. In the years of counter-revolution that followed the defeat of the Revolution, the monarchy, with the support of the bourgeoisie, had attempted to reform and modernise the army. But these reforms remained incomplete in 1914, when Russia faced a far more serious test.

Every army is a reflection of the society out of which it arises and the Russian army was no exception. There were some very talented Russian officers, men like Aleksei Alekseyevich Brusilov. Years later the British Field Marshal Bernard Montgomery expressed the opinion that Brusilov was one of the seven outstanding fighting commanders of World War I. But for every capable officer in the Russian army there were a dozen idle, cowardly and inept aristocrats, promoted to leading positions of authority by virtue of favouritism and family connections.

The deep contradictions in society were enormously exacerbated by the war, which not only turned the common soldiers and NCOs against their officers, but even drove a section of the latter to go over to the side of the Bolsheviks in the Civil War. The former tsarist junior officer Tukhachevsky, the hero of the Civil War, was to become the most prominent leader of the Red Army. After the October Revolution, Brusilov himself helped to organise the Red Army and served the Revolution loyally throughout the Civil War. When he died in Moscow in 1926, he was given a state funeral with full honours by the Bolsheviks. Tukhachevsky was not so fortunate. He was framed and murdered by Stalin in the notorious Purges of 1937.

Throughout the First World War, at every step, the army leadership was affected by the poisonous influence of the Court clique, particularly the tsarina, who constantly manipulated and intrigued to remove able men and replace them with her favourites.

THE RUSSIAN OFFENSIVE

Under the command of the Grand Duke Nicholas, the Russian Army entered the War with a total strength of 1.5 million men with 3 million reservists – numerically more than a match for the German Army. In August 1914, two Russian armies marched into Germany through East Prussia and Austria via the Carpathians. In the beginning, the Russian Army was successful against both the Germans and Austrians.

No one could doubt the courage of the Russian soldiers who, when they ran out of ammunition, fought with their bayonets. But in modern warfare the courage of the individual soldier is not necessarily the decisive factor. Despite all their bravery, the Russian soldiers were little more than cannon fodder. Their initial successes only served to mask profound problems in the Russian Army.

The real relation of forces in modern warfare is determined not by numbers alone but by equipment and supplies, modern weapons, the training of the troops and the quality of the officers and NCOs. These factors in turn are determined by the relative level of industrial, technological and cultural development of each country. Russia's less-developed industrial base and ineffective military leadership was glaringly exposed in the events that unfolded.

Initially, the Russian attack caused panic among the German civilian population. On all sides the cry went up: 'The Cossacks are coming!' The alarm soon spread to the German General Staff, who moved two divisions from the Western Front to the Eastern Front. This helped give the French the breathing space they needed at the Marne to stop the Germans' advance on Paris. But the Germans need not have been so worried.

Thousands of Russian troops were sent to the front without proper equipment. They lacked everything: weapons, ammunition, boots and bedding. As many as a third of Russian soldiers were not issued with a rifle. In late 1914, Russia's general headquarters reported that 100,000 new rifles were needed each month, but that Russian factories were capable of producing less than half this number (42,000 per month). The Russian Army had sixty heavy artillery batteries while the German Army had 381. Russia had two machine guns per battalion, Germany had thirty-six. The soldiers, however, were well armed with prayers, as Russian Orthodox bishops and priests worked diligently to bless those about to go into battle, showering them generously with holy water from a bucket.

By December, 1914, the Russian Army had 6,553,000 men. However, they only had 4,652,000 rifles. Untrained troops were ordered into battle without adequate arms or ammunition. And because the Russian Army had about one surgeon for every 10,000 men, many of its soldiers died from wounds that would have been treated on the Western Front. With medical staff spread out across a 500-mile front, the likelihood of any Russian soldier receiving any medical treatment was close to zero.

The backwardness of Russian capitalism was shown by the deficiencies of military supplies and finances and the lack of munitions. The number of factories was simply too small for their production, while the lack of railway lines impeded the transportation of troops and supplies.

THE BATTLE OF TANNENBERG
The two Russian armies in East Prussia were under the command of generals Rennenkampf and Samsonov. Rennenkampf's First Army was to converge with the Samsonov's Second Army to give a two-to-one numerical superiority over the German Eighth Army. The plan began well. But relations between the two Russian generals were bad and communications between them poor.

The German Army under Ludendorff counter-attacked and, by 29 August, the Russian centre, amounting to three army corps, was surrounded by Germans and trapped in the gloomy and impenetrable depths of the Tannenberg forest with no means of escape. The Battle of Tannenberg lasted three days. General Samsonov attempted to retreat but found himself encircled by an immense German cordon that held the Russian forces in a vice-like grip. Most of his troops were slaughtered or captured. Only 10,000 of the 150,000 Russian soldiers managed to escape. Stunned by the extent of the catastrophe, General Samsonov shot himself.

The conduct of the Russian General Staff at Tannenberg was indescribably appalling. Battle plans were sent out uncoded over the radio and the Russian generals leading the offensive, Samsonov and von Rennenkampf, refused to communicate with each other. The Germans outmanoeuvred the Russians and were able to take on one Russian army at a time through the incompetence of Russian generals and the backwardness of Russian communications and transportation. At Tannenberg, the Russians lost 100,000 men in a single day. By the end of the battle, the Germans had annihilated practically the whole of the Russian Second Army.

The Germans, who lost only 13,800 men in the battle, were able to take more than 92,000 Russian prisoners. The German victory at Tannenberg set the stage for the First Battle of the Masurian Lakes one week later, where the reinforced German Eighth Army now faced only the Russian First Army and inflicted a crushing defeat on it. Despite a more-than-threefold numerical superiority in the region (250,000 Germans against 800,000 Russians), Russian losses were nine times larger than the German.

Among the Russian dead were a large number of officers who obligingly went into battle wearing their ceremonial uniforms, providing excellent targets for German snipers and machine gunners. By 1915, a Russian officer had an eighty-two per cent chance of being killed. In some parts of the front their life expectancy was only four or five days. A German machine gunner wrote in a letter: "they just kept coming and we just kept shooting. Periodically, we had to push the bodies aside in order to fire at the fresh waves."

The German Ninth Army led by August von Mackensen attacked the Russian Second Army, under General Smirnov, near the Polish village of Bolimów, lying on the railway line connecting Łódź and Warsaw. This battle saw the first attempt at the large-scale use of poison gas. On New Year's Eve the Germans fired eighteen thousand xylyl bromide gas shells at the Russians. But the poisonous cloud was blown back towards their own lines. The gas caused few, if any, casualties because the cold weather caused it to freeze, rendering it ineffective. But a fatal precedent had been established.

The failure of the gas attack caused the German commanders to call it off. In response, the Russians launched a counter-attack with eleven divisions. They were cut to pieces by the German artillery, suffering a further 40,000 casualties. No army could withstand the huge number of casualties that Russia suffered in the first ten months of the war. In total, they lost around 350,000 men – more than an entire army – as well as vast amounts of military equipment. Thus, the Russian offensive in East Prussia ended in a disgraceful rout.

THE FALL OF WARSAW

Russian offensives on the south-western front were more successful, allowing them to push across the Carpathians and into Galicia. These spectacular celebrated victories were in stark contrast to the catastrophic debacles on the other fronts. But here the Russian army was facing Austro-Hungarian, rather than German troops. The

Russian successes against Austria-Hungary, however, are explained rather by the feebleness of Austria-Hungary than the strength of Russia.

The success of the Russian offensive led by General Brusilov was short-lived. The army of the Austro-Hungarian Empire was one thing. But the mighty German war machine was another matter altogether. The arrival of German reinforcements in May 1915 again forced the Russians to fall back. By the spring of 1915, the Russians had retreated to Galicia, and, in May, the Central Powers smashed their way through Poland's southern frontiers. On 5 August, they captured Warsaw and forced the Russians to withdraw from Poland.

The invasion of East Prussia was a bloody failure for the Russians. But worse was to come. On the Eastern Front, the next phase of the combined Austro-German offensive against the Russians commenced in northern Poland, with the Austro-Germans advancing toward Warsaw. The Russian Army was now growing weaker by the day as a result of chronic supply shortages and declining morale.

Within five days of the beginning of the offensive, the Austro-German troops broke through the Russian lines and pushed the Russian Third and Eighth Armies further eastward. Russian casualties soon surpassed 400,000. On 5 August, 1915 Warsaw itself was taken by Austro-Germans troops, putting an end to a century of Russian control of the city. Buoyed up by their successes, the Austro-German forces went on to capture Ivangorod, Kovno, Brest-Litovsk, Bialystok, Grodno and Vilnius. By the end of September, the Russian troops were driven out of Poland and Galicia, far behind the original lines from which they had begun the war in 1914.

The Russian attack ended in disaster, but it served to relieve pressure on the French Army and undoubtedly played a major role in halting the German advance on Paris. The Head of French Intelligence Colonel Dupont wrote: "their debacle was one of the elements of our victory". For the time being, the battered Russian Army was effectively eliminated as an offensive threat on the Eastern Front, freeing the Germans to concentrate once more on the Western Front. In reality, the Russian Imperial Army was acting as mere cannon fodder for the

Allies. The Russian soldiers began to think and even to express the thought: "they are all ready to fight to the last drop of my blood."

CRISIS ON THE HOME FRONT

The combined Russian losses of the Austro-German offensives in Galicia and Poland were over 1,800,000 casualties, 1,250,000 of whom were captured. Capture rates were the most evident symptom of disaster. In order to replace these appalling losses, barely trained recruits had to be called up for active duty, a process repeated throughout the war as the losses continued to mount.

A similar change affected the officer class, especially in the lower echelons. The gaps left by the loss of qualified officers and NCOs were quickly filled by raw soldiers rising up through the ranks, usually of peasant or working-class backgrounds. Many of these were to play a large role in the politicisation of the troops in 1917. On the front, Russian soldiers were without rifles, which they could only get from fellow soldiers after they were killed or wounded. *Only on 1 July, 1915 did Russia create a Central War Industries Committee to oversee production and address a severe shortage of artillery shells and rifles.*

News of the military catastrophe caused panic in the ruling circles. Trotsky quotes the words of the Russian War Minister Polivanov, answering his colleagues alarmed at the situation at the front: "I place my trust in the impenetrable spaces, impassable mud, and the mercy of Saint Nicholas Mirlikisky, Protector of Holy Russia." That was on 4 August, 1915. One week later General Ruszky confessed to the same ministers: "The present-day demands of military technique are beyond us. At any rate we can't keep up with the Germans." That was the plain truth.

What became known as the Great Retreat frequently turned into a disorderly rout. Desertion, plunder and chaotic flight were common. The Russian generals made the peaceful population pay for their own criminal incapacity. They issued a cruel order for a total evacuation of the Polish civilian population. This caused terrible suffering for the people as they were forced to leave their homes and head eastward, clogging the roads and hampering the movement of Russian troops. Enormous tracts of land were violently laid waste. As always in such cases bloody pogroms were unleashed against the Jews as a convenient way of diverting the anger of the soldiers away from the real authors of their misery.

The fleeing mass of Russian troops and civilians from Poland poured fuel on the smouldering flames of political and social unrest in Russia, which was increasingly directed against the tsar and his degenerate and corrupt court clique. The tsar expressed his outrage at the defeat by removing his army commander-in-chief, Nicholas Nikolayevich, and taking command of the army himself, although he had no practical experience of strategic warfare or commanding infantry and artillery in combat. Egged on by his wife, Nicholas proceeded to the front.

By assuming personal command of the Russian Army, Nicholas was hoping to rally his demoralised troops. However, this decision did not have the slightest effect on Russia's war effort, since the tsar rarely intervened or countermanded the decisions of his battlefield generals. What it did do was to make him personally responsible for every military failure. It also placed the government of Russia, at a time of growing social and political crisis, in the hands of his ambitious and scheming wife, Alexandra. The stench of corruption and incompetence in the Imperial government began to circulate in the population. The notorious influence of the drunken, debauched 'Man of God' Grigori Rasputin over the Imperial family was common knowledge, exposing the inner rottenness at the heart of the tsarist regime.

The devastation of war did not only affect the soldiers at the front. By the end of 1915, there were clear signs that the economy was breaking down under the unbearable strains of wartime demands. There were food shortages and rising prices. Inflation eroded incomes at an alarmingly rapid rate, and even such things that could be afforded were in short supply, especially in St. Petersburg, where distance from supplies and poor transportation networks made matters even worse.

Russia was further weakened economically by the loss of Poland's industrial and agricultural production. The conscription of millions of men produced a labour shortage on peasant landholdings and a resultant decline in food production. Large numbers of peasants were also moved to the industrial sector, which generated a slight rise in production, but nowhere near enough to meet Russia's war needs. As a result, agricultural production slumped and civilians had to endure serious food shortages. Shops were running out of bread, sugar, meat and other provisions, and there were long queues for what remained. It became increasingly difficult to afford food, or even to find it.

The outbreak of war in August 1914 had initially served to suffocate the growing social and political protests, focusing hostilities against a common external enemy, but this false patriotic unity did not last long. As the war dragged on with no end in sight, the fog of patriotic intoxication began to clear from people's minds as war-weariness gradually bean to take hold of the masses.

It was the wives of the workers who had to bear the heaviest burden. Working-class women in St. Petersburg reportedly spent about forty hours a week shivering in the cold while queuing for food. To feed their hungry children, many were compelled to turn to begging or prostitution. Tearing down wooden fences to keep stoves heated against the freezing cold of the Russian winter, they cursed the rich and the government and its wars that meant only misery and endless suffering for them, their children and their husbands at the front. When would it all end?

Public morale and support for the war was dwindling and the people became more receptive to anti-war propaganda. On 17 September, 1915, Alexei Kuropatkin, former Minister of War and Commander of the Grenadier Corps, wrote: "The lower orders began the war with enthusiasm; but now they are weary, and with the continual retreats have lost faith in a victory." From the middle of 1915 the number of strikes increased inexorably. The stage was being prepared for revolutionary developments.

8. TURKEY JOINS THE WAR

At the turn of the twentieth century, the Ottoman Empire was in a state of terminal decline. In 1908, Austria-Hungary annexed Bosnia and Herzegovina. Three years later, the Italian bourgeoisie proclaimed its colonial ambitions by grabbing Libya in North Africa from the Ottomans. Later, they seized the islands of Rhodes and Kos. A year after that, a league of Balkan nations drove the Ottomans from their last foothold in Europe.

The Empire was now facing revolts of Christians in the north and growing discontent among Arabs. On its northern border the vast power of the Russian Empire posed an ever-present threat. Its breakup was confidently expected in St. Petersburg, where the Russian imperialists were hovering like hungry vultures waiting to tear the flesh off their dying victim.

In 1908, the Young Turks – a movement of ambitious, discontented nationalist junior army officers – had seized power with the aim of modernising and strengthening the Empire. Enver Pasha, supreme commander of the Ottoman armed forces, was ambitious and dreamed of re-conquering central Asia and areas that had been lost to Russia previously. However, his military skills were not equal to his rhetoric and the Russian armies were successful in their struggle with Turkey for domination of the Caucasus.

TURKEY JOINS THE CENTRAL POWERS

The Young Turks entered World War I on the side of the Central Powers, the secret Ottoman-German Alliance having been signed in August 1914. In fact, the backward semi-feudal Ottoman Empire was in no shape to wage war. After several crushing defeats, it had lost territories and its economy was in a state of collapse, its people and army demoralised and exhausted. But the outbreak of world war made it impossible for the Ottoman Empire to stand aside.

The Italo-Turkish War and Balkan Wars had exhausted the Empire's resources in both weaponry and financial reserves. Its only option was to enter into an alliance with a European power; and it did not really matter which one. In the words of Talaat Pasha, the Minister of Interior:

> Turkey needed to join one of the country groups so that it could organise its domestic administration, strengthen and maintain its commerce and industry, expand its railroads, in short to survive and to preserve its existence.

An alliance with Russia was ruled out in advance, since Russia was its main adversary and aimed to exercise domination over the disintegrating Ottoman Empire. And since France was allied to Russia there could be no question of entering an alliance with it. London showed no interest in coming to the help of Constantinople. But Berlin was very interested indeed.

Since the first German military mission to the Ottoman Army after the Russo-Turkish War of 1877-8, German officers had often been attached to the army in an advisory or training role and some of the best Ottoman officers had attended staff colleges in Germany. Ottoman officers admired the German Army's professionalism and traditions, and, like many foreign observers at the time, were convinced that it was the best in the world. Therefore, pro-German sentiment was widespread in the Ottoman Army, at least among its officers, reflecting the close professional ties between the Ottoman and German officer corps.

The powerful War Minister, Enver Pasha, was pro-German. Invited to Berlin, where he witnessed the impressive spectacle of a parade of disciplined and well-armed Prussian soldiers, he was dazzled by Germany's military might. But this admiration was not mutual. The German General Staff was unimpressed by the military potential of the decaying Ottoman Empire and sceptical about the advantages to Germany of an alliance. But nevertheless, the Turks were the traditional enemy of Russia, and the old saying proved to be decisive: "The enemy of my enemy is my friend".

Germany had been steadily pursuing its march to the east. Ever since 1889 the Orient Express had run directly to Constantinople, and before the First World War the Sultan had accepted a German plan to extend it through Anatolia to Baghdad. This would strengthen the Ottoman Empire's link with industrialised Europe, while also giving Germany easier access to its African colonies and to the lucrative markets of British India.

Another element came into the strategic calculations of Berlin. The Kaiser and his clique were convinced that in order to deal a decisive blow against Britain it was necessary to strike at its Empire by stirring up a revolt of the Muslim populations of India and Afghanistan. The Kaiser thought that Muslim Turkey would be a valuable ally in this scheme. Even before the outbreak of war, enraged by England's diplomatic manoeuvres and proposals for peace, he is reported to have exclaimed:

> Now the whole scheme must be ruthlessly exposed, the mask of Christian readiness for peace, which England has shown to the world, must be rudely torn off, and her Pharisaic protestation of peace pilloried! And our consuls in Turkey and India, our agents, &c., must rouse the whole Mohammedan world to a wild rebellion against this hated, deceitful, unscrupulous nation of shopkeepers. If we are to bleed to death, England shall at least lose India.

At first, the German alliance was kept secret. Apart from anything else, there were sharp divisions in Constantinople over this question. It is known that Sultan Mehmet was against it. Fearing the effects of entering a war on his fragile Empire, he was trying to keep out of it. His signature was not on the agreement. But the real power in Constantinople was not in his hands but in those of Enver Pasha.

Constantinople was seething with German agents. On 5 August 1914, one day after declaring war on Germany, the British government decided to requisition two Ottoman battleships that were being built in British shipyards. Since the ships had already been paid for by public subscription, the decision provoked the fury of the Turks. A few days later, two German warships, the *Goeben* and the *Breslau*, fleeing from the French and British fleets, requested passage through the straits to Constantinople.

One week later, the two warships, complete with their German crews, their identity thinly disguised by wearing the Turkish fez on their heads, were renamed the *Yavuz Sultan Selim* and *Midilli* and 'transferred' to the Ottoman Navy. The British refused to recognise the transfer unless the German crews were removed, and to back up their demand, the Royal Navy blockaded the entrance of the Dardanelles: a warlike action that was bound to provoke a hostile reaction.

Although the Ottoman Empire was still ostensibly neutral at this point, Enver Pasha was growing impatient and Berlin was pressing him to commence hostilities. A series of open provocations followed. The German naval commander of the *Goeben* and *Breslau* was put in command of the Ottoman Navy and the Germans were given the responsibility of shoring up the coastal defences of the Gallipoli Peninsular.

The Ottoman Empire finally entered the war in October when Enver Pasha, without consulting any of his ministerial colleagues, ordered the Ottoman fleet, including German-crewed ships, into the Black Sea to attack the Russians. The fleet carried out surprise raids on Theodosia, Novorossiysk, Odessa and Sevastopol, sinking a Russian minelayer, a gunboat and fourteen civilian ships.

On 2 November, Russia declared war on the Ottoman Empire. France and the British Empire, Russia's wartime allies, followed suit. Enver Pasha had succeeded in bringing the Ottoman Empire into the First World War on the side of the Central Powers, Germany and Austria-Hungary. Whether he would be as successful in achieving his principal war aim – pan-Turkic expansion into Central Asia and the Caucasus at Russia's expense – was another question.

WAR WITH RUSSIA

Russian tsarism cynically used the small oppressed nationalities for its own expansionist purposes. Shortly after Russia's entry into the war, Nicholas II issued a statement aimed at the Armenian population of the Ottoman Empire, which said:

> From all countries Armenians are hurrying to enter the ranks of the glorious Russian Army, with their blood to serve the victory of the Russian Army… Let the Russian flag wave freely over the Dardanelles and the Bosporus, let you will the peoples [Armenian] remaining under the Turkish yoke receive freedom. Let the Armenian people of Turkey who have suffered for the faith of Christ receive resurrection for a new free life.

The tsar of all the Russians forgot to mention that other small nations were almost as oppressed by his regime as the Armenians were by the Turkish Pashas.

The Germans were putting heavy pressure on Enver Pasha to launch a land attack against Russia. In December 1914, the Turkish army launched an offensive against the Russians in the Caucasus with an army of 100,000 troops. The aim of attacking Russia in the Caucasus was to capture the city of Baku, with its huge oil reserves. Enver Pasha insisted on a frontal attack against Russian positions that were dug in on the mountains. At first, the Russians fell back in panic. But the harsh conditions of winter soon took a heavy toll on the Turkish soldiers, most of them poor peasants from Anatolia.

Without adequate footwear or clothing, many of them were soon crippled by frostbite. The result was the loss of 25,000 men, many of whom froze to death in the snow before they had even made contact with the Russians. Many others deserted. Those who remained found that their weapons had been made useless by the freezing conditions. Piles of Turkish corpses lay on the mountainside, where remains of bodies with staring eyes were torn to pieces by starving dogs.

The Russians then began a multi-pronged invasion of the Ottoman Empire from the Caucasus. On 6 January, the Third Army headquarters found itself under fire. Hafiz Hakki Pasha ordered a total retreat. On

7 January, the remaining forces began their march towards Erzurum. The resulting Battle of Sarikamish was a shattering defeat for the Turks who lost eighty-six per cent of their forces. Only ten per cent of the army managed to retreat back to its starting position.

This was a military catastrophe and a national humiliation of extraordinary proportions. As a result, the architect of the disaster, Enver Pasha, desperately needed to find a scapegoat for his defeat and found one in the Christian Armenians. Armenian volunteer units played a role in the success of the Russian forces, a fact that was used by ruling circles in Constantinople to stir up feelings against the Armenian population. On the eve of World War One, there were 2 million Armenians living in the Ottoman Empire. By 1922, there were fewer than 400,000. The others – some 1.5 million – were dead.

THE ARMENIAN GENOCIDE

For generations in the Ottoman Empire minority religious communities, like the Christian Armenians, were allowed to maintain their religious, social and legal structures, though they were often subject to extra taxes or other measures. Largely concentrated in eastern Anatolia, many of them merchants and industrialists, Armenians appeared markedly better off than their Turkish neighbours in many ways, most of whom were small peasants or low-paid government functionaries and soldiers.

As was also the case with the Jews, the relative prosperity of the Armenians provoked the envy of their neighbours. The fact that they were of a different religion made them objects of suspicion and resentment. But it was the outbreak of war that turned these elements into an explosive mixture of hate and fear. The defeats of the Turkish army on the Caucasian front threw petrol on the flames of religious and national hatred. Armenians were presented by official propaganda as agents of the Russians and blamed for the military setbacks.

It is true that there were Armenian nationalists who acted as guerrillas and co-operated with the Russians. In fact, they briefly seized the city of Van in the spring of 1915. But the great majority of Armenians

8. TURKEY JOINS THE WAR

played no part in such things. They merely wished to be left alone to live their lives in peace. But this was not to be. The Young Turks began a campaign to portray the Armenians as a kind of fifth column, a threat to the state.

The Young Turks, who called themselves the Committee of Unity and Progress, launched a set of measures against the Armenians, including a law authorising the military and government to deport anyone they 'sensed' was a security threat. Another law later allowed the confiscation of 'abandoned' Armenian property. The day of 24 April, 1915, marks the fatal date when several hundred Armenian intellectuals were rounded up, arrested, and later executed. This was the start of the Armenian genocide, a bloody massacre which lasted until 1917.

Armenians were ordered to turn in any weapons that they owned to the authorities. Those in the army were disarmed and transferred into labour battalions where they were either killed or worked to death. Innocent people were executed and thrown into mass graves. Even worse was the fate of those men, women and children who were forced to go on death marches across the baking, waterless Syrian Desert to concentration camps. Many of these poor creatures perished along the way of a combination of exhaustion, exposure and starvation, or else were murdered by Turkish troops and bandits.

There had been other massacres of Armenians in 1894, 1895, 1896, 1909, and this was to be repeated again between 1920 and 1923. But in its scope and ruthlessness nothing can compare with the mass slaughter of 1915-17, which is correctly described as genocide. In his excellent book *A Peace to End All Peace* David Fromkin describes the terrible fate of the expelled Armenians:

> Rape and beating were commonplace. Those who were not killed at once were driven through mountains and deserts without food, drink or shelter. Hundreds of thousands of Armenians eventually succumbed or were killed.

Thousands of sick and hungry people, men, women and children, were driven to their deaths in this way. Those few pitiful human skeletons who managed to survive the march of death across the mountains into Turkish-occupied Syria did not live to tell the tale. The pretty ones were handed over to the Turkish soldiers for their amusement. The others died of starvation or were murdered.

These terrible atrocities were quite well documented at the time by Western diplomats, missionaries and others, creating widespread wartime outrage against the Turks in the West. Although its ally, Germany, was silent at the time, German diplomats and military officers wrote to Berlin expressing horror at what was going on. Later, the Turkish authorities tried to downplay these horrors as merely 'abuses' committed by 'some officials'. But the American ambassador, Henry Morganthau Sr. wrote in his memoirs:

> When the Turkish authorities gave the orders for these deportations, they were merely giving the death warrant to a whole race; they understood this well, and in their conversations with me, they made no particular attempt to conceal the fact.

Following the surrender of the Ottoman Empire in 1918, the three Pashas fled to Germany, where they were given protection. But the Armenian underground formed a group called Operation Nemesis to hunt them down. On 15 March, 1921, one of the Pashas was shot dead on a street in Berlin in broad daylight in front of witnesses. The gunman pleaded temporary insanity brought on by the mass killings and a jury took only a little over an hour to acquit him.

WINSTON CHURCHILL AND THE GALLIPOLI ADVENTURE

With the war stalled on the Western Front by 1915, the Allied Powers were considering going on the offensive in another region of the conflict, rather than continuing with attacks in Belgium and France. Early that year, Russia's Grand Duke Nicholas appealed to Britain for aid in countering the Turkish invasion in the Caucasus.

On learning of this request, the French imperialists immediately demanded that they should be included. This was not an act of gallantry on their part. The gentlemen in Paris had no wish to see the British navy controlling the Mediterranean. They were, moreover, extremely anxious not to be left out of the division of the spoils when the Middle East was carved up after the war.

Finally, the British and French decided to launch a naval expedition to seize the Dardanelles Straits, that narrow passage connecting the Aegean Sea to the Sea of Marmara in north-western Turkey. If successful, the capture of the Straits would have allowed the Allies to link up with the Russians in the Black Sea, where they could work together to knock Turkey out of the war.

The most enthusiastic advocate of this campaign was the first lord of the British Admiralty, an ambitious young politician called Winston Churchill. However, his plan met with the strong opposition of Admiral John Fisher, head of the British Navy, who mistrusted Churchill and correctly doubted his military and naval qualifications. But Churchill's colossal ego more than made up for his lack of military training and experience and he pushed the plan through anyway.

With his characteristic arrogance, Churchill immediately began to interfere in strategic and operational matters. He reasoned that, since the western front was in a state of deadlock, the Allies should look for a weaker target. And he believed he had found it in Turkey. This belief led to one of the greatest catastrophes of World War One. The link-up between Germany and Turkey did not only represent a threat to Russia's Caucasian territories, it also threatened Britain's communications with India via the Suez Canal.

As a fanatical advocate of Britain's imperial role, Churchill saw this threat to the Suez Canal as a powerful reason to attack Turkey. Moreover, if Turkey could be knocked out of the war, it would alter the balance of forces in the Balkans to the detriment of Austria and therefore alter the whole course of the war. It all seemed very fine – on paper. But in practice it turned out very differently.

Not long ago Winston Churchill was voted the most important figure in British history. The reason is that people in Britain have always been encouraged to believe that he was a great war leader. In fact, Churchill was an opportunist and an adventurer, whose main interest in life was self-promotion. He had no understanding of war and was responsible for some of the greatest military disasters in both the First and Second World Wars. He overlooked the small detail that the weak and decaying Ottoman Empire had the backing of mighty German imperialism. Churchill's 'soft underbelly' turned out to be a very tough proposition indeed.

THE ATTACK BEGINS

The attack on the Dardanelles began on 19 February, 1915, with a long-range bombardment by British and French battleships. Turkish forces abandoned their outer forts, but met the approaching Allied minesweepers with heavy fire, stalling the advance. On 18 March, an Anglo-French force involving eighteen battleships attacked the Dardanelles. However, they suffered heavy losses when Turkish fire sank three ships in one day and severely damaged three others. They were sitting ducks for the Turkish guns onshore.

Despite the evident fact that the Anglo-French naval bombardment had ended in total failure, preparations began several weeks later for large-scale troop landings on the Gallipoli Peninsula. Troops from Australia, New Zealand and the French colonies assembled with British forces to carry this out. However, the element of surprise had already been lost and the Ottomans, under the command of experienced German officers, had plenty of time to strengthen their defences in preparation for the attack.

General Liman von Sanders stationed Ottoman troops along the shore where he expected the landings would take place. On 25 April the allied troops waded ashore at five beaches at Gallipoli. The Ottoman troops were waiting for them. The troops walked right into an inferno. The bombardment was intense. Many Allied soldiers did not even succeed in leaving the landing vessels before being cut down. Under the withering hail of machine guns, men fell like ripe corn before a deadly scythe.

Despite suffering heavy casualties, Australian and New Zealand troops managed to establish two beachheads: at Helles on the peninsula's southern tip, and at Gaba Tepe on the Aegean coast. The latter site was later dubbed Anzac Cove, in honour of the men who fought with great courage against a determined Ottoman defence. However, after the landing, the Allies were not able to advance much further from their initial landing sites, while the Allied officers showed excessive caution in ordering the men to dig trenches. This tardiness allowed the Ottomans time to bring in fresh troops in ever increasing numbers from Palestine and the Caucasus. With neither side able to gain a decisive advantage, the situation turned into yet another bloody stalemate.

In an attempt to break the stalemate, the Allies made another major troop landing on 6 August at Suvla Bay, combined with a northward advance from Anzac Cove towards the heights at Sari Bair and a diversionary action at Helles. The surprise landings at Suvla Bay advanced, meeting only light opposition, but the vacillations of Allied commanders slowed their progress, allowing Ottoman reinforcements to arrive and shore up their defences in all three locations.

The Allies had badly underestimated the fighting qualities of the Ottoman soldiers, who were fighting a defensive war to defend their homeland against foreign invaders. These peasants in uniform fought like tigers despite taking heavy casualties. The Allies found themselves trapped.

The Gallipoli front became a vicious deadlock, just like the western front in France. On 19 May, the Ottomans launched a major attack to force the Allies out of Gallipoli, but suffered heavy casualties. On 6 August, hoping to break the stalemate at Gallipoli, the British renewed the offensive. An additional 20,000 troops were landed, but their attack was hampered by poor communications and logistical problems. The Ottomans, led by Mustafa Kemal, responded by rushing in two divisions, issuing the famous order to his troops: "I do not order you to attack: I order you to die!" The British offensive was beaten back.

The Allied soldiers suffered the torment of heat, thirst, flies and sickness. Pinned down on the coast and subject to a constant bombardment of shells and machine gun fire, they were being killed in large numbers. When winter came, they suffered from cold. In November, 15,000 troops were evacuated from Anzac Cove for frostbite, trench foot and exposure. With Allied casualties mounting, the British commander Hamilton, encouraged by Churchill, petitioned the war secretary Kitchener for 95,000 reinforcements. But the men in London were already beginning to doubt the success of the Gallipoli adventure and offered him barely a quarter of that number. The venture was already doomed to failure.

DECISION TO EVACUATE GALLIPOLI

By mid-October the situation of the Allies had not improved. The idea of an evacuation was in the air, but Hamilton (backed, naturally, by Churchill) stubbornly opposed withdrawal, arguing that an evacuation would cost up to fifty per cent casualties. London was not impressed, and Hamilton was subsequently recalled. His replacement, Sir Charles Monro, took one look at the situation and proposed that the remaining 105,000 Allied troops should be evacuated. The evacuation began from Suvla Bay on 7 December, 1915, and the last troops left Helles on 9 January, 1916. It is an irony that the most successful episode in the entire campaign was the evacuation. Contrary to Hamilton's dire warnings, the Ottomans did not attempt to slaughter the retreating soldiers. They were just relieved to see them depart.

The Gallipoli campaign ended in a humiliating defeat for the Allies. Accepting his responsibility for the disastrous Dardanelles Campaign, Winston Churchill resigned his post as First Lord of the Admiralty and re-joined the army as a battalion commander. He lost his job. But the soldiers he sent to their deaths lost a lot more. In all, some 480,000 Allied forces took part in the Gallipoli Campaign, at a cost of more than 350,000 casualties, including some 46,000 dead.

On the Ottoman side, the campaign also cost an estimated 250,000 casualties, with 65,000 killed. But, for the Turks, this was a great national victory. Masses of people danced and sang on the streets of Constantinople. Eight years later, the man who had led the Ottoman troops to victory stood at the head of the new nation called Turkey that emerged from the ashes of the Ottoman Empire. He became known to history as Kemal Atatürk (the Father of the Turks).

9. VICTIMS AND AGGRESSORS

While the armies of the Great Powers were busy slaughtering each other in Flanders, Tannenberg and Gallipoli, their weaker brethren were watching with keen anticipation from the sidelines, like hyenas waiting to gorge themselves on the corpses of the defeated party. As long as it remained unclear which of the big bandits would prove the stronger, the little bandits had to be patient and wait for their opportunity to arrive.

On 26 April, 1915, Italy suddenly announced its entry into the war on the side of the Allies. This announcement provoked fury in Berlin and Vienna. Because Italy had been allied with the German and Austro-Hungarian Empires since 1882 as part of the Triple Alliance, the Germans and Austrians felt they had been tricked, and so they had. Unknown to their former partners, the Italians had already signed a secret treaty with the Entente.

As early as 1902, when Italy was still a member of the Triple Alliance (with Germany and Austria), the government of Rome had signed a secret pact with France that effectively nullified its alliance with the Central Powers. But even then, the Italian diplomats manoeuvred to hedge their bets. At the outbreak of war, Italy refused to commit troops, arguing that the Triple Alliance was 'defensive' and that Austria-Hungary was an 'aggressor'. This semantic argument was really cynicism of the most exquisite refinement, since the men in Rome were already preparing a little aggression of their own.

The weakness of the Italian bourgeoisie meant that they had to compensate with cunning what they lacked in military might and economic weight. The gentlemen in Rome were worthy disciples of Machiavelli and had their own agenda to pursue. Since this involved design on Austrian territory in Trentino, the Austrian Littoral, Fiume (Rijeka) and Dalmatia, the break with Austria and Germany was perfectly logical from their point of view. And what was a broken promise or two, or some treaty or other, compared to a few thousand acres of land and a substantial amount of plunder?

Alarmed by a potential threat to its southern borders, the Austro-Hungarian government hastened to open negotiations to purchase Italian neutrality by offering them the French colony of Tunisia in return. Of course, since France had not yet been defeated and was still in secure possession of its North Africa colony, the value of this offer was somewhat relative. No, the rulers of Italy were men of honour and therefore were not prepared to sell themselves at such an absurdly low price. Like a man haggling over the price of herrings in the market, they turned their backs on one stall and moved on to the next.

On 16 February, 1915, while negotiations with Austria were still continuing, the Italian Prime Minister, Antonio Salandra, sent a representative to London under the cloak of utmost secrecy to suggest, with respect, to the British government that Italy might possibly be open to an offer from the Entente, provided, of course, that it was sufficiently generous. The gentlemen in London did not deceive their expectations. They made a most tempting counter-offer: Italy would receive the Southern Tyrol, Austrian Littoral and territory on the Dalmatian coast – but, of course, only after the defeat of Austria-Hungary.

The final choice was aided by the arrival of news of Russian victories in the Carpathians in March and the Allied invasion of Turkey in April. The Italians began to think that victory for the Entente was imminent, and were naturally anxious not to arrive too late for a share in the plunder. In order to expedite matters, Salandra instructed his envoy in London to drop some of the earlier demands and reach agreement as quickly as decently possible. The Treaty of London was concluded on

26 April, binding Italy to fight within one month. But it was not until 4 May that Salandra denounced the Triple Alliance in a private note to its signatories. Italy declared war on Austria-Hungary on 23 May. Fifteen months later it declared war on Germany.

ITALY ATTACKS AUSTRIA

From a military point of view, things did not look at all bad for Italy. The Italian army enjoyed a numerical superiority over the opposing Austrian forces. But this apparent advantage took no account of the difficult terrain in which fighting took place, or the mule-like stupidity of the Italian commander, Field Marshal Luigi Cadorna. Cadorna dreamed of a triumphant Italian army smashing its way onto the Slovenian plateau, seizing Ljubljana and even marching up to the gates of Vienna itself.

Cadorna, who seemed to see himself as a reincarnation of Julius Caesar, was an enthusiastic proponent of the frontal assault. His army must always advance. The number of soldiers who were lost in the process was a matter of little or no interest to him. What he did not see were the frightful difficulties posed by the rugged Alpine and Karstic terrain, the freezing temperatures, or the new conditions created by trench warfare.

Full of optimism, the Italians launched offensives along the 400-mile common border between Austria and Italy, a region with some of the highest mountains in Europe. Unfortunately for Cadorna, and even more unfortunately for his soldiers, the better equipped Austrians took advantage of the mountainous terrain to establish strong defensive positions all along the border. There was to be no triumphal march to the gates of Vienna but only a series of bloody battles, long lists of casualties and an inglorious stalemate.

Fighting at such high altitudes in harsh and brutal conditions was a new kind of hell for the soldiers on both sides. The Italian *alpinisti* (mountaineers) had to scale sheer rock faces under a barrage of enemy fire. The Austrians fought with ferocious tenacity in what were frequently bloody hand-to-hand battles. A single hand grenade could cause an avalanche in which hundreds could be buried alive or hurled into the abyss. An even more terrible threat was that posed by mining. The Austrians and Italians dug caves in the mountainsides, where twentieth century men lived like Stone Age troglodytes. Both sides tried to dig under the enemy's caves and plant explosives to blow them sky-high. The constant fear of such explosions drove men mad.

More than 30,000 casualties in this campaign were ethnic Slovenes, the majority of them being drafted into the Austro-Hungarian army. Many thousands of Slovene civilians from the Gorizia and Gradisca region were forcibly resettled in refugee camps where they were treated as state enemies by the Italians, and several thousand were starved to death.

The Italians shifted the focus of their attacks on the mountain passes at Trentino and the valley of the Isonzo (Soča) River, northeast of Trieste. On the Trentino front, the mountainous terrain was advantageous to the Austro-Hungarian defenders. Owing to the difficult terrain, mules could not be used and so the unfortunate Italian soldiers had to haul heavy artillery up frozen mountains, plagued by frostbite, hunger and exhaustion and all the time under a continuous barrage of fire from the enemy who held the summit.

On 23 June, the First Battle of Isonzo began as Italian troops attacked Austrian defences. Initial gains by the Italians were soon repulsed by the Austrians with heavy casualties for both sides. Three additional battles were fought through the end of 1915 with similar results, totalling 230,000 casualties for the Italians and 165,000 for the Austrians.

Throughout the summer, the Austrian *Kaiserschützen* and *Standschützen* fought the Italian *Alpini*. The Italian army was bleeding to death, but general Cadorna knew only one command: 'advance!' Cadorna mounted a total of eleven offensives on the Isonzo front. All eleven offensives were repelled by the Austro-Hungarians with frightful losses.

In the summer of 1916, after the Battle of Doberdò, the Italians captured the town of Gorizia. After this minor victory, the front remained static for over a year, despite several Italian offensives. Then disaster struck. In the autumn of 1917, thanks to the improving situation on the Eastern front, the Austro-Hungarian troops received

9. VICTIMS AND AGGRESSORS

large numbers of reinforcements, including German Stormtroopers and the elite *Alpenkorps*. The morale of the Austrians received a great boost from the arrival of the Germans, who were fresh and optimistic.

On 26 October, 1917, the Central Powers launched a crushing offensive spearheaded by the Germans. They achieved a decisive victory at Caporetto (Kobarid). By now the morale of the Italian soldiers was near breaking point. Mutinous moods found their expression in mass surrenders. Thousands of Italian troops handed themselves over to the Germans without firing a shot. Those officers who attempted to resist were shot by their own men.

In the winter of 1917, approximately 300,000 Italian soldiers surrendered to the Germans, while a similar number joined the mass of civilian refugees fleeing from the war zone. When asked why they were retreating, they would reply that they had been told to do so. When asked who had told them, they just shrugged their shoulders.

So heavy were the losses of the Italian Army in the Battle of Caporetto, that the Italian Government called to arms the so-called '99 Boys (*Ragazzi del '99*): that is, all males who were eighteen-years-old or older. But time was not on the side of Austro-Hungary. By the start of 1918, the tide of the War in Europe was turning against the Central Powers. The Austro-Hungarians made a desperate attempt to break through in a series of battles on the Piave River but were defeated in the Battle of Vittorio Veneto in October of that year.

Exhausted by its losses, Austria-Hungary surrendered in early November 1918. The Italian gamblers lost no time in scrambling to collect the winnings that had been promised to them by the London Pact. On 3 November, the Italians occupied Trieste. By mid-November 1918, the Italian military occupied the entire former Austrian Littoral, and seized control of the entire portion of Dalmatia.

Just to make sure there was no objection from the Slovenes, Croats, and Serbs, who were creating Yugoslavia out of the wreckage of the Empire, the Italian Navy destroyed much of the Austro-Hungarian fleet stationed in Pula, preventing it from being handed over to the new State. Italy was showing its weaker neighbours that a new bully-boy had arrived on the block.

BULGARIA JOINS IN THE FIGHT

For the first ten months of 1915, Austria-Hungary used most of its military reserves to fight Italy. But while that life-and-death struggle was being fought in the Alps, new and deadly manoeuvres were taking place on the diplomatic chessboard. The struggle between Germany and Austria and Russia was portrayed in Berlin as a racial struggle between Teutons and Slavs. This was a fact that conveniently overlooked the fact that a large part of the Austro-Hungarian Empire was also composed of Slavs (Czechs, Slovaks, Slovenes and Bosnians) and this was reflected in the mixed composition of the Austro-Hungarian army.

The immediate cause of the War was precisely the struggle of the Habsburgs to maintain their domination of the Balkans against the young and thrusting power of Serbia, with Russia standing behind it. Balkan wars have always been accompanied by a particular ferocity, fuelled by national hatreds. These feelings were systematically fanned by the ruling circles as a means of mobilising the darkest passions for the sake of territorial ambitions and satiating their greed. The bloody Balkan Wars of 1912 and 1913 drove the Turks from the Balkans but also ended in catastrophe for Bulgaria.

After bearing the bulk of the fighting against the Ottoman forces, Bulgaria was stabbed in the back by its supposed allies, Serbia and Greece. Together with Romania, they seized huge swaths of territory that they had agreed should be given to Bulgaria. Bulgaria's participation in the Balkan Wars crippled its public finances and ruined its economy. A predominantly peasant country, Bulgaria's agricultural production fell by about nine per cent compared to 1911. The loss of Southern Dobrudja, which had accounted for twenty per cent of Bulgarian grain production before the wars dealt a mortal blow to Bulgarian agriculture. Thousands of peasants and agricultural workers were killed in the wars. The number of available horses, sheep, cattle and other livestock was twenty per cent and forty per cent lower.

Bled white by the heavy loss of life, isolated and surrounded by hostile neighbours, deprived of the support of the Great Powers, stripped of a large part of its territory and economically ruined, Bulgaria was seized by deep feelings of resentment. This inevitably found an expression in

9. VICTIMS AND AGGRESSORS

a desire for revenge in the ruling circles in Sofia. It was only a matter of time before this accumulation of combustible material would lead to a new explosion.

When war broke out in August 1914, the Bulgarian ruling clique declared the country's neutrality. Its strategic geographic location and strong army made Bulgaria a desirable ally for the Entente, for Germany and particularly Austro-Hungary. But Bulgarian aspirations included territorial claims against four Balkan countries. If it had just been a question of Serbia, it would have been a simple matter for the Central Powers to have won Bulgaria to their side. But an open alliance with Bulgaria would have alienated Romania and Greece, countries that Germany and Austria Hungary were also attempting to woo.

King Ferdinand of Bulgaria, who was incidentally born in Vienna and whose full name was Ferdinand Maximilian Karl Leopold Maria of Saxe-Coburg and Gotha, had stated, "the purpose of my life is the destruction of Serbia." That was music to the ears of the men in Vienna who, up until this moment, had tried three times, and shamefully failed each time, to conquer Serbia. However, outside the aristocratic ruling clique and the patriotic middle-class riff-raff, there was no popular enthusiasm in Bulgaria for entering the war.

The Bulgarian workers and peasants had already suffered enough from wars and were mostly in favour of neutrality. This was a major element in forcing Prime Minister Radoslavov to stay out of the war, while at the same time carefully exploring the willingness of both sides to satisfy Bulgarian territorial ambitions. The ruling clique was waiting to see which one of the sides would win a decisive military advantage and who would give cast-iron guarantees for the fulfilment of 'Bulgarian national ideals'.

As the war dragged on, the Central Powers decided they had no alternative but to give in to the demands of the ruling clique in Sofia. German and Austro-Hungarian diplomats pulled off a major coup by persuading Bulgaria to join the attack on the common enemy, Serbia. As soon as the Central Powers offered to give them what they claimed, the Bulgarians entered the war on their side. It seemed to be a sound decision. The Allies were losing the Battle of Gallipoli and the Russians had suffered a major defeat at Gorlice. So, it was with high hopes that King Ferdinand signed a treaty with Germany on 23 September, 1915, and Bulgaria began mobilising for war.

With Germany and Bulgaria now on their side, the Austrians resumed their plan of conquest with a new spirit of optimism. The Slav provinces of the Austro-Hungarian Empire (Slovenia, Croatia and Bosnia) provided troops for the Austro-Hungarian invasion of Serbia, while only little Montenegro allied itself with Serbia. The Germans and Austro-Hungarians crossed the Danube and moved on to take Belgrade. The Serbs fought like tigers in vicious street fighting, but in two days the capital fell, overwhelmed by superior forces. Then came a further crushing blow. On 14 October, Bulgaria sent 600,000 troops into Serbia. The Bulgarian Army attacked from two directions, from the north of Bulgaria towards Niš and from the south towards Skopje.

The Bulgarian attack rendered the Serbian position completely untenable; the main army in the north (around Belgrade) could either retreat, or be surrounded and forced to surrender. In the Battle of Kosovo, the Serbs made a last and desperate stand, but in the end were forced to retreat. Beset by enemies on all sides, Serbia was overrun in a little more than a month. Faced with the prospect of annihilation, the Serbian generals decided to retreat into Albania. The army had to deal with snowstorms and intense cold, with impassable roads and almost no supplies or food, whilst they trudged across steep mountains together with the tens of thousands of civilians fleeing from a merciless enemy. Many soldiers and civilians did not make it to the coast. They perished of hunger, disease, the attacks of enemy forces and ambushes by Albanian bandits.

Britain and France talked about sending troops to Serbia, but nothing was done until it was too late. At the end of 1915, a Franco-British force landed at Salonika in Greece, to offer assistance to the Serbs and to pressure the Greek government to declare war against the Central Powers. The answer of the pro-German King Constantine I was to overthrow the pro-Allied government of Eleftherios Venizelos before the Allied expeditionary force arrived.

9. VICTIMS AND AGGRESSORS

The British puppet Venizelos set up a provisional government in Salonika where he was protected by the bayonets of the Entente. Greece was split into two camps, which nearly came to blows before the King of Greece resigned in favour of his son Alexander, who joined the war on the side of the Allies. But the Greek army did nothing. French and Serbian forces retook limited areas of Macedonia by recapturing Bitola on 19 November 1916 following a costly offensive. For most of the time, however, what was known as the Macedonian Front was a picture of impotent inactivity.

Only after most of the German and Austro-Hungarian troops had been withdrawn in September 1918 did the French finally make a breakthrough, when the Bulgarians suffered their only defeat of the war at the Battle of Dobro Pole. Two weeks later, on 29 September 1918, Bulgaria surrendered to the Allies and, as a consequence, lost not only the additional territory it had fought for in the major conflict, but also the territory it had won after the Balkan Wars, giving access to the Aegean Sea.

Bulgaria had suffered a second national catastrophe, which shaped its national consciousness just as the agonising Calvary of the Serbs has been burned into the collective memory of that people. These tragedies have played an important part in creating a sense of victimhood that lasted for generations. Serbs and Bulgarians, Greeks and Albanians, Croats and Macedonians – all saw themselves as victims.

That is the problem. In the Balkans everyone sees themselves as a victim and nobody as an aggressor. That is the great tragedy of the Balkans. The question that must be asked is: who are the victims and who are the aggressors? The ordinary Serbs, Greeks, Bulgarians and Albanians have always been victims – victims of their own ruling class. The ordinary people did not engage in diplomatic intrigues. They did not spread lying propaganda in the press. They did not declare war against anybody. And they did not order thousands to march to their deaths.

It is the poor peasants and workers, who were driven like sheep to the slaughter in wars against other poor peasants on the other side of imaginary and meaningless borders. They, and nobody else, are always the victims of somebody else's war. As for the rulers of the Balkan states, history shows us that yesterday's victim becomes tomorrow's aggressor and yesterday's hanged man becomes tomorrow's executioner. And so it goes on, a never-ending dance of death and hate, until the workers and peasants rise up against their own landlords and capitalists, tear down the artificial frontiers, and create a Balkan Socialist Federation on the principles of freedom, equality and justice. Only then can we put an end to this whole bloody business.

10. THE USA: WAR IS GOOD FOR BUSINESS

Somebody once said to Lenin war is terrible, to which he replied: "yes, terribly profitable". The European war suited the American industrialists rather well. Capitalism in the USA had developed with whirlwind speed in the last decades of the nineteenth century. At the beginning of the war in Europe, America was already a powerful young nation with a mighty industrial base. In this war it played the role of chief usurer and quartermaster to the European belligerents.

For most of the war the United States remained formally neutral and, even when it eventually intervened, the costs it had to bear were insignificant when measured against its huge resources and the colossal profits it derived. America's main competitors in the world market, Britain, Germany and France, were too busy slaughtering each other to present an alternative to the Transatlantic Colossus.

A Europe that was tearing itself apart now presented itself as a huge market of millions of consumers prepared to buy anything and everything the USA had to sell, and was willing to pay any price the American government and big business saw fit to charge. As a result, US exports soared to two-and-a-half times greater than the highest pre-war level. Moreover, most of these exports were no longer agricultural produce as in the past, but manufactured goods.

Yes, war was definitely good for business. American companies that had been facing ruin in the economic crisis that preceded the outbreak of war were now working flat out supplying the belligerents with the shells, bombs and bullets they required to blow themselves to bits. This fact reveals a new relationship between the Old World and the New. In effect, the United States was placing Europe on rations.

A country that, just over a hundred years earlier, had been a European colony now emerged as a new and powerful imperialist nation. In the words of Hegel, things become transformed into their opposite. While the sclerotic and already somewhat senile European bourgeoisie was wasting its precious resources in a cannibalistic war between the pygmy states of that continent, the productive forces of America, with its vast spaces and almost limitless human and material resources, were booming. Between 1914 and 1917, American industrial production increased thirty-two per cent and GNP increased by almost twenty per cent.

Bethlehem Steel, which had suffered from the economic recession before the war, was now making handsome profits pouring out the steel that Europe needed to build tanks, guns and artillery shells. By the end of the war, Bethlehem Steel had produced 65,000 pounds of forged military products and 70 million pounds of armour plate, 1.1 billion pounds of steel for shells, and 20.1 million rounds of artillery ammunition for Britain and France.

The entry of the USA into the war in 1917 gave Bethlehem Steel an additional boost. It was now producing sixty per cent of the weapons used by the US army and forty per cent of the artillery shells used in the war. Even after President Wilson imposed price controls and a lower profit margin on manufactured goods, the profits Bethlehem Steel made from its wartime sales continued to soar, turning it into the third-largest manufacturing company in the country.

US exports to belligerent nations rose rapidly during the years of the war from $824.8 million in 1913 to $2.25 billion in 1917. All this was aided by generous grants to business by the US government. The link between big business and government, the fusion of the big banks and monopolies with the bourgeois state, one of the most prominent features of imperialism, was already very firmly established.

What was true of industry was even truer for finance capital, the real heart of imperialism. Loans from American financial institutions to the Allied nations in Europe experienced a sharp increase during the war. The House of Morgan provided the necessary funds for the wartime financing of Britain and France. From 1914 onwards the House of Morgan's bank in New York was designated as the primary financial agent to the British government, and later played a similar role in regard to France. But as the war raged on with no end in sight, relations between the House of Morgan and the French government became strained as the falling value of the Franc gave rise to doubts as to its ability to pay. When all is said and done, democracy is democracy, but profits are profits.

WOODROW WILSON

All these facts show that, from the very beginning, America was a major participant in the war through its economic and financial might. Yet, formally speaking, it remained a neutral state until 1917. The reasons for this 'pacifism' are not difficult to see. It was dictated by the same cynical calculations that motivated the foreign policy of British imperialism before the summer of 1914.

The British imperialists thought that they could remain aloof from the European conflict, confining themselves to providing just enough aid to Russia and France to halt the triumphal march of Germany. Later, when the belligerents had bled themselves to the point of exhaustion, Great Britain could step in as the almighty arbiter and obtain total domination. This is the real explanation for the apparent 'pacifism' and supine inactivity of men like Sir Edward Grey up to and even beyond the assassination in Sarajevo.

But the calculations of the British Foreign Office proved to be mistaken. The colossal power of German militarism soon proved itself on the battlefields of Belgium and France, and Britain was compelled to come off the fence and intervene in the war to prevent Germany from achieving complete victory. In the end, it was the United States that inherited the role that Great Britain had hoped to play. Its 'pacifism' was dictated, not by morality or humanitarianism, but by naked self-interest.

That does not necessarily mean that the opponents of America's entry into the war were not personally convinced that they were motivated by the highest ideals. In every historical period, the needs of different classes are expressed with greater or lesser coherence by individual men and women. These 'great individuals' seem to anticipate and dominate events, but more often than not, they are dominated by them. They do not themselves understand the real content and significance of the idea they are advocating. But a given idea can correspond closely to the interests of certain classes or groups in society. This is what explains their success at a given moment, and also their failure at a later stage when conditions have changed and new ideas are needed.

Onto the stage of history strides Thomas Woodrow Wilson. He was known to his contemporaries as a 'schoolmaster in politics', which was a very apt description. With his acidic facial expression, tightly pursed lips and pince-nez perched on a long and aquiline nose, he resembled a hybrid between a retired headmaster and the vicar of a sleepy rural parish. The history books depict him as a high-minded idealist, whose ideals were shattered against the pitiless rock of a cruel world. The truth, as usual, is more complex.

A devoted Presbyterian, Wilson gave up a promising academic career that took him to the presidency of the prestigious Princeton University to enter the rough and tumble of American and international politics. Determined to become a statesman, he studied law for a year and then became a candidate for the Democratic Party. The change did not really suit him.

It is one thing to deliver lectures on morality and good behaviour to a lecture hall full of bright-eyed and obedient students. It is quite another to deliver the same lectures to hard-headed politicians engaged in the single-minded pursuit of power. And when these same politicians and statesmen are engaged in the serious business of war, lectures on peace, morality and justice are received with as much enthusiasm as a speech on the virtues of vegetarianism at a cannibals' dinner party.

In 1910, Wilson accepted the Democratic nomination for governor of New Jersey. He stood on a progressive agenda, based on the idea of protecting the public from exploitation by rapacious trusts and won a landslide victory. This earned him national recognition, and in 1912 he won the Democratic nomination for President. Wilson's 'New Freedom' platform, based on the need to revitalise the American economy, then in a deep recession, won him the Presidency.

From his desk in the White House, President Wilson continued his Holy Crusade against corrupt trusts. But the outbreak of War in 1914 changed everything. From the very beginning there was pressure from all sides for the USA to enter the war, but the peace-loving Woodrow Wilson firmly maintained American neutrality. In the 1916 election Wilson campaigned on the slogan 'He kept us out of war!' He warned that a Republican victory would mean war with both Mexico and Germany. He won again.

Public opinion in the USA was divided on the question of the war. The sizable German-speaking population was obviously pro-German and many other Americans were against entering the war. There were also pronounced regional differences, with the South firmly opposed. There were sharp divisions within the American ruling class as to whether the USA should participate in a 'European war'.

Three broadly distinct groups can be discerned. There were the 'pacifists', who wanted to keep America out of the war at all costs. They included Secretary of State, William Jennings Bryan; the Republican, Senator Robert M. La Follette, Sr.; and Henry Ford, who was a Democrat. Then there were those who wanted to forge an alliance with Britain, led by former President Theodore (Teddy) Roosevelt. Finally, there was the group represented by President Woodrow Wilson and former president William Howard Taft.

However, behind the façade of 'pacifism' were concealed the real material interests of American capitalism. Wilsonian pacifism lasted only as long as it served those interests, and the moment it ceased to do so, the smiling mask of pacifism was cast off to reveal the ferocious physiognomy of bellicose imperialism. One year after fighting an election on a 'no war' platform, Wilson draped himself in the Stars and Stripes and led the USA into the war on the side of the Allies.

'PREPAREDNESS'

Behind the smokescreen of 'pacifism', step by step, American public opinion was being prepared for war. A major step towards this end was the launching of the so-called Preparedness movement, which emerged in 1915. It argued that the United States needed to immediately build up strong naval and land forces 'for defensive purposes'. The unspoken assumption was that the US would have to enter the war sooner or later. In addition to Roosevelt, many of the nation's most prominent bankers, industrialists, lawyers and scions of prominent families backed the movement.

The Preparedness movement had no time for the kind of woolly idealism favoured by the President. Causes like democracy and national self-determination for small nations and similar idealistic baloney were not for them. These hard-headed men and women advocated a far-more realistic philosophy of world affairs. As true-blue American patriots, they firmly believed that economic strength and military muscle were vastly preferable to sentimental speechifying. And they were determined to put this philosophy into practice. They were looking for a new world role for America when the war had ended, and nothing would be allowed to stand in the way.

Again and again, they complained about the weak state of national defences. They protested that America's 100,000-man Army (even if one included the 112,000 National Guard) was outnumbered twenty to one by the German Army, although Germany had a smaller population. They demanded universal military training, or UMT. They advocated the establishment of a national service programme in which every male citizen who reached the age of eighteen would be required to spend six months in military training, and afterwards be assigned to reserve units. The small regular army would serve mainly for training purposes. Woodrow Wilson firmly opposed it – after all, he was a pacifist and a man of high principles. Later, however, he changed his principles and embraced the very same programme that had previously earned his most severe moralistic condemnation.

Anti-militarists and pacifists protested and opposed the plan, which they said would turn the USA into a militaristic society like Germany.

The Socialist Party, which initially held an anti-war position, correctly branded the European conflict as an imperialist war. Eugene V. Debs, the leading figure in the US socialist and labour movement, explained that the war was a result of capitalism: "A bayonet", he said, "was a weapon with a worker at each end". But just as in Europe, so in the United States, the labour movement soon divided into right-wing pro-war and left-wing internationalist wings.

In 1914, Samuel Gompers, the extreme opportunist leader of the AFL unions, at first denounced the war as "unnatural, unjustified, and unholy". That was safe enough to do, since it was in line with the official position of American Big Business and the President. But already by 1916, Wilson was edging away from that line. In the 1916 election, the US union leaders supported Wilson for President and kept very quiet about the war question, sensing that a change was in the air. Soon after, Gompers became a supporter of the Preparedness programme, despite the protests of the radical union rank and file.

When Wilson changed his mind and led America into the War, the AFL leaders predictably hastened to fall into line with the bourgeoisie, becoming the most rabid pro-war 'patriots'. However, old Debs remained an implacable opponent of the War and conducted a sharp struggle against the opportunist wing of the SP and the unions. The anti-war socialists were viciously persecuted under the Anti-Espionage Act 1917 and many, including Debs, were arrested for their alleged treason. In 1920, Debs received almost a million votes while he was locked up in a prison cell.

THE SINKING OF THE *LUSITANIA*

The reason for America's entry into the war was exactly the same as the one that compelled Britain to intervene in 1914: to prevent Germany from winning the war and uniting the entire European continent under its domination. This would be a serious threat to the interests of US imperialism and it had to be stopped at all costs, as Trotsky explained:

> In relation to Europe as a whole the United States assumed the role which England had taken in previous wars and which she tried to take in the last

war in relation to the continent, namely: weakening one camp by playing it against another, intervening in military operations only to such an extent as to guarantee her all the advantages of the situation. According to American standards of gambling, Wilson's stake was not very high, but it was the final stake, and consequently assured his winning the prize. (Trotsky, L., *The First Five Years of the Communist International*, Vol. 1, p. 20.)

However, by 1917 there seemed to be a serious possibility that Germany would win the war and achieve total domination of Europe. This represented a serious threat to the interests of the American bourgeoisie. They now decided that the time was ripe to throw all the material and military might of the United States onto the side of the Entente. But there was a problem. In 1916, the majority of Americans were still opposed to entering the war.

However, the ruling class has a thousand ways of conditioning people's thinking and moulding what is known as 'public opinion' in its own interests. At the beginning of every war a pretext is needed – some kind of act of aggression by the other side – that can justify the call to arms. The key turning point in changing the mood of American public opinion was provided by the sinking of the *Lusitania* in 1915.

For some time, the Atlantic had been as much a battleground in the war as the fields of Flanders and the Somme. In order to starve Germany into submission, the British navy implemented a blockade, halting and boarding merchant ships to prevent the shipment of war supplies and food to Germany. This included stopping and searching the ships of neutral nations, including American ones. But the British naval blockade of the Atlantic was a minor irritation for the American bourgeois who, in any case, were deriving fat profits from the European slaughter. In private, Washington sent signals to London and Paris that America too was on the side of 'democracy', while publicly maintaining a stance of hypocritical neutrality.

Unable to challenge the powerful British navy in an open conflict, Admiral Alfred von Tirpitz launched the submarine war in the Atlantic. Since Britain depended on imports of food, raw materials, and manufactured goods by sea, this was a way of defeating it by slow strangulation. "England wants to starve us", he said. "We can play the same game. We can bottle her up and destroy every ship that endeavours to break the blockade". German submarines carried out their campaign with ruthless efficiency and total disregard for human life. Merchant ships were torpedoed without warning, and sailors and passengers drowned. Berlin argued that it was too dangerous for submarines to surface to rescue survivors as most merchant ships carried guns that could sink a submarine.

In February 1915, the United States warned Germany about the activities of its submarines. On 7 May, 1915, a German submarine sank the British passenger liner *RMS Lusitania* with the loss of 1,198 civilian lives, including 128 Americans. The sinking of a large, unarmed passenger ship, combined with the previous atrocity stories from Belgium, shocked Americans and was used to stir up hostility towards Germany, although not yet sufficiently to unleash a US military intervention. Wilson issued a warning to Germany that it would face "strict accountability" if it sank any more neutral US passenger ships. This was a big step in preparing the road to America's entry into the war.

The prospect of US intervention caused alarm in Germany. The men in Berlin cursed under their breath and ordered their submarines to avoid passenger ships. But the damage had been done. On the basis of a massive propaganda campaign, the US government was already beginning to mobilise for war. In 1917, determined to win the war of attrition against the Allies, Germany announced the resumption of unrestricted warfare in war-zone waters.

On top of this, there was the revelation of the Zimmermann Telegram, in which Germany offered Mexico its support for winning back the states of Texas, New Mexico and Arizona from the US if it became a German ally. It was a clear attempt to divert America's attention from the War in Europe by provoking war between the United States and Mexico. The United States broke diplomatic relations with Germany, but Wilson continued to plead for peace: "We are the sincere friends of the German people and earnestly desire to remain at peace with them," he said. "We shall not believe they are hostile to us unless or until we are obliged to believe it".

But the men in Berlin were no longer listening. Convinced that the USA was preparing to declare war, in March the Germans sank several more American ships. Teddy Roosevelt raged against Wilson's inactivity: "If he does not go to war, I shall skin him alive". Fortunately, he was soon relieved of that disagreeable necessity. On 20 March, Wilson called a cabinet meeting, which voted unanimously for war. On 2 April, the President appeared before Congress calling for a declaration of war against Germany. Four days later, his request was granted.

On 26 June, the first 14,000 US infantry troops landed in France. Significantly, the US did not sign a formal alliance with Britain or France but operated as an 'associated power'. That is to say, the US imperialists wanted to keep their hands free and not become entangled in formal alliances. It was in their interests to prevent a German victory, but it was not at all their intention to subordinate themselves to the British and the French, whom they were aiming to displace as masters of the world once Germany had been disposed of.

AMERICA'S IMPERIALIST AMBITIONS

The First World War was a war to decide which of the Great Powers would achieve world domination. The old imperial powers of Europe had already succeeded in carving the world up into colonies, protected markets and spheres of influence. Germany, which had arrived late on the scene, was determined to bring about a radical redistribution of the world. But while Britain, France and Germany were engaged in a bloody and prolonged slogging match, the new and powerful rival across the Atlantic was flexing its muscles.

The imperialist ambitions of the American ruling class had already been tested in the war with Spain in 1898, which led to the de facto annexation of Cuba by the USA. Long before that the Monroe Doctrine proclaimed to the world the determination of the US to dominate the whole of Latin America, to the exclusion of all other powers. This claim was reinforced by the forcible annexation of huge swathes of Mexican territory in Texas and California. The USA continually interfered in Mexico's internal affairs and intervened militarily during the Mexican

Revolution, during which it occupied Vera Cruz and even staged an invasion of Mexican territory in a failed attempt to capture Pancho Villa in 1916.

But US imperialism had its eyes fixed on targets far from the shores of the New World. It had far more ambitious aims in mind in Asia and the Pacific. This was shown by its seizure of the Philippines after a cruel war that lasted three years and resulted in the death of over 20,000 Filipino combatants. The US Marines distinguished themselves by the extreme barbarity with which they slaughtered thousands of Filipinos like animals. As many as 200,000 Filipino civilians died from violence, famine, and disease in this vicious conflict by which America first staked its claim to the colonial domination of Asia.

In 1915, while the world's attention was focused on the battlefields of Europe, the USA set out to conquer yet another small and defenceless country. The United States was increasingly concerned about growing German activity and influence in Haiti. At the beginning of the twentieth century, the German presence in the country increased as German merchants began establishing trading branches there, quickly dominating commercial business in the area. Using the assassination of the Haitian president Jean Vilbrun Guillaume Sam as an excuse, the pacifist President Wilson sent the US Marines to Haiti, claiming the invasion was an attempt to prevent anarchy. In reality, the Wilson administration was protecting the assets of US business in the area and forestalling a possible German invasion.

The truth is that the United States government had been interested in Haiti for decades prior to its occupation. As a potential naval base for the United States and other imperialist powers, Haiti was of great interest to Washington. As early as 1868, President Andrew Johnson suggested the annexation of the island of Hispaniola, made up of Haiti and the Dominican Republic, to secure a US defensive and economic stake in the West Indies. From 1889 to 1891, Secretary of State James Blaine unsuccessfully sought a lease of Mole-Saint Nicolas, a city on Haiti's northern coast strategically located for a naval base. In 1910, President William Howard Taft granted Haiti a large loan in order to tie that country firmly to Washington and Wall Street.

The invasion ended with the Haitian-American Treaty of 1915. The articles of this agreement created a Haitian gendarmerie, which was essentially a military force made up of Americans and Haitians under the effective control of the US Marines. The United States gained complete control over Haitian finances, and the right to intervene in Haiti whenever the government in Washington deemed it necessary. Overnight, to all intents and purposes, the existence of Haiti as an independent nation was abolished.

The US government then consolidated its control by forcing the election of a new President, Philippe Sudré Dartiguenave, an American stooge, by the Haitian legislature. The 'election' under the bayonets of the US army of a President who did not represent the choice of the Haitian people led to increased unrest in Haiti. The gendarmerie's brutality and unpopular policies – including racial segregation, press censorship and forced labour – led to a peasant rebellion from 1919 to 1920. In 1929, a series of strikes and uprisings forced the United States to begin withdrawal from Haiti, and the occupation was ended in 1934. But, even after that, Washington maintained its influence over the country, together with the former imperial power France, which ruled through the agency of brutal and corrupt dictators. These actions tell us quite a lot about the true nature of President Wilson's pacifist beliefs, his policy of 'non-interventionism' and his respect for the cause of self-determination of small nations.

'THE WHOLE WORLD FOR AMERICA'

After three years of bloody stalemate on the western front, the entry of America's well-equipped forces into the conflict marked a major turning point in the war and helped the Allies to win a decisive victory. When the war finally ended, on 11 November, 1918, more than 2 million American soldiers had served on the battlefields of Western Europe, and some 50,000 of them had lost their lives. These losses, however, were small when compared with those suffered by Germany, Austria, France, Britain and Russia. The Great Powers of Europe emerged from the fighting with ruined economies and enormous debts.

In the space of seven years there was a complete reversal in the sphere of world division of labour. The United States had grown at the expense of Britain far more than Britain had benefited from the defeat of Germany. The United States was challenging Britain's domination of the seas. Before the war, Great Britain possessed more than half of the world tonnage, and the United States only five per cent, but by the end of World War One that relationship had been transformed. Britain now accounted for no more than thirty-five per cent, while the United States possessed thirty per cent of the world shipping tonnage. Similarly, the United States attained domination of the coal market, which Britain once had.

The World War compelled the United States to abandon the old continental conservatism that goes under the name of isolationism. As Trotsky put it: "The programme of an ascending national capitalism – 'America for the Americans' (the Monroe Doctrine) – has been supplanted by the programme of imperialism: 'The Whole World for the Americans'." By waiting until the last moment before throwing its sword onto the scales, US imperialism gained tremendously at the expense of Europe, thus preparing the path for America's future world domination. As Trotsky later explained:

> For four-odd years Europe became converted into a sheet of fire fed, not only by Europe's income, but also by her basic capital, while the American bourgeoisie warmed its hands at the flames. America's productive capacity has grown extraordinarily but her market has vanished because Europe is impoverished and can no longer buy American goods. It is as if Europe had first done everything in her power to help America climb to the topmost rung and then pulled the ladder out. (Trotsky, L., 'Manifesto to the Third World Congress', *The First Five Years of the Communist International*, Vol. 1, pp. 193-196.)

Before the war, French finance capital was dominant. The whole world was in debt to France, including America. By the end of the war, however, Europe's combined debts to the United States amounted to 18 billion gold dollars and these debts were constantly increasing.

Almost one-half of the world's gold reserves were now in the hands of the United States. Europe's accumulated debts to America amounted to $18 billion.

After draining the blood from its European rivals and turning them into its supplicants and debtors, America's intervention in the war tipped the scales decisively in favour of the Entente, bringing about Germany's defeat. All this meant that the USA became the arbiter of Europe's destiny and a major factor in world politics.

One of the central planks of Wilson's 'Fourteen Points' was, of course, the right of self-determination. This right, long before proclaimed by Lenin, was achieved in Soviet Russia through revolution. But one and the same slogan can have very different contents according to who says it, under what concrete circumstances, and in whose interests. On the lips of Woodrow Wilson, the demand for self-determination was intended, not to give small nations power over their destinies, but rather, to break up the old European Empires and bring about the Balkanisation of Europe, thus increasing the power of US imperialism.

The imperialists always play with small nations as if they were just so much small change in their pockets. In the hands of the imperialists, far from playing a progressive role, the slogan of self-determination merely leads to new conflicts, wars and insoluble contradictions. During the war, all the Great Powers proclaimed the liberation of the colonies – of their enemies. After the war, the victorious imperialists of the Entente carved out isolated, small national states from the territories of their defeated enemies. And they did so while quoting from that part of Wilson's 'Fourteen Points' that suited them: the 'right to self-determination'.

Actually, there was not even a semblance here of the democratic principle of self-determination. In order to obtain points of support, imperialism created a chain of small and weak vassal states. The old empires were split up to create Hungary, Poland, Yugoslavia, Bohemia, Finland, Estonia, Latvia, Lithuania, Armenia, Georgia etc. While creating the impression of independence, France and Britain dominated them through the banks and monopolies, creating the conditions for endless friction and bloody wars.

The League of Nations, Wilson's brain child, served as a convenient cover to disguise its drive for world domination. For a while, Woodrow Wilson became a hero for many people in Europe, who saw him (and the Almighty Dollar that he held in his hands) as a saviour who would mend all of Europe's ills. As Trotsky put it:

> The President of the United States, the great prophet of platitudes, has descended from Mount Sinai in order to conquer Europe, 14 Points in hand. Stockbrokers, cabinet members and businessmen never deceived themselves for a moment about the meaning of this new revelation. But by way of compensation the European 'Socialists,' with doses of Kautskyan brew, have attained a condition of religious ecstasy and accompanied Wilson's sacred ark, dancing like King David.
>
> When the time came to pass to practical questions, it became clear to the American prophet that, despite the dollar's excellent foreign exchange rate, the first place on all sea lanes, which connect and divide the nations, continued as heretofore to belong to Great Britain, for she possesses a more powerful navy, longer transoceanic cables and a far older experience in world pillage. Moreover, on his travels, Wilson encountered the Soviet Republic and Communism. The offended American Messiah renounced the League of Nations, which England had converted into one of her diplomatic chancelleries, and turned his back upon Europe. (Trotsky, L., *The First Five Years of the Communist International*, Vol. 1, pp. 103-5.)

President Wilson was bitterly disappointed when confronted with the ugly reality that was born out of the ruin of his Fourteen Points. Returning to his country a broken man, he faced hostility from a new mood of isolationism. He suffered a stroke and died a few years later. But in reality, the age of American isolation had ended forever. The road to world domination by the United States was laid during the First World War. The Second World War turned it into reality. But that is another story.

11. BIG BANDITS AND SMALL BANDITS

In 1915, while Churchill was preparing his disastrous Gallipoli adventure, British diplomacy was attempting to win allies for its war against the Turks in the Balkans. The British mission in Sofia reported that Bulgaria might be prepared to attack Turkey, although this hope was soon dashed when Bulgaria joined the Central Powers to attack Serbia instead. In early March, Churchill received more encouraging news from Athens. The Greek Prime Minister, Venizelos, promised to send three army divisions to Gallipoli. He assured a gleeful Churchill that the King Constantine, known to be pro-German, would not object.

But Churchill's joy was premature. Greek politics were a tangle of contradictions, in which promises were broken as soon as they were made, and intrigue and back-stabbing were a normal part of life. The Greek bourgeoisie, like all the other ruling cliques in the Balkans, had its own expansionist agenda. But it was split over which group of imperialist bandits to support. Venizelos was inclined to the Entente, while the King and his clique preferred the Germans as allies. The only question was: which side would guarantee them the biggest amount of loot.

The Germans aimed to control the Turks and prepare the ground for a German Empire in the East that would rival the British Raj in India.

The construction of the Baghdad Railway before the war was a key part of this plan. But in order to succeed, Berlin needed to have both Turkey and Bulgaria on its side.

Russia wanted to seize Constantinople, get control of the Dardanelles and turn the Black Sea into a Russian Lake. Russia had put pressure on the British to launch an attack on the Turks. But the men in St. Petersburg were worried that, if the British got hold of Constantinople, they might be tempted to hang onto it. The Greek bourgeoisie also cast its hungry eyes on Constantinople, but the problem for the men in London was that, once the Greek army entered Constantinople, it might not be in any hurry to leave.

If the Greeks seized Constantinople it would mean conflict with Russia. That was one reason why the Greek King looked to Berlin rather than London and Paris. Meanwhile, in Rome, the Italian bandits were also looking forward to grabbing chunks of Turkish territory in the Balkans, even before they had entered the war. They were all sharpening their knives in anticipation of the great feast to come.

In this complex diplomatic game, the French and British imperialists did not want Russia to have Constantinople. The French feared that a Russian naval presence in the Mediterranean would present a challenge to their own power, while the British saw a potential threat to Egypt and the Suez Canal – that is, to British India. They planned to lead Russia by the nose during the war and then betray it at the post-War Conference table.

All of them had one eye on the enemy and the other firmly fixed on their 'Allies'. The British Prime Minister Asquith told his cabinet that the discussions about the division of the Ottoman Empire "resembled that of a gang of buccaneers." The comparison was very apt, but Asquith then added that if "we were to leave other nations to scramble for Turkey without taking anything ourselves, we should not be doing our duty." (Quoted in Fromkin, D., *A Peace to End All Peace*, p. 142.)

THE NATIONAL SCHISM

The ambitions of the Greek bourgeoisie for a Greater Greece found its expression in what was called the Big Idea or Megali Idea. In the

Second Balkan War in 1913, Serbia and Greece had seized the lion's share of Macedonia, which they had earlier promised to Bulgaria. Under the Treaty of Bucharest of 1913, Greece increased its territory by seventy per cent in size and its population grew from 2,700,000 to 4,800,000. The Greek state, which had hitherto been more or less ethnically homogeneous, was now in possession of the 'new lands' with populations of Muslims, Slavs and Jews.

The upheavals of war produced a massive exchange of populations. People who had lived together peacefully for centuries found themselves uprooted and forced from their homes. Greeks fled from Eastern Thrace, Asia Minor and Bulgaria into Greek Macedonia, while Muslim and Bulgarian inhabitants of the same region fled in the opposite direction. The 'new lands' of the Greek kingdom provided new material and human resources but only at the cost of increasing antagonism with its neighbours. But these successes fuelled the expansionist ambitions of the Greek bourgeoisie. Under the guise of liberating the Greek people, who remained under Turkish rule, they were preparing a war with Turkey that ended up as a national catastrophe.

An atmosphere of hatred was created that poisoned relations between Athens, Sofia and Constantinople. Serbian politicians and military men carried out even greater propagandist activity, setting their sights on western Greek Macedonia, where there was a large Slavic population, part of which wished to be united with its fellow Slavs. Constantine's refusal to provide Serbia with military aid led to an increase of Serbian propagandist activity, although it diminished after Venizelos' return as prime minister and Greece's official entry into the war.

The war produced deep contradictions within the Greek political class, which came to the surface in early 1915. When Britain and France requested Greek military aid in the Gallipoli campaign in return for vague promises of future concessions in western Asia Minor, Venizelos agreed immediately and even offered limited territorial concessions to Bulgaria. But the Greek General Staff were implacably opposed to sending troops to the Dardanelles. They were more concerned with strengthening their stranglehold on 'new lands' in the northern region.

They were also doubtful about the campaign's chances of success – doubts that were soon shown to be well founded.

Relations between Prime Minister Venizelos and Crown Prince Constantine (later King Constantine I) deteriorated to the point of producing a rift in the country's political regime. The result was a serious internal political crisis known as the National Schism. The split between the monarchist clique and the bourgeoisie over the control of power spread to the Greek officer corps. Mass mobilisations of supporters from both camps threatened civil war.

The leading members of the monarchist faction were pro-German. Constantine sided with the General Staff, and Venizelos was forced to resign. On that very day, however, the first Allied troops landed in Salonika. The aim of the so-called Macedonia campaign was partly to put pressure on Greece to enter the war on the side of the Entente and partly to support the Serbian army against the Bulgarian threat. In reality, neither objective was achieved. But on 26 June, 1917, backed by the Allies, Venizelos returned to Athens and resumed his post as Prime Minister. He then proceeded to purge the state machinery and the armed forces of royalists.

Soon after, the war came to an end. Bulgarian resistance finally collapsed with the fall of Skopje on 29 September, 1918. Crushed by the weight of war, Bulgarian peasants and soldiers rose in revolt behind the lines and Bulgaria was forced to capitulate. The war in the Balkans ended with the collapse of both the Ottoman and Habsburg Empires. Like the Serb, Bulgarian and Romanian ruling cliques, the rulers of Greece, greedy for expansion, attempted to exploit the decline of the Ottoman Empire and the antagonisms between the Great Powers in order to implement their own imperialist programme.

By a lucky accident, Greece found herself on the side of the victors of the Great War. She was pampered by the Allies for her services (although, truth to tell, they were minimal). Under the Treaty of Neuilly (1919), Greece was permitted to annex still more Bulgarian lands (Western Thrace) and received even greater concessions from the collapsing Ottoman Empire under the Treaty of Sèvres (1920).

However, it was not at all ruled out that Greece might have entered the war on the side of Germany.

Turkey's defeat in the war hastened the inevitable collapse of the Ottoman Empire, which was divided amongst the victorious Entente powers with the signing of the Treaty of Sèvres on 10 August, 1920. During the war a number of secret agreements were made regarding the partitioning of the Ottoman Empire. In order to entice potential allies to the side of the Triple Entente, they had made contradictory promises about post-war arrangements. But when the time arrived to cash these promissory notes, the would-be recipients were frequently disappointed.

All of them – big bandits and small – were interested in grabbing territory from a disintegrating Ottoman Empire. During the war the British had promised Palestine to both the Arabs and the Jews, thus preparing the ground for decades of wars and bloodshed in the future. In the event, the British gave Palestine neither to the Jews nor the Arabs but kept it for themselves. The British and French imperialists seized large chunks of territory in the Middle East – including Syria, Lebanon and Iraq – that had been previously been under Ottoman rule.

A GREEK TRAGEDY

The collapse of the Ottoman Empire led to a new revolution in Turkey with the seizure of power by Kemal Atatürk, a republican general who had successfully fought the Allies in Gallipoli. Although he was a ruthless anti-Communist who murdered and imprisoned the leaders of the Turkish Communist Party, he launched a progressive programme of modernisation in an attempt to drag Turkey into the twentieth century.

The victorious Allies, particularly British Prime Minister David Lloyd George, who had promised Greece territorial gains at the expense of the Ottoman Empire, encouraged the Greek Army to invade Turkey. At Versailles, Venizelos pressed hard for his Great Idea, which would hand the large Greek-speaking communities in Northern Epirus, Thrace and Asia Minor over to Greece.

The Allies had already promised Greece territorial gains at the expense of the Ottoman Empire, including Eastern Thrace, the islands of Imbros (Gökçeada) and Tenedos (Bozcaada), as well as parts of western Anatolia around the city of Smyrna, which contained large ethnic Greek populations. Now Athens was determined to cash its promissory notes in full. Lloyd George informed the Greek leaders that, if they decided to attack Turkey, Britain would not stand in their way. This was giving the green light to the Greeks. It was also the start of a terrible Greek tragedy. The men in Athens were not slow to take the hint. In 1919 the Greek army invaded Turkey.

This was a predatory war, a war of expansion that ended in disaster. The English historian Arnold J. Toynbee wrote:

> The war between Turkey and Greece, which burst out at this time, was a defensive war for safeguarding of the Turkish homelands in Anatolia. It was a result of the Allied policy of imperialism operating in a foreign state, the military resources and powers of which were seriously underestimated; it was provoked by the unwarranted invasion of a Greek army of occupation.

Initially, the Greeks' advance appeared to be unstoppable. But then disaster struck. In August 1922, the Turkish forces counter-attacked, forcing the invaders into a disorderly retreat. Faced with a military disaster, the Greek government appealed to the Allies for help, but no help came. Having encouraged the Greeks to attack, the British and French promptly left them in the lurch. The Italian and French troops evacuated their positions, leaving the Greeks exposed.

The Greek leaders underestimated the Turkish response to an attack on their homeland. It stirred the fires of Turkish patriotism, just as the Gallipoli adventure had done. The Turkish counter-attack is known to the Turks as the 'Great Offensive' (Büyük Taarruz). The major Greek defence positions were swiftly overrun. On 30 August, the Greek army suffered a decisive defeat at the Battle of Dumlupınar, when half of its soldiers were captured or killed, and its equipment entirely lost.

All these predatory wars were caused by the greed of the ruling cliques in all the Balkan countries, their insatiable thirst for land and loot. But, in every case, it was the poor civilians and soldiers – Greeks,

Turks, Serbs, Bulgarians, Montenegrins and Macedonians – who paid the price. And it was a very heavy one. The Greek army had perpetrated atrocities on the Turks, burning villages, driving families from their homes and murdering civilians. Now the advancing Turkish army inflicted a terrible revenge on the Greek population of Asia Minor.

The Greek archbishop of Smyrna wrote to Venizelos, pleading for help. But no help ever came for these poor people. The archbishop himself was literally cut to pieces in a barbers' shop. As a result, more than a million terrified local Greeks who had lived there for thousands of years were forced to abandon their ancestral lands. The Greek bourgeoisie's dream of expansion had come to an end in a ghastly nightmare.

Approximately 2 million people (around 1.5 million Anatolian Greeks and 500,000 Muslims in Greece) were forced from their homes and turned into rootless refugees. The hauntingly sad music that the Greeks of Asia Minor brought with them is a tragic reflection of the plight of these dispossessed, despairing masses who ended up in the slums and tavernas of Salonika and Athens. It is the voice of people with no work, no home, no hope and no future.

At the end of the period, Greece emerged twice as big as before both in terms of territory and population, but at a terrible cost. The deep wounds inflicted on Greek society were never healed, creating the conditions for new and bloody conflicts that poisoned the political life of the country for most of the twentieth century. The policy of expansionism had led to endless wars, ethnic cleansing, massacres, diplomatic crises, political instability and constitutional chaos. It created misery for millions of Greeks and non-Greeks alike and prepared the way for future tragedies.

ROMANIA, HUNGARY AND TRANSYLVANIA

Romania was yet another country with important strategic value for the Big Powers. The Romanian ruling clique had two contradictory war aims: to seize Bessarabia from Russia and Transylvania from Hungary. A difficult dilemma, since one would bring it into conflict with the Entente and the other with Austro-Hungary! But, in the end it obtained both objectives through a mixture of treachery and counter-revolutionary violence.

The King of Romania, Carol I of Hohenzollern, had signed a secret treaty with the Triple Alliance in 1883, which stipulated that Romania would be obliged to go to war only in the event Austro-Hungarian Empire was attacked. Carol wanted to enter World War I as an ally of the Central Powers, but the Romanian public and the political parties were in favour of joining the Entente. Thus, in 1914, King Carol, with many a tear and sigh, was compelled to inform Czernin, the Austrian ambassador, that Romania was unable to fulfil its agreed obligations.

Bucharest declared its neutrality on the diplomatic pretext that, since Austria-Hungary had itself declared war on Serbia, Romania was under no obligation to join in. In reality, the Romanian ruling clique was waiting to see which side would prevail, and, more importantly, who would offer them the biggest slice of the cake when the fighting was over. In the end, it was the Entente Powers who proved more generous.

According to some American military historians, Russia delayed approval of Romanian demands out of worries about Romanian territorial designs on Bessarabia, claimed by nationalist circles as part of the Romanian land. According to British military historian John Keegan, before Romania entered the war, the Allies had secretly agreed not to honour the territorial expansion of Romania when the war ended. Yet again, the wheels of bourgeois diplomacy were well oiled with hypocrisy and duplicity.

Nevertheless, the British and French continued to entice the Romanians with the promise of a large slice of eastern Hungary (Transylvania and Banat), which had a substantial Romanian population, if it would declare war on the Central Powers. In the end, the Romanian government took the bait and renounced its neutrality. On 28 August, 1916, King Ferdinand issued a Proclamation, written in the true bombastic heroic style:

> Romanians!
>
> The war which for the last two years has been encircling our frontiers more and more closely has shaken the ancient foundations of Europe to their depths.

11. BIG BANDITS AND SMALL BANDITS

It has brought the day, which has been awaited for centuries by the national conscience, by the founders of the Romanian State, by those who united the principalities in the war of independence, by those responsible for the national renaissance.

It is the day of the union of all branches of our nation. Today we are able to complete the task of our forefathers and to establish forever that which Michael the Great was only able to establish for a moment, namely, a Romanian union on both slopes of the Carpathians.

For us the mountains and plains of Bukovina, where Stephen the Great has slept for centuries. In our moral energy and our valour lie the means of giving him back his birth right of a great and free Rumania from the Tisza to the Black Sea, and to prosper in peace in accordance with our customs and our hopes and dreams.

Romanians!

Animated by the holy duty imposed upon us, and determined to bear manfully all the sacrifices inseparable from an arduous war, we will march into battle with the irresistible élan of a people firmly confident in its destiny. The glorious fruits of victory shall be our reward. Forward, with the help of God!

Ferdinand

In fact, this 'heroic' Proclamation was a bit late. Twenty-four hours before the ink was dry on the paper it was written on, the Romanian Army, without warning and with limited Russian support, had launched an attack against Austria-Hungary, advancing through the Carpathians and into Transylvania.

The defection of Romania was a major blow to the Austro-German Alliance, particularly to Austria. It not only deprived the Central Powers of an important spear directed against Russia's southern flank, but also created a serious opening, threatening Austria-Hungary on the great Danubian Plain. However, against the armies of the Central Powers, the Romanian Army proved to be a paper tiger. Despite its size (over 650,000 men in twenty-three divisions), it suffered from poor training and equipment when compared to its German counterparts.

The Romanian offensive was initially successful, pushing back the Austro-Hungarian troops, but a counter-attack by the forces of the Central Powers drove the Russo-Romanian forces back in disorder. The Romanians suffered a crushing defeat and the Central Powers occupied Bucharest on 6 December, 1916. Romania was forced to sign an armistice with the Central Powers on 9 December, 1917.

Fighting in Moldova continued in 1917, resulting in a costly stalemate for the Central Powers. But the entire situation was transformed by revolutionary developments in Russia. The October Revolution, which was fought under the banner of peace, bread and land, ended Russia's participation in the war. After the successful offensive on the Thessaloniki front, which put Bulgaria out of the war, the Romanian ruling clique saw its chance and hastily re-entered the war on 10 November, 1918 – just one day before it ended in Western Europe.

The minor robbers in Bucharest were in luck. Despite its inglorious performance in the fighting and the blatant opportunism of its 're-entry' after the Central Powers had already been defeated, Romania got considerably more than its fair share of the booty when the big robbers assembled at Versailles to share out the loot. As we have seen, they had intended to deceive Romania and renege on their promises in order to satisfy Russia. But the Russian Revolution had changed all that. The French and British imperialists were terrified of the spread of Bolshevism in Europe.

Germany was also in the throes of revolution. In 1919, a Soviet Republic was set up in Bavaria. More serious still, a Soviet Republic was declared in Hungary. This had to be crushed, and the most obvious candidate for the role of the hangman was Romania. The Versailles robbers, therefore, hastily threw a bone in the direction of Bucharest in the shape of Bukovina, which they handed over to Romania, utilising, as usual, the convenient slogan of the 'right of national self-determination'.

11. BIG BANDITS AND SMALL BANDITS

The Romanian bandits took the hint and proceeded to invade the territory of the Hungarian Soviet Republic, seizing control of Transylvania in the process. But the 'right of self-determination' overlooked the inconvenient fact that Transylvania was the ancestral home of a Hungarian-speaking population of 1,662,000 (31.6 per cent, according to the census data of 1910). As is so often the case, what is 'self-determination' for some becomes national oppression for others.

The Hungarian Soviet government lasted for 133 days, falling on 1 August, 1919. The Romanian army attacked Hungarian territory from the east, while the Serbs, egged on by the Allies, invaded southern Hungary, and the 'democratic' Czech bourgeois also joined in, attacking in the west with troops commanded by French and Italian officers. When the Romanian army entered Budapest, it launched a reign of terror against the Hungarian working class.

The landlords and capitalists took their revenge for the fright they had experienced. Wounded Red Army soldiers were dragged from the hospitals and murdered. The Whites used the most barbarous, medieval methods of torture, with 5,000 people losing their lives in this period. And the Pontius Pilates of reformism, those labour leaders who had protested loudly at the alleged 'excesses' of the workers and peasants now looked the other way, justifying murder and repression in the most cowardly way in return for the retention of their jobs and privileges. When it came to slaughtering workers and peasants, they showed no qualms of conscience about 'ruthless acts of cruelty'.

The short-lived Hungarian Soviet Republic was drowned in a river of blood by the combined efforts of the White armies of Romania, Czechoslovakia and the Kingdom of Serbs, Croats and Slovenes, all of them shouting the slogan of 'self-determination'. Hungary was occupied for a while by the counter-revolutionary Romanian forces, acting at the behest of their masters in Versailles. Only in early 1920 did the Romanian army finally leave Hungary, having sated itself with plunder. The question of Transylvania has poisoned relations between Hungary and Romania ever since, yet another toxic inheritance of what they used to call the Great War.

12. UNDER FIRE – THE REAL FACE OF WAR

Paradis says to me, "That's war."
"Yes, that's it," he repeats in a far-away voice, "that's war. It's not anything else."
"It is that, that endless monotony of misery, broken, by poignant tragedies."
"Beautiful? Oh, hell! It's just as if an ox were to say, 'What a fine sight it must be, all those droves of cattle driven forward to the slaughter-house!' He spat out mud from his besmeared mouth, and his unburied face was like a beast's.
"Let them say, 'It must be,'" he sputtered in a strange jerky voice, grating and ragged; "that's all right. But beautiful! Oh, hell!"

Under Fire: The Story of a Squad (French: *Le Feu: journal d'une escouade*) by Henri Barbusse was written in December 1916. It was one of the first novels about the First World War to be published and was based on Barbusse's personal experiences as a soldier in the French Army on the Western Front. *Le Feu* made an immediate impact, winning the prestigious *Prix Goncourt* the same year it was published. It remains one of the great novels about the 'war to end all wars'.

In stark contrast to the heroic visions of the official propaganda, the authentic experience of trench life is here depicted with brutal reality.

We follow their progress through the gigantic mincing machine that is war. Some will live. Most will die. One by one, they disappear into the infernal meat grinders: some killed in battle, others lost in no man's land, others wounded.

Barbusse's depiction of the lives of the ordinary French soldiers or 'poilus' is rendered even more graphic and poignant because, from the beginning, we are introduced to the members of the squad as individuals, men with names and families, real individuals with families, lives, good points and bad, hopes and fears.

But the first sight we have of these characters is of a kind of amorphous mass slowly emerging out of the trenches like primeval sub-human creatures from the depths of the earth:

> I see shadows coming from these sidelong pits and moving about, huge and misshapen lumps, bear-like, that flounder and growl. They are 'us'.

Who are 'us'!? The soldiers who are sent to the front are all poor farmers, workers and employees:

"Our ages? We are of all ages." […]

"Our races? We are of all races; we come from everywhere." […]

Our callings? A little of all – in the lump. In those departed days when we had a social status, before we came to immure our destiny in the molehills that we must always build up again as fast as rain and scrap-iron beat them down, what were we? Sons of the soil and artisans mostly. Lamuse was a farm-servant, Paradis a carter. Cadilhac, whose helmet rides loosely on his pointed head, though it is a juvenile size – like a dome on a steeple, says Tirette – owns land. Papa Blaire was a small farmer in La Brie.

The men are dressed in all kinds of rags, using old tyres and anything they can find to try to keep off the rain that penetrates their uniforms and soaks them to the skin. The trenches themselves resemble filthy bogs where men live in animal-like conditions amidst rubbish, rats and excrement, sometimes dead bodies. From the beginning, Barbusse creates a strong sense of class:

12. UNDER FIRE – THE REAL FACE OF WAR

We are fighting men, we others, and we include hardly any intellectuals, or men of the arts or of wealth, who during this war will have risked their faces only at the loopholes, unless in passing by, or under gold-laced caps.

Yes, we are truly and deeply different from each other. But we are alike all the same. In spite of this diversity of age, of country, of education, of position, of everything possible, in spite of the former gulfs that kept us apart, we are in the main alike. Under the same ways and habits, the same simple nature of men who have reverted to the state primeval.

The same language, compounded of dialect and the slang of workshop and barracks, seasoned with the latest inventions, blends us in the sauce of speech with the massed multitudes of men who (for seasons now) have emptied France and crowded together in the North-East.

Here, too, linked by a fate from which there is no escape, swept willy-nilly by the vast adventure into one rank, we have no choice but to go as the weeks and months go – alike. The terrible narrowness of the common life binds us close, adapts us, merges us one in the other. It is a sort of fatal contagion.

MONOTONY

The title of the novel is somewhat ironical, since for most of the time there is no fighting at all. Only in chapter twenty do we finally get a terrifying picture of what war meant for these men. Until then, the men are shown in a state of hopeless tedium, hunting for lice that infest their clothes while waiting, always waiting, for some thing or another, mainly for the food that always arrives late, waiting for the order to dig trenches or to move on, but always waiting. This is a truthful depiction of the realities of war, when battles are punctuated by long periods of mind-numbing inactivity:

> We are waiting. Weary of sitting, we get up, our joints creaking like warping wood or old hinges. Damp rusts men as it rusts rifles; more slowly, but deeper. And we begin again, but not in the same way, to wait. In a state of war, one is always waiting. We have become waiting-machines.

The monotony is broken by the arrival of food that momentarily acts as a soporific drug to deaden the pain. They wait and curse the slowness of the orderlies that are always late. When they finally arrive, even this small pleasure is spoiled by the fact that the wine ration is short – according to those who carried it to the trenches, "it got spilled on the way" – a story that is received with grim scepticism by the men in the trenches.

The little things that we take for granted in everyday life suddenly assume an enormous importance: a box of matches or an egg are luxuries that must be pursued with determination and when found are regarded as trophies far more valuable than medals. The misery of the soldiers is somehow reflected in the utter desolation of a blasted landscape:

> There are trees here; a row of excoriated willow trunks, some of wide countenance, and others hollowed and yawning, like coffins on end. The scene through which we are struggling is rent and convulsed, with hills and chasms, and with such sombre swellings as if all the clouds of storm had rolled down here. Above the tortured earth, this stampeded file of trunks stands forth against a striped brown sky, milky in places and obscurely sparking – a sky of agate.

And the rain that falls ceaselessly, drenching the poor wretches who are crowded, trembling with the cold, into a draughty barn full of holes that they try to plug with leaves and twigs – a futile exercise. The men sleep on soaking straw that stinks of liquid manure.

Barbusse presents us with some moving little cameos that sum up the condition of the men. A soldier who does not have enough money to obtain wine he desperately needs to deaden his senses returns empty handed to the barn where he must sleep. He looks into the mournful eyes of a dog that has been adopted by the squad and sees himself in the reflection of a dumb beast that has also given up all hope and pays no attention even to the food that is on the plate before him. Man and beast are reduced to the same level of utter hopelessness.

LEAVE

> They are not soldiers, they are men. They are not adventures, or warriors, or made for human slaughter, neither butchers nor cattle. They are labourers and artisans whom one recognises in their uniforms. They are civilians uprooted, and they are ready. They await the signal for death or murder; but you may see, looking at their faces between the vertical gleams of their bayonets, that they are simply men.

Even on those rare occasions when the men get leave, there is not much relief. They are obliged to go from house to house in a village, pleading to be given shelter (which they obtain – at a price). They are shamelessly fleeced by greedy peasants, who are growing rich and wish the war would go on forever. They consider themselves lucky to find a dirty old shed where they achieve their dream – to be able to eat "on a table", or to be more accurate, an old door supported on heaps of bricks.

These are the slaves and drudges at the bottom of the social pile. In times of peace they are what the Bible calls the "hewers of wood and drawers of water". In wartime they are merely cannon fodder for the generals. They watch as other slaves in uniform return from the front line, some wounded, some grim-faced, some smiling because they are still alive, all exhausted. They have been brought back from the jaws of hell to be rested, patched up, and then sent back to the slaughter house.

There is little or no hatred for the Germans, who, they imagine, are slaves and cannon-fodder just like themselves. But there is a burning hatred of the rich, the parasites, the speculators and those who avoid being drafted through money and connections. Above all there is a hatred of the scroungers in the rear:

> Besides, there are too many rich and influential people who have shouted, "Let us save France! – and begin by saving ourselves!" On the declaration of war, there was a big rush to get out of it, that's what there was, and the strongest succeeded. I noticed myself, in my little corner, it was especially those that jawed most about patriotism previously. Anyway, as the others

were saying just now, if they get into a funk-hole, the worst filthiness they can do is to make people believe they've run risks. 'Cos those that have really run risks, they deserve the same respect as the dead.

HELL

Finally, the fatal hour arrives when the squad has to move into action. Barbusse's description of the horrors of war read like the *Inferno* of Dante Alighieri: descent into hell in which each circle is more frightful than the last.

The battle commences in the dead of night, when the sky is lit up by dazzling lights that resemble a devilish firework display. In spite of themselves, the men of the squad are dazzled by this display of pyrotechnics that strikes them as having a strange sort of beauty. But this initial sense of wonder soon gives way to very different sensations:

> Abruptly, across all the width of the opposite slope, lurid flames burst forth that strike the air with terrible detonations. In line from left to right fires emerge from the sky and explosions from the ground. It is a frightful curtain which divides us from the world, which divides us from the past and from the future.

Eventually the order comes down the line: the sergeant blows a whistle and the soldiers, like blind automata, clamber up the ladders that the sappers have placed against the slippery walls of the trenches. Now they are outside the relative safety of the trench, advancing into no man's land, a barren, blasted terrain of mud, criss-crossed with barbed wire entanglements, churned up by exploding shells and raked with deadly machine gun fire. Men stumble and sink into the mud, fall into shell-holes and are cut in half by machine gun bullets or hurled into the air by explosions. It is hell on earth.

There is no possibility of escape: to halt or to retreat is to die. The only possibility is to advance, to keep advancing while your comrades are falling all around you. There is only one idea in your head: to keep going until you reach the objective: the enemy trench – to keep on going with bayonets at the ready with which to rend and pierce the entrails of other men, who like you are staring death in the face. The final slaughter is carried out without thinking, a senseless mechanical act that is as automatic and inevitable as every other action in this terrible shambles.

In the heat of battle men sometimes forget to be afraid. Other emotions take over. The unconscious mind develops strategies for blotting out the horror, for objectifying a terrible reality and reducing it to a kind of tranquillising banality. The men become experts in distinguishing the sounds of different high explosive shells, taking a peculiar pleasure in their respective powers of observation. This kind of mental activity provides a necessary antidote to the realisation that sooner or later one of these flying missiles of death will find its target, landing on a trench and blowing all its occupants to pieces.

The enemy trench is taken. It is filled with the dead bodies of men in both blue and grey uniforms, each corpse caught in the same grotesque attitudes with which it left the world of the living. The squad has realised its objective. It is time for the exhausted men to rest. But there is no rest – for after this trench there is another, and another and yet another trench to conquer. There is no end to the slaughter. It is as infinite as the fields that stretch before one's gaze, as infinite and as barren as the landscape of the moon.

The stretcher teams are struggling to rescue the wounded and carry away the dead, but this task is too much for human beings to perform. The vast numbers of shattered bodies, dead or living, overwhelms the efforts of the rescuers. The central figure of the novel (one cannot speak of heroes in such a context) is ordered to assist a wounded comrade to a place where he can receive some medical attention (nor can one speak of a hospital).

Crossing the field of battle in the cold light of day, they witness countless horrors that had been mercifully hidden by the darkness of the night. An old man they both knew, grievously wounded, begs them not to leave him, but they have to press on, promising to return. When they look back, he is already dead.

What passes for a field hospital is like the final circle of the *Inferno*: a dark, foul-smelling cave full to bursting with broken minds and bodies that are clinging to life as a drowning man clings to a straw. The darkness is broken only by the faint glimmering of candles; the silence is broken by the groans of the dying and the howls of pain. Even this intolerable suffering is not complete. The hospital receives a direct hit from an enemy shell.

The torrential rain has turned the battlefield into a sea of mud into which men fall and drown. *"The rain is raging and the sound of its streaming dominates everything – a horror of desolation. We feel the water on our flesh as if the deluge had washed our clothes away."* Crossing this nightmarish landscape, the horrified members of the squad are unable to see whether the bodies they discover are French or German, alive or dead:

> Quite near, we notice that some mounds of earth aligned along the ruined ramparts of this deep-drowned ditch are human.
>
> Are they dead – or asleep? We do not know; in any case, they rest.
>
> Are they German or French? We do not know.
>
> I once used to think that the worst hell in war was the flame of shells; and then for long I thought it was the suffocation of the caverns which eternally confine us. But it is neither of these. Hell is water.

DAWN

The last chapter bears the title of the novel entitled Dawn, a word pregnant with symbolism. One normally associates it with the hope and joy that springs from the dawning of a new day. But dawn over the trenches is never a moment of hope or happiness but merely the commencement of another day of misery, suffering and death.

Here, however, dawn has a different significance: it is the dawn of consciousness, the first tentative steps of men's minds towards the idea that things can be different, that another world is possible. Between one offensive and another, the men begin to reflect on what they have seen and done. "What is it all for?" Gradually, ideas begin to crystallise, ideas that point the way to revolution against an intolerable state of affairs:

I listened, leaning on a stick and towards him, drinking in the voice that came in the twilight silence from the lips that so rarely spoke. He cried with a clear voice – "Liebknecht!"

He stood up with his arms still crossed. His face, as profoundly serious as a statue's, drooped upon his chest. But he emerged once again from his marble muteness to repeat, "The future, the future! The work of the future will be to wipe out the present, to wipe it out more than we can imagine, to wipe it out like something abominable and shameful. And yet – this present – it had to be, it had to be! Shame on military glory, shame on armies, shame on the soldier's calling, that changes men by turns into stupid victims or ignoble brutes. Yes, shame. That's the true word, but it's too true; it's true in eternity, but it's not yet true for us. It will be true when there is a Bible that is entirely true, when it is found written among the other truths that a purified mind will at the same time let us understand. We are still lost, still exiled far from that time. In our time of today, in these moments, this truth is hardly more than a fallacy, this sacred saying is only blasphemy!"

A kind of laugh came from him, full of echoing dreams – "To think I once told them I believed in prophecies, just to kid them!"

I sat down by Bertrand's side. This soldier, who had always done more than was required of him and survived notwithstanding, stood at that moment in my eyes for those who incarnate a lofty moral conception, who have the strength to detach themselves from the hustle of circumstances, and who are destined, however little their path may run through a splendour of events, to dominate their time.

"I have always thought all those things," I murmured.

"Ah!" said Bertrand. We looked at each other without a word, with a little surprised self-communion. After this full silence he spoke again. "It's time to start duty; take your rifle and come."

AFTER THE BATTLE

After the battle, the few surviving members of the squad wander aimlessly through the streets of a town that seems a million miles removed from the nightmare through which they have lived:

The commercial people are shutting up their shops with complacent content and a smile for both the day ended and for the morrow, elated by the lively and constant thrills of profits increased, by the growing jingle of the cash-box. They have stayed behind in the heart of their own firesides; they have only to stoop to caress their children. We see them beaming in the first starlights of the street, all these rich folk who are becoming richer, all these tranquil people whose tranquillity increases every day, people who are full, you feel, and in spite of all, of an unconfessable prayer.

The conclusion becomes inescapable: here are two worlds inhabited by two classes of people: those who fight wars and those who profit by them; those who work and those who enjoy the fruits of the labour of others; those who create and those who exploit:

> The sight of this world has revealed a great truth to us at last, nor could we avoid it: a Difference which becomes evident between human beings, a Difference far deeper than that of nations and with defensive trenches more impregnable; the clean-cut and truly unpardonable division that there is in a country's inhabitants between those who gain and those who grieve, those who are required to sacrifice all, all, to give their numbers and strength and suffering to the last limit, those upon whom the others walk and advance, smile and succeed.

One of the survivors, the indomitable Volpatte draws his own conclusions:

> "It isn't one single country, that's not possible," suddenly says Volpatte with singular precision, "there are two. We're divided into two foreign countries. The Front, over there, where there are too many unhappy, and the Rear, here, where there are too many happy."

Another says:

> "We're made to live, not to be done in like this!"

"Men are made to be husbands, fathers – men, what the devil! – not beasts that hunt each other and cut each other's throats and make themselves stink like all that."

"Two armies fighting each other – that's like one great army committing suicide!"

For understandable reasons, the central message is a fiercely anti-war sentiment. But this is not the usual sentimental pacifism, but a message where the struggle against war is inseparably linked to the class war. The discussion among the men already begins to take on a revolutionary content:

> When it had passed, and we saw the volley take flight across the plain, seizing and shaking its muddy plunder and furrowing the water in the long gaping trenches – long as the grave of an army – we began again.
>
> "After all, what is it that makes the mass and the horror of war?"
>
> "It's the mass of the people."
>
> "But the people – that's us!"
>
> He who had said it looked at me inquiringly.
>
> "Yes," I said to him, "yes, old boy, that's true! It's with us only that they make battles. It is we who are the material of war. War is made up of the flesh and the souls of common soldiers only. It is we who make the plains of dead and the rivers of blood, all of us, and each of us is invisible and silent because of the immensity of our numbers. The emptied towns and the villages destroyed, they are a wilderness of our making. Yes, war is all of us, and all of us together."
>
> "Yes, that's true. It's the people who are war; without them, there would be nothing, nothing but some wrangling, a long way off. But it isn't they who decide on it; it's the masters who steer them."
>
> "The people are struggling to-day to have no more masters that steer them. This war, it's like the French Revolution continuing."
>
> [...]

"Then we'll have to go on fighting after the war?"

"Yes, p'raps –"

"You want more of it, do you?"

"Yes, because I want no more of it," the voice grunted. "And p'raps it'll not be foreigners that we've got to fight?"

"P'raps, yes –"

BARBUSSE AND COMMUNISM

Henri Barbusse became a Communist, like many others, inspired by the Russian Revolution. He described the birth of Soviet Russia as "the greatest and most beautiful phenomenon in world history." He left France in January 1918, and moved to Moscow, where he married a Russian woman and joined the Bolshevik Party.

Later on, Barbusse became a Stalinist. Before Stalin's rise to power, he had dedicated a book to Leon Trotsky, but he later he wrote a book eulogising Stalin, for which Trotsky castigated him. Barbusse's former comrade, Victor Serge, called him a hypocrite, who wanted to be on the winning side. This was a harsh verdict but not an unjust one.

Henri Barbusse died of pneumonia in Moscow on 30 August, 1935. Despite his sharp criticism of Barbusse for his capitulation to Stalinism, Trotsky had a high opinion of *Le Feu*, which remains perhaps the greatest novel of the First World War. It should be read by all who wish to have a real understanding of what the Great Slaughter really meant for those who fought and died in it.

We will leave the final word to one of the characters of *Le Feu*, in reality, Barbusse himself:

> The peoples of the world ought to come to an understanding, through the hides and on the bodies of those who exploit them one way or another. All the masses ought to agree together.
>
> All men ought to be equal.

12. UNDER FIRE – THE REAL FACE OF WAR

The word seems to come to us like a rescue.

After all, why do we make war? We don't know at all why, but we can say who we make it for […] whole nations go to slaughter marshalled in armies in order that the gold-striped caste may write their princely names in history, so that other gilded people of the same rank can contrive more business, and expand in that way of employees and shops.

[…]

Ah, you are right, poor countless workmen of the battles, you who have made with your bands all of the Great War, you whose omnipotence is not yet used for well-doing, you human host whose every face is a world of sorrows, you who dream bowed under the yoke of a thought beneath that sky where long black clouds rend themselves and expand in dishevelled lengths like evil angels – yes, you are right. There are all those things against you. Against you and your great common interests which as you dimly saw are the same thing in effect as justice, there are not only the sword-wavers, the profiteers, and the intriguers.

There is not only the prodigious opposition of interested parties – financiers, speculators great and small, armour-plated in their banks and houses, who live on war and live in peace during war, with their brows stubbornly set upon a secret doctrine and their faces shut up like safes.

There are those who admire the exchange of flashing blows, who hail like women the bright colours of uniforms; those whom military music and the martial ballads poured upon the public intoxicate as with brandy; the dizzy-brained, the feeble-minded, the superstitious, the savages.

There are those who bury themselves in the past, on whose lips are the sayings only of bygone days, the traditionalists for whom an injustice has legal force because it is perpetuated, who aspire to be guided by the dead, who strive to subordinate progress and the future and all their palpitating passion to the realm of ghosts and nursery-tales.

With them are all the parsons, who seek to excite you and to lull you to sleep with the morphine of their Paradise, so that nothing may change.

There are the lawyers, the economists, the historians – and how many more? – who befog you with the rigmarole of theory, who declare the inter-antagonism of nationalities at a time when the only unity possessed by each nation of today is in the arbitrary map-made lines of her frontiers, while she is inhabited by an artificial amalgam of races; there are the worm-eaten genealogists, who forge for the ambitious of conquest and plunder false certificates of philosophy and imaginary titles of nobility. The infirmity of human intelligence is short sight. In too many cases, the wiseacres are dunces of a sort, who lose sight of the simplicity of things, and stifle and obscure it with formulae and trivialities. It is the small things that one learns from books, not the great ones.

How many are the crimes of which they have made virtues merely by dowering them with the word 'national'? They distort even truth itself. For the truth which is eternally the same they substitute each their national truth. So many nations, so many truths; and thus, they falsify and twist the truth.

Those are your enemies… all those who for one reason or another cling to the ancient state of things and find or invent excuses for it – they are your enemies!

13. 1916-17: THE TURNING OF THE TIDE

Dialectics explains how, sooner or later, things can change into their opposite. The First World War is a very good example of this. In the first period of the war, reaction was firmly in the saddle.

In 1914, the popular mood was determined by a tidal wave of patriotism and war fever, fanned by optimistic news of successful military operations in the government-controlled media. But, as the war dragged on and conditions worsened, a mood of disillusionment set in. Everybody hoped that war would end soon, but the optimistic predictions of a decisive breakthrough were postponed time and time again.

Popular disillusionment and war-weariness was manifested in growing labour unrest and food riots, which were becoming increasingly common. Conversations on the street corner, in the marketplace, and in the factories turned to the injustice, not just of the war, but of an economic system that put all the burdens on the shoulders of the poor and the working class while the rich got ever richer. Talk of everybody making sacrifice sounded hollow to a woman standing in the bread queue while the rich drank champagne and went to parties.

The thick curtain of censorship and propaganda, which downplayed or denied defeats were regarded increasingly with scepticism or ridicule.

Soldiers on leave told a very different story, and they were believed. The loss of life and the growing economic hardship now shaped the popular consciousness far more than the official propaganda.

For the men in the trenches, life was hard: harsh discipline and brutal punishments, bad food, low wages, insanitary living conditions, substandard weapons and uniforms, and few opportunities for recreation. The danger of being sent to be slaughtered like cattle for a cause that seemed increasingly pointless was ever-present. All the ingredients were present for an explosion.

In the beginning, morale was maintained by a constant stream of patriotic propaganda. The soldiers of every army were told that the war would soon be over, that the enemy would crumble and fall. Later, the message was that 'one last push' would settle the matter. But the result of every 'final push' was always the same: a few metres of ground lost or won at the cost of thousands of dead and wounded.

The war had an enormous economic, political, and human cost. Some 65 million men were mobilised; of those, over 8 million were killed and another 21 million wounded over fifty-two months, from August 1914 to November 1918. It dislocated economic life, destroying the means of production on a massive scale and condemning millions to hunger and privation.

It resulted in the dissolution of the Austrian, Ottoman, German, and Russian empires, and culminated in a wave of revolutions between 1917 and 1920. Sailors and soldiers mutinied, while massive strikes broke out everywhere: from Berlin to Vienna, from Paris to Brussels to Glasgow, and stretching across the Atlantic to Chicago, San Francisco, and Canada.

The World War prepared the ground for world revolution.

VERDUN

The year 1916 can be seen as a turning point. Civilian morale was undermined by the stark contrast between the huge loss of life at the front and the meagre results achieved. The first cracks in domestic morale appeared in Italy, tsarist Russia and the Ottoman Empire during the winter of 1916-17. At the same time, in France and Germany, the

13. 1916-17: THE TURNING OF THE TIDE

social truce was coming under increasing strain as soldiers on leave brought back dispiriting news from the front.

The Western Front forces were locked in an endless war of attrition at the start of 1916. Here the war was characterised by a particularly bloody and brutal stalemate. To break it, the Germans launched an offensive on a series of forts around the town of Verdun. This was yet another 'final push' that was supposed to knock France out of the war, leaving Britain isolated. It turned out to be the longest single battle of World War One, lasting for nine long months and characterised by unparalleled savagery.

Verdun was targeted by General Erich von Falkenhayn, the Chief of the General Staff and Germany's principal strategist, because of its position on the Allied line and its psychological significance to the French people. Convinced by 1916 that the war could only be won on the Western Front, he hoped that the French would throw huge resources into defending it, only to be annihilated. Then he could turn his attention to the British.

The excessively optimistic Falkenhayn thought that this attack would not require big German forces. The opening bombardment would be sufficient to liquidate the French defences. During the first eight hours alone, the Germans fired 2 million shells. Tens of millions more were fired over the course of the following 300 days. But as so often happens in war, the plans of the generals did not work out as expected. Verdun proved to be a hard nut to crack.

The battle for Verdun became a matter of national prestige for the German General Staff, but for the French it was a question of national survival. With their backs against the wall, fighting with the courage of desperation, they put up unexpectedly stiff resistance. The fighting often degenerated into ferocious hand-to-hand combat that resembled the butchery of medieval battlefields, as desperate men lunged with their bayonets at other men's bodies. German losses piled up, little territory was gained, and Falkenhayn was forced to throw many more men into the meat-grinder.

Divisions began to appear in the top echelons of the German army as the conflict ground on. The Kaiser's son, Crown Prince Wilhelm, wanted to call a halt, while others urged Falkenhayn to keep attacking. In July, Falkenhayn finally halted the offensive and resigned. He was replaced by Paul von Hindenburg and Erich Ludendorff. They upheld the decision to suspend attacks at Verdun, but decided to defend the positions they had won. The conflict therefore dragged on for four more bloody months.

Paris put heavy pressure on Russia to launch an attack on the Eastern Front to relieve some of the pressure on the French Army. The tsar duly obliged his French creditors, ordering an offensive under the command of General Aleksei Brusilov in June and July. But this latest sacrificial offering of Russian lives for French gold did not halt the slaughter at Verdun, which lasted from 21 February until 19 December 1916.

In the end, the Germans had to admit that they had failed to break through. It is estimated that the battle of Verdun cost more than 700,000 casualties – dead, wounded, and missing. But neither side had much to show for the losses incurred. The largest area of territory gained amounted to a mere five miles. France was pronounced the victor. But the word 'victory' had a hollow sound when France had paid for it with the flower of her youth.

THE SOMME

While the French army was being bled white at Verdun, the French General Staff was angrily demanding that the British launch a new offensive on the banks of the River Somme. They complained bitterly that their allies were leaving all the fighting to the French. Stung by this criticism, General Haig, British Commander-in-Chief, decided that the time had come for him to fight to the last drop of his men's blood.

Thus began one of the largest and bloodiest conflicts of World War One. It was supposed to be part of a massive joint offensive by the Allies on their fronts in France, Italy, and Russia. Following the same erroneous idea as his German counterparts, Haig hoped to end the deadlock on the Western Front with 'one last push'. He was convinced that a massive artillery bombardment would silence the German guns and allow his infantry to break through. The Allies used their eighteen-pounder field guns to blast the German trenches with high explosives

13. 1916-17: THE TURNING OF THE TIDE

for seven days, after which 100,000 men would attack the German lines with little or no resistance – or so it was hoped.

A bombardment on such a scale had never yet been seen in modern warfare. To the British troops waiting anxiously in their trenches for the whistle that would send them 'over the top,' it seemed as though nothing could have survived that inferno. What they did not know was that the German troops, buried deep in underground bunkers, had mostly escaped destruction. The artillery barrage did not even succeed in cutting through the barbed wire defences, and the British troops had to cross masses of barbed wire under enemy fire to attack impregnable defences.

To make matters worse, the British artillery, which was meant to be covering the advance, fired too far ahead and also ceased firing too soon. This enabled the Germans to clamber out from their underground bunkers, ready to fight for their lives. The British soldiers advancing across 'no man's land' were easy targets for the German machine gun fire and shrapnel. Most of them were cut down before they got anywhere near the enemy trenches.

The first of July, 1916, was a disaster for the British Army. On that day, 720 men of the Eleventh East Lancashire battalion went into action, and 584 became casualties. Many other units suffered a similar fate. By the end of the day 20,000 were killed, British casualties amounted to some 60,000 – the biggest scale of losses in British military history.

The carnage on the muddy fields of the Somme, as in Verdun, dragged on for months. It finally drew to a close as the winter downpours turned the battlefield into a muddy swamp, officially ending on 18 November. The British had advanced just seven miles in 141 days. They had failed to break through the German defences. And every metre of ground that was conquered was paid for by thousands of lives. In total, the Battle of the Somme cost over 1 million killed, wounded, or captured.

REACTION AGAINST THE WAR

On all sides, the strains of the war were now showing. Acute manpower shortages forced governments throughout Europe to begin deploying women in what were hitherto male-only jobs in industry and agriculture. Strikes broke out to protest against low wages and exploitation.

A fresh supply of young blood was needed to make up for the colossal loss of life. Ever more lambs were being driven to the European slaughterhouse. Britain, the only major combatant with a volunteer army, was forced to introduce conscription in early 1916. This was the spark that ignited the Irish powder keg, the Easter Rising in Dublin, brutally suppressed by the British Army.

While Britain and France were formally democracies, Germany and the other Central Powers were open or partially disguised dictatorships. The same was true of tsarist Russia. Even sharper were the contradictions in those states. They were the same contradictions that existed everywhere. Governments increased surveillance on the population, fearful of popular unrest.

In Germany the authorities prepared secret monthly reports (*Monatsberichte*) on civilian attitudes (*Stimmungsberichte*) and morale (*Geist*). They acquired their information from an army of paid informers, spies, and military and police officials. Public mood was categorised by nationality by the censorship boards of the Austro-Hungarian Empire, fearing, justifiably, that the non-German citizens of the Empire were not entirely loyal to the ruling Habsburg monarchy.

In Russia the tsarist authorities compiled the detailed reports of spies. They categorised the mood of the population as 'patriotic', 'depressed', 'indifferent', and so on. The agents of the Okhrana penetrated every nook and cranny of society, infiltrating political movements (including the Bolsheviks) even at leadership level. Italy and France also developed their own surveillance systems, spy networks, and censorship boards. But in the moment of truth, all these measures proved to be completely ineffectual.

MUTINY

The discontent in society was reflected in the armies, and expressed itself as a series of mutinies. The disasters suffered by the French army in 1916 produced a collapse of morale, which French Commander in Chief Joffre obstinately refused to see. He promoted Robert Nivelle to commander of the armies of Northern and North-Eastern France, despite the fact that he had only six months of experience as an army commander.

Nivelle, like Joffre, had big ideas. He planned a massive Allied offensive for spring 1917. But French troops refused to obey the order to advance when a new offensive was ordered in April. This was the signal for a wave of mutinies, which the French officers preferred to describe as "collective acts of indiscipline." The mutinies spread like wildfire until they affected nearly half the French frontline forces.

Philippe Pétain, the hero of Verdun and future head of the pro-German Vichy regime in the Second World War, was brought in to replace Nivelle and restore order. The ringleaders were court-martialled, and 554 death sentences were handed out to French soldiers, though only forty-nine were actually executed. Measures were taken to improve the men's living conditions, and a gradual return to order was achieved.

In the end, French soldiers chose to obey orders and return to the trenches, with a tacit agreement that no further futile offensives would be launched. Fearful of the mood of his men, Pétain kept his soldiers' losses to a minimum by engaging in only limited engagements. The French army conducted no further major offensives in 1917. There were mutinies in the Italian army, which Cadorna described as "naked treason."

The situation was becoming critical in Germany by the end of 1916. Allied naval blockades of the North Sea and the Adriatic caused food shortages. Bread, meat, sugar, eggs, and milk were rationed. For the first time, signs of internal unrest were noticeable. Hindenburg told the Chancellor that "the military position could hardly be worse than it is."

A British military historian described the situation thus: "The fear lurking everywhere in the minds of the rulers was of revolution through war weariness." As the Austrian Foreign Minister Czernin had put it, "The bow was being strung too tight." The bowstring finally snapped in Russia.

THE YEAR 1917

The war created an ever-more unbearable situation for the masses. Upon the nightmare of war was superimposed the horrors of a deep economic crisis. Tsarist Russia was the first to fall. Military defeats, class conflict, economic exhaustion, war-weariness, and the national question all combined to produce an explosive cocktail. In the words of Lenin, in Russia, capitalism broke at its weakest link.

Thirty-nine Petrograd factories were at a standstill for lack of fuel by December 1916, and eleven more because of power cuts. The railways were on the point of collapse. There was no meat, and a shortage of flour. Bread queues became a normal condition of life. To all this must be added the constant news of military defeats and the whiff of scandal emanating from the court, the Rasputin clique, and the Black Hundred monarchist-landlord government.

A regime dominated by aristocratic crooks, speculators, and assorted riff-raff openly paraded its rottenness before an increasingly disaffected people. On Thursday 23 February, meetings were held to protest against the war, the high cost of living and the bad conditions of women workers. This in turn developed into a new strike wave.

The women played a key role. The first day of the revolution was 23 February [in the Old Style calender, 8 March in the New Style calender], International Working Women's Day. Working women, driven to despair by their hard conditions, prey to the torments of hunger, were first to come out on to the streets demanding 'bread, freedom, and peace'. They marched on the factories, calling the workers out. Mass street demonstrations ensued. Flags and placards appeared with revolutionary slogans: 'Down with the war!' 'Down with hunger!' 'Long live the revolution!'

Street orators and agitators appeared as if from nowhere. Many were Bolsheviks, but others were ordinary workers, both men and women, who had discovered suddenly they had a tongue in their head and a mind that thinks, after years of enforced silence. Within a few days, from 25 to 27 February, Petrograd was in the grip of a general strike.

On paper, the regime had ample forces at its disposal. But in the moment of truth, these forces just melted away. The desperate calls for reinforcements went unanswered. Fraternisation between troops and strikers was widespread. Workers went to the barracks to appeal to their brothers in uniform. Most of the capital was in the hands of the workers and soldiers after 27 February, including bridges, arsenals, railway stations, the telegraph and the post office.

The workers had power in their hands, but, as Lenin explained later, were not conscious and organised sufficiently to carry the revolution through to the end. This was the central paradox of the February Revolution. It required a further nine months of experience, combined with the tireless work of the Bolsheviks under the leadership of Lenin and Trotsky, for the abortion of dual power to be brought to an end by the October Revolution.

The discontent erupted simultaneously all over Europe. The war exacerbated social tensions that were already at the point of exploding. The same tendencies made themselves felt in France in April-November and even more so in Italy in the spring and summer. Unrest culminated among workers and peasants in the Turin insurrection in August 1917. Workers' strikes also shook the French and British governments.

AUSTRIA-HUNGARY

Alexis de Tocqueville wrote a famous maxim: "The most dangerous moment for a bad government is when it begins to reform." On 21 November, 1916, the old Emperor Franz Josef died. His successor, Karl I, promised to institute reforms, but his efforts merely opened the floodgates to disorder and dissent.

Count István Tisza, Hungarian Prime Minister, was a prominent defender of the Austro-Hungarian dualist system of government. He opposed voting reform in Hungary and was a loyal supporter of the monarchy and its alliance with Germany. Consequently, he was associated in the mind of the Hungarian public with a war effort that most people saw as hopeless.

On 1 May, 1917, socialists and revolutionaries staged mass demonstrations on the streets of Budapest, together with supporters of Karolyi. Fearing revolution in Hungary, the emperor asked Count Tisza to stand down, which he did on 22 May. He was later assassinated by members of the Red Guard. Tisza was succeeded by Moritz Esterhazy, who expressed his desire to build 'Hungarian democracy' – a clear attempt to prevent revolution from below by making reforms from the top. But by now, events were moving fast.

The state struggled to prevent soldiers in the field from learning of the discontent on the home front. Letters from home that mentioned food shortages and hunger were confiscated so as not to 'endanger the discipline of front troops and negatively affect their spirits'. The press censors were working overtime. Left-wing newspapers often appeared with large 'white spaces'. But all these measures were in vain. Discontent was already approaching boiling point on the home front.

Shortages, combined with war-weariness and political discontent, fuelled revolutionary and national agitation in Germany and Austria-Hungary. Vienna was suffering from severe food scarcity. Ration cards introduced for various foodstuffs were originally supposed to supply 1,300 calories per day, but by 1917 this had fallen to a mere 830 calories. By the end of the war, a medical study found that ninety-one per cent of Viennese school-children were mildly to severely undernourished.

Scarcely a week had passed since Count Tisza's resignation when the first of a series of mutinies broke out in the army. The first mutiny, led a group of Slovenes, was suppressed, but then others broke out, led by Serbs, Rusyns (or Ruthenians), and Czechs.

The sailors, being mainly drawn from the proletariat, were particularly active as a revolutionary force, not only in Russia but also in Austria-Hungary and Germany. The warships were like floating factories, and close contact with the officers bred a class hatred that was all the more intense for that. In Austria-Hungary, the first naval revolts began in July 1917 over a disruption of food supplies. An Austrian submarine defected to Italy in October 1917, provoking fear that Austro-Hungarian forces might succumb to the revolutionary moods that affected the Russians.

In early 1918, a series of workers' strikes broke out in Austria. Daimler plant employees struck in Wiener, Neustadt, after the flour ration was drastically reduced on 14 January. Then 113,000 workers struck in Vienna, 153,000 in Lower Austria, and 40,000 in Styria. Two waves of strikes in January and June threatened to paralyse Austrian industry.

Revolutionary sailors actively supported the striking workers at the Pola arsenal. The Slovene, Serbian, Czech, and Hungarian troops in the armed forces mutinied. In February, a naval mutiny broke out at Cattaro in which the captain of the cruiser, Sankt Georg, was shot in the head. Mutineers demanded better food and a 'just peace' based on President Wilson's Fourteen Points.

The arrival of three light battleships forced the mutineers to surrender, but the uprising was a warning signal to the government. More than 400 sailors were imprisoned for their role in the mutiny, four of whom were executed.

A memo sent to the Emperor from the Interior Ministry attributed the labour unrest to insufficient food supplies, but warned that it was spreading into the "political realm." This prediction was vindicated when 550,000 workers from around Austria took part in anti-war demonstrations. The strikes were mainly spontaneous, and not necessarily welcomed by the labour leaders.

New and hitherto unorganised layers of the working class were moving into action. As in Russia, the women workers were in the vanguard. In one huge demonstration, the shocked Socialist Party leaders complained that there were elements "unknown to the Party" and comprised of agitated, "sensation-hungry womenfolk."

The hardships caused by the war enormously exacerbated the tensions between the different nationalities in the Austro-Hungarian Empire. The introduction of government rationing in Hungary in 1915 caused serious food riots. A foreign press account from February 1915 noted, "Travelers from Austria… report that they have witnessed riots and demonstrations at Budapest, Prague, and other smaller towns of Hungary and Bohemia, against the continuation of the war."

Price inflation hit the poor and working class hard. Between 1915 and 1916, workers' wages rose by fifty per cent, but food prices rose more than 100 per cent. Demonstrations, bread riots, and strikes were increasingly common in Hungary. In the autumn of 1917, a new wave of strikes paralysed rail transportation for a week. The petty bourgeoisie was being drawn to the side of the workers. There were reports that middle-class organisations were beginning to behave like trade unions, demanding improvements. Sections of the avant-garde artists and intellectuals also found common cause with workers. This widespread social and national ferment was laying the basis for the Hungarian Revolution of 1918-19.

The situation was similar in the Czech-speaking part of the Empire. By August 1917, potatoes, fruits, and vegetables were no longer available in Bohemia. The weekly meat, milk, and bread ration could also not be covered fully. On 13 April, two days after the new ration had been implemented, angry crowds destroyed the mayor's house, the food depot, restaurants, and hotels, or anywhere else where food could be found.

Prague erupted into massive, violent, and widespread demonstrations that the police were unable to control when further flour rationing was announced in August. The disturbances quickly spread to the factories. Soon, all the major factories in the Prague area were on strike, and the municipal transit system had to be shut down. There were instances of sabotage on the railways as workers began to destroy equipment and trains.

INTRIGUES BETWEEN ROBBERS

When Karl came to the throne, he promised to take Austria-Hungary out of the war as soon as possible. Faced with a desperate position at home and at the front, the new emperor decided to stake everything on a gambler's throw of the dice. In complete secret (he did not even inform Foreign Minister Czernin), he made approaches to the Allies, with the aim of getting a deal that would enable Austria-Hungary to extricate itself from the war.

President Poincaré demanded not only the restoration of Alsace-Lorraine, but also that France should be given the German Saar and Landau territories. In fact, the French had recently arrived at a secret deal with Russia, unknown to Britain, that would give them not only the above-mentioned territories, but also the much-coveted Left Bank of the Rhine, which would provide France with a new frontier and a buffer zone against Germany in the future.

The reason Britain was not informed of this deal was that London was not very keen on strengthening France at Germany's expense.

Lloyd George was even ambivalent about giving Alsace-Lorraine back to France, although he kept his opinions to himself in public. To please their friends in St. Petersburg, Poincaré also demanded that Constantinople should be handed over to Russia – one of the prime objectives of tsarist Russia in the war.

The terms he offered were highly tempting to the British and French, who were eager to detach Austria-Hungary from Germany. Feeling the fire under his backside, Karl was only too pleased to agree to almost all their demands – almost, but not quite. For Lloyd George and Poincaré had a little problem, and that problem was called Italy.

When Italy agreed to join the war on the side of the Entente in 1915, it did so on the basis of a series of promises that were contained in the Treaty of London. Now Italy wanted its pound of flesh. The men in Rome wanted the Tyrol and several other big slices of Karl's lands. In vain, the British and French attempted to persuade the Italians to accept Somaliland in exchange for dropping their demand for Trentino, Tyrol, and Istria. The Italian Foreign Minister, with admirable frankness, said that Italy had entered the war to destroy Austria, and could not be expected to help her.

Emperor Karl did not mind giving away territory belonging to Germany or the Ottoman Empire. But his spirit of generosity suddenly vanished when it was a matter of giving away the lands of the Austro-Hungarian Empire. He was not prepared even to consider Italy's demands. Nor was he prepared to declare war on Germany, as the Allies were pressing him to do. The whole purpose of his intrigues with the Allies was to get out of the war, not to start another, even more dangerous one.

The Austrian Foreign Minister had no idea that the Emperor was planning to ditch Germany, and he would have been horrified if he had known. He thought that the idea was to negotiate a general peace. But he was wrong. Karl would have sacrificed his own grandmother if he could only save his throne. Thus, he was quite prepared to sacrifice the interests of the men in Berlin, whom he did not like in any case. Who did those Prussian upstarts think they were, anyway? They were always giving orders and sneering at the fighting qualities of his armies.

To stab the German Kaiser in the back would be sweet revenge for all the insults and humiliations he had suffered. But Karl was mortally afraid of the men he secretly despised and detested. And he was right to be afraid. The German General Staff was seriously considering declaring war on Austria-Hungary at one point, fearing that it was about to drop out of the war or change sides. That proved unnecessary in the end. The Austrian peace plan fell to pieces, shattered by the violence of inter-imperialist rivalries, as a boat with rotten timbers is shattered by the waves.

14. THE MIDDLE EAST AND THE SYKES-PICOT TREATY: A POISONOUS LEGACY

The frontiers of the Arab world today are the product of a secret plan drawn in pencil on a map of the Levant in May, 1916, in a deal struck between British and French imperialism at the height of the First World War. Worked out 100 years ago, the Sykes-Picot agreement is now synonymous with imperial deceit, cynicism and treachery.

The authors of this notorious document were Sir Mark Sykes and François Georges-Picot, appointed by the British and French governments respectively to decide how to carve up the Ottoman Empire after the War. Hovering in the background was the Russian foreign minister, Sergei Sazonov, anxious to ensure that Constantinople would be handed over to Russia as part of the deal.

During the War, Britain made different offers to different countries. The French, the Arabs and the Jews were all promised things that the British imperialists had no intention of giving them. Arab historian, George Antonius, called this document the product of "greed allied to suspicion and so leading to stupidity". It was a messy solution that prepared the way for future disaster.

The Turks had miscalculated badly when they entered the war on the side of Germany and the Central Powers. Now their lands were up for grabs. The only question was: who would grab what? Like rival gangs the bandits of the Entente were already arguing over how to split up the goods of the man they planned to murder. But there was a slight problem. Their intended victim was not yet dead.

At the time, the war was not going well for the Allies. The Gallipoli adventure launched on the initiative of Winston Churchill ended in disaster. In January 1916, while a ferocious battle was being fought in Verdun, the British had been forced into an ignominious withdrawal. A few months later the British were about to suffer a humiliating defeat in Mesopotamia.

OIL

Even at this early stage the presence of oil was a decisive factor in the calculations of imperialism. What was the right of self-determination when compared to this black gold? Before 1914, Britain already controlled large parts of what is today called Iraq, bribing the local sheikhs to obtain influence, such as in the case of the Sultan of Kuwait. The importance of this was to secure the Shatt Al-Arab, the name given to the point where the waters of the Euphrates and Tigris are joined. This was a key port for British Indian trade.

The construction of the Anglo-Persian oil pipeline that ran along the banks of the river made it even more important for Britain to secure the region. The Anglo-Persian Oil Company was the company that kept the Royal Navy supplied with oil, a fundamental strategic consideration. Just before the outbreak of war the British government had secured a controlling interest in the company. The vast profits thus obtained rivalled those of the Suez Canal Company. There was money in oil. And there was blood also.

All this was ultimately related to the British control of India. In theory, British interests in Mesopotamia were protected by the British forces in India. But, in reality, the latter were not sufficient. The attention of the Foreign Office in London was drawn to the possibility of provoking an Arab uprising against the Turks.

The Arabs suffered oppression under Turkish rule and many were restive. The politicians in London saw in this an opportunity. They imagined that, if the Turks could be driven out of Basra, the Arabs would be inclined to rise against them and support the British in their war against the Ottoman oppressors. But in practice this turned out to be a mirage.

In the words of one British military historian:

> British policy was not free from an unpleasing Machiavellianism for, while the Arabs were urged to throw off Turkish allegiance, no pledge was given against their ultimate return to the vengeance of their ferocious masters. (*A History of the Great War*, pp. 339-40.)

The author adds, as if to excuse himself: "Doubtless, however, our action was regarded as a fair counter to Turko-German intrigues in India, for which Mesopotamia was regarded as a useful base."

"MARCH ON TO BAGHDAD!"

A British force composed partly of Indian troops was sent into Mesopotamia. The Political Officer of this expedition, Sir Percy Cox, was considered to be a great expert on the region. He argued enthusiastically in favour of marching on Baghdad. There would be little or no opposition, he thought. But he thought wrong.

The military planners had left out of account several factors, one of the most important being the climate: one of the most unforgiving and extreme in the world. The British and Indian forces suffered the torments of heat and thirst, plagued by flies and struck down by diseases. Later, they suffered from the cold. The field hospitals were, to say the least, inadequate, and an increasing number of soldiers were beginning to fall. Wounded men were spending up to two weeks on boats before reaching any kind of hospital. This was a warning of the horrors yet to come.

Sir John Nixon, Commander of the British forces in Mesopotamia, was unmoved by any of these little local difficulties. It is hard to say whether his conduct was the product of naivety or megalomania. Cromwell once said: "No man goes so far as he who knows not wither he is going." Overcome by his irrepressible optimism, Nixon only seemed to know one word of command, and that word was 'Advance!'

Appetite comes with eating, and the British were getting greedy. At first things appeared to go well. By late September 1915, Nixon's forward divisional commander, Sir Charles Vere Ferrers Townshend, had already occupied the Mesopotamian province of Basra, including the town of Kut al-Amara. From there, they attempted to move up the Tigris and Euphrates Rivers toward Baghdad.

General Townshend seems to have been a very vain and arrogant man, his ego having been inflated by some military successes against tribal guerrillas in northern India. Like Nixon he was absurdly self-confident. That self-confidence cost many lives. He was reckless, taking ridiculous risks while neglecting the most elementary precautions. The end result was catastrophe.

The easy victory in Basra filled the British with a fatal sense of complacency. But all too often in war the ability of advancing leaves out of account the desirability of so doing. In the end, the Arab population did not turn out to be as friendly to the British as the men in London had hoped. Often, the Turkish forces were backed by huge numbers of Arabs, who also began sabotaging the oil pipelines. For these actions, the local population were subjected to a 'severe chastisement' by their British saviours.

From a military point of view, the occupation of Baghdad did not make any sense. To carry out such an operation successfully would have required a very large number of troops and huge amounts of supplies, river transport, field hospitals and artillery. Instead of this, the British force consisted of only 12,000 men, who were sent marching through desert country with no roads and inadequate supplies. But Sir John pressed on regardless.

The Sixth (Poona) Division advanced upriver, leaving a very thinly stretched supply line of hundreds of miles behind them. Nixon deceived himself and deceived the British government with his bragging tone. He told Chamberlain: "I am confident that I can beat Nur-ud-Din and occupy Baghdad without any addition to my present force." In London, the Cabinet hummed and hawed, wrote memos and then wrote other memos, and finally, swayed by the confident assurances of 'the men on the ground', they decided to send reinforcements to the invading force (Kitchener voted against).

14. THE MIDDLE EAST AND THE SYKES-PICOT TREATY

The vast majority of the British Empire's forces in this campaign were recruited from India. But the British authorities in India were becoming increasingly alarmed by the deteriorating situation on the turbulent north-western frontier with Afghanistan. They were also beginning to be concerned at the success of the very efficient and tenacious German agents, who were increasingly active in Tehran. It was feared that Persia might enter the war on Germany's side at any moment. The Government of India reluctantly decided to try to scrape together some reinforcements. But it was a case of too little and too late.

What they did not know in London or New Delhi was that this tiny force of 12,000 veterans was about to walk into a trap. In late November, at Ctesiphon (or Selman Pak), sixteen miles outside Baghdad, they collided with an army of 20,000 Turks.

THE CATASTROPHE OF KUT

The battle was fought with great ferocity and casualties were high on both sides. Being outnumbered by the Turks two-to-one, Townshend's troops were rebuffed, with the loss of 4,500 men. The Turks lost about twice that number, but Townshend was in far worse shape than them, having lost forty per cent of his infantry and half his British officers. A ragged and dispirited army began the retreat back to Kut al-Amara. On 5 December, Turkish and German troops began to lay siege to that city.

In the beginning, the seriousness of their position had not yet penetrated the thick skull of Sir Charles Townshend. In the officers' mess they dined almost as well as in the exclusive clubs for gentlemen in London. They drank toasts to King and Country in champagne and consumed quantities of excellent whiskey. Nobody saw the terrible end that was staring them in the face.

Convinced that they would soon be relieved, they saw no reason to worry. But heavy winter rains had swollen the Tigris River, making it difficult to manoeuvre troops along its banks. Consequently, the anticipated relief force did not appear. Townshend sent whinging, at times hysterical, demands for help.

The British attempted to break the Turkish siege four times during the winter, only to be driven back. Townshend made no effort to support the relief efforts by organising a sortie from the besieged city, but merely remained passive. The number of casualties suffered by the relieving forces was around 23,000 – almost twice the strength of the entire remaining forces inside Kut.

As the siege dragged on, food became scarce. Sickness began to strike down on the men who were weakened by exhaustion and hunger. The situation was even worse for Indian soldiers, who were forbidden by their religion to eat horse meat. Morale sank along with dwindling supplies.

Now desperate, Townshend pleaded with the British government negotiate a grubby deal with the Ottomans. They attempted to buy off the enemy with a huge bribe. A team of officers (including the notorious 'Lawrence of Arabia') was sent secretly, offering £2 million (the equivalent of £122,300,000 in 2016), promising they would not fight the Ottomans again, in exchange for Townshend's troops. The Turkish leader Enver Pasha contemptuously turned this offer down.

Although reinforcements were not so far from the city, instead of waiting, Townshend suddenly surrendered on 29 April, 1916. The general and his 13,000 men were taken prisoner. This was the single largest surrender of troops in British history and it dealt a shattering blow to British prestige. British historian James Morris has described the loss of Kut as "the most abject capitulation in Britain's military history."

Townshend and most of the other British commanders involved in the failure to relieve Kut were removed from their command. But they got off lightly compared to the grisly fate of the men under them. C.R.M.F Cruttwell writes:

> Townshend [went] into an honourable and almost luxurious interment, the officers into endurable prison camps. The men were herded like animals across the desert, flogged, kicked, raped, tortured and murdered. Though the Germans gave them tokens of humanity and kindness almost wherever they met them, more than two-thirds of the British rank and file were

14. THE MIDDLE EAST AND THE SYKES-PICOT TREATY   189

dead before the war ended. Halil, the Turkish commander, had cynically promised that they would be 'the honoured guests of his government.' The relieving force had suffered 23,000 casualties. Mainly composed of young barely trained troops, it had nobly endured every kind of avoidable and unavoidable hardship and suffering. (*A History of the Great War*, pp. 348-9.)

The class divisions in society persist even in prisoner of war camps.

BETRAYAL OF THE ARABS
When Turkey entered the war on the side of the Central Powers, London immediately declared Egypt a British 'protectorate'. The people of Egypt merely exchanged one imperial master for another. Naturally, their opinion on the matter was never consulted.

During the war, British agents worked tirelessly to whip up an Arab revolt against the Turks. The exploits of one of these agents, T.E. Lawrence, was made famous in the film *Lawrence of Arabia*, which presents these activities in a most flattering light. In fact, this was part of a cynical plan to use the Arabs against the Turks, winning over the tribal chiefs and sheikhs by a mixture of vague promises of territorial expansion for the future and very tangible monetary bribes for the present.

The men in London believed they had scored a great success in persuading Emir and Sharif of Mecca, Hussein bin Ali, to proclaim a rebellion against the Ottoman rule. In fact, this action, which he took with great reluctance, was not the result of British diplomacy, but the fact that he had discovered a German plot to get rid of him. Without this bit of encouragement, his preference would have been to continue the easier and highly profitable policy of accepting generous bribes from both sides.

The revolt in the Hejaz was declared in June 1916. Displaying his usual good business sense, Hussein had already pocketed £50,000 from the Turks to finance a campaign against the British and a further substantial down payment from the British to finance a campaign against the Turks. His commitment to Arab nationalism was, in fact, only a fig leaf to cover his own territorial ambitions – a fact that was not lost on the British. David Hogarth, the head of the Arab Bureau in the Foreign Office, commented acidly: "It is obvious that the king regards Arab Unity as synonymous with his own kingship."

The revolt of the Hejaz, despite its glorification in the film *Lawrence of Arabia*, was of a mainly fictitious character. The British spent about £11 million to subsidise it. That would be £1 billion in modern money. But they did not get much of a return on their investment. Hogarth was forced to admit:

> That the Hejaz Bedouins were simply guerrillas, and not of good quality at that, had been amply demonstrated even in the early stages; and it was never in doubt that they would not attack nor withstand Turkish regulars. (Quoted in Fromkin, D., *A Peace to End All Peace*, p. 223.)

If London did not get a good return on their investment, Hussein got even less for his. The right of self-determination of small nations is merely the small change of imperialist diplomacy. Subsequent events showed that Britain regarded Arab Unity as synonymous with rule from London. The Arabs had been led to expect a great Hashemite kingdom ruled from Damascus. Instead they were handed a few puny little kingdoms, mainly consisting of deserts.

The Hashemites were unceremoniously evicted from Syria by the French. They also lost their ancestral fief of the Hejaz, with the holy cities of Mecca and Medina. This was handed over to the British stooge Abdel Aziz bin Saud, a chieftain from the Nejd, who founded Saudi Arabia in cahoots with his Wahhabi religious zealots, the authentic fathers of today's fundamentalists.

One branch of the Hashemites went on to rule Iraq. Another branch still survives in the Hashemite Kingdom, Jordan (which was then called Transjordan), sliced off from Palestine by the British.

THE SYKES-PICOT DEAL

Secret diplomacy is not the exception but the rule in dealings between imperialist powers. This is entirely logical, since the purpose of diplomacy is to deceive both the enemy and public opinion about one's real intentions and disguise the most sordid interests with honeyed phrases about humanitarian missions, preserving peace, defending democracy and upholding the rights of small nations. Diplomacy is both politics and war by other means. It is cynicism raised to the level of a work of art.

The military setbacks in Gallipoli and Mesopotamia did not for one moment interrupt the normal workings of civilised diplomacy. Hidden from the public view, the Allied robbers busied themselves with the noble and lucrative task of dividing up the spoils. Even before the First World War, Egypt, North Africa and stretches of the Arabian Gulf had already been divided up as colonies or protectorates of the European imperialist powers. Now the latter could finish the job.

In late 1915 and early 1916, a young British politician, Sir Mark Sykes, chief adviser to the Asquith government on the Near East; and a French lawyer-turned-diplomat, François Georges-Picot were haggling the terms of a secret deal to carve up the Arab lands of the Ottoman Empire like two men arguing over the price of herrings in a market place. Haggling is a complicated business. It consists essentially in a conflict of wits that has for its aim to deceive, mislead and cheat the other party into accepting a deal that is essentially contrary to his or her interests. It is like a game of chess or, more correctly, poker. Only the stakes tend to be far higher, and the danger to the loser comparably higher.

Sykes actually had a high regard for the cultured Turkish rulers of the Ottoman Empire. By contrast, he held the Arabs, whom the British were attempting to rouse against the Turkish yoke, in complete contempt. He described the town Arabs as "cowardly", "vicious yet despicable", while the Bedouin Arabs were "rapacious… greedy animals." Here we can hear the authentic voice of imperialism, in which contempt for the lower classes becomes mingled with overt racism.

By contrast, Sykes' admiration for the Turks is the expression of a kind of upper-class solidarity. The representative of British imperialism had no problem identifying with the Turkish overlords who had enslaved millions of Arabs, just as the British ruling class has enslaved millions of Indians and Africans. Slaves deserve to be slaves and rulers are destined to be rulers. Naturally, Sykes' good opinion of the men in Constantinople did not prevent him from preparing to rob them of all their land and assets. Solidarity between robbers can only be stretched so far...

Between the French- and British-ruled blocs, large, mostly desert areas were apportioned to the two powers' respective spheres of influence. Later, in 1917, Italian claims were added, but they arrived too late at the table of the victors, after the main course had been served, and got only the left-overs.

A POISONOUS LEGACY

The only aim of the negotiations was the dismemberment of the Ottoman Empire. At one point, there was the possibility of reaching a deal with the Turks that satisfied both the British and Russians. But the French put a stop to that. They demanded not only control of Syria but of Turkey itself.

In the end, it was agreed that Russia would get Constantinople, the territories adjacent to the Bosporus strait (thus giving Russia the sea passages from the Black Sea to the Mediterranean) and four provinces near the Russian borders in east Anatolia (including Armenia). The British would get Basra and southern Mesopotamia (modern Iraq) and the French would get a slice in the middle, including Lebanon, Syria and Cilicia (in modern-day Turkey). Palestine would be an 'international territory' – whatever that might mean.

Italy was given control of Turkey's southwest and Greece was allocated control of Turkey's western coasts. But as always, the final result would be decided not by a scrap of paper but by the unpredictable fortunes of war, and, in the end, the Greek Army was defeated by the new Turkish state.

The result was the barbaric expulsion of the Greek population of Asia Minor, which generated feelings of mutual hatred and fear between Greeks and Turks that has poisoned relations between the peoples for generations. In the same way the bloody conflict between Arabs and Jews can be traced back to these dirty deals of the First World War.

14. THE MIDDLE EAST AND THE SYKES-PICOT TREATY

During the war, Britain had promised Palestine to both the Arabs and the Jews. In the end, neither got what they wanted. Even while Britain was negotiating with Hussein bin Ali, the foreign secretary, Arthur Balfour, wrote a letter to Baron Walter Rothschild, a close friend of Zionist movement leader Chaim Weizmann, promising to establish "a national home for the Jewish people" in Palestine (2 November, 1917).

The standpoint of imperialism was clearly expressed by the British Prime Minister Lloyd George in a secret session of the House of Commons on 10 May 1917, when he shocked the House by his bluntness:

> The Prime Minister intended to deny France the position that Sir Mark Sykes had promised her in the post-war Middle East, and took the view that the Sykes-Picot agreement was unimportant; that physical possession was all that mattered. Regarding Palestine, he told the British ambassador to France in April 1917 that the French would be obliged to accept a *fait accompli*. *"We shall be there by conquest and shall remain"*. (Fromkin, F., op. cit. p. 267, my emphasis, AW.)

One could not wish for a clearer exposure of the brutal reality of imperialist politics and diplomacy: might is right; what we have we hold. It was expressed far more eloquently long ago by Heraclitus when he said: "War is father of all and king of all; and some he manifested as gods, some as men; some he made slaves, some free"

As Lloyd George had predicted, Palestine was pocketed by Britain, along with a huge slice of the former Arab territories of the Ottoman Empire. France got most of what was left. Mosul was at first apportioned to France, but finally was handed over to Britain, which joined it to the future Iraq. The Jews got a slice of Palestine, but not the Jewish homeland that the British had promised them. As for the unfortunate Kurds, who aspired to a state for themselves, their claims were completely ignored and they were split up between four countries (Syria, Iraq, Turkey and Iran).

To keep the French quiet, Syria was handed over to them. They also had effective control of Greater Lebanon, although it was nominally in the hands of the Maronite Christians. Given the complex mixture of faiths and ethnic groups in that small country, that was a recipe for future instability and chaos.

After the October Revolution, the Bolsheviks found a copy of the Sykes-Picot agreement in the government archives. Leon Trotsky published a copy of the agreement in *Izvestia* on 24 November, 1917, exposing the real plans of the great powers to carve up the Ottoman Empire. Lenin called it "the agreement of colonial thieves." There is not a lot one could add to that accurate and succinct definition.

The consequences of all this are still with us today. By dividing this most volatile region into artificial states cutting across through ethnic and religious boundaries, the Sykes-Picot agreement guaranteed a future plagued by wars and conflicts. The crimes of imperialism have left a poisonous legacy, which has reduced the most promising parts of the Middle East to a pile of smoking ruins. In the words of the Roman writer Tacitus: "They have created a wilderness and they call it peace."

15. HOW REVOLUTION ENDED THE FIRST WORLD WAR

For the soldiers, the war was a seemly unending nightmare; for the civilians on the home front, especially the women, hardly less so. In the end, large tracts of Europe lay wasted, millions were dead or wounded. The great majority of casualties were from the working class. Survivors lived on with severe mental trauma. The streets of every European city were full of limbless veterans. Nations were bankrupt – not just the losers, but also the victors.

This bloody conflict was brought to an end by revolution – a fact that has been buried under a mountain of myths, pacifist sentimentality, and lying patriotic propaganda. By 1917, in all the belligerent states, the discontent of the masses was growing.

BREST-LITOVSK

Internationally, the Bolshevik Revolution of 1917 had a profound effect. In the factories and trenches it sounded a clarion call. An urgent priority for the Bolsheviks was to get out of the war. The Russian army was disintegrating. On the Eastern Front, there was mass fraternisation between Russian and German soldiers. They met together in no man's land and exchanged caps and helmets, shared vodka and schnapps, embraced and danced together. Even some officers joined the festivities.

But the party was not allowed to last. The German General Staff realised the danger of this fraternisation and ordered a new advance. The Russian Army was in no position to resist. The war-weary peasants in uniform threw away their rifles and deserted *en masse* to return to their villages. The Russian army was rapidly collapsing. The Germans pushed deep into Russian territory. A truce was hastily called, followed by a peace conference that ended Russia's participation in the war.

The conference opened in December at Brest-Litovsk (now in Belarus), where the German Army had its headquarters. As leader of the Bolshevik delegation, Leon Trotsky skilfully used the negotiations as a platform to launch revolutionary propaganda directed at the soldiers and workers of the belligerent powers. Trotsky strove to stretch the discussions out in the hope of a revolution in Germany and Austria, which would come to Russia's aid. His speeches, which were translated into German and other languages and widely distributed, did have a considerable effect.

The revolutionary events in Russia transformed public opinion in Austria-Hungary. The rebellious mood was reflected in a wave of factory strikes, which forced the government to attend to the workers' grievances, improving working conditions and easing wartime controls. They had a tremendous effect on the ranks of the army and especially the navy. But the development of the revolution in Austria-Hungary and Germany needed time and, for the Russian Revolution, time was running out.

At one point, as a sign of impatience with Trotsky's delaying tactic, General Hoffmann placed his jackboots on the table. In his memoirs Trotsky later commented that Hoffmann's jackboots were the only thing that was real in that room. The Bolsheviks had no army to defend the Soviet power. The old tsarist army had practically ceased to exist and the Red Army had not yet been created. Threatened by enemies on all sides, the Bolshevik Revolution was in danger of being throttled at birth.

The German army advanced and seized control of Poland, the Baltic States, and the Ukraine. The Allied powers also intervened: the French in Odessa, the British in Murmansk, and the Japanese in the Russian Far East. Under these circumstances, the Bolsheviks were compelled to accept the harsh conditions imposed by German imperialism at Brest-Litovsk. This was a blow, but it gave the Bolsheviks some breathing space, to allow time for the revolution to develop in Europe. They did not have long to wait.

On 27 October, 1918, in the final days of the war, unrest again broke out after the Austro-Hungarian Army collapsed in the face of an Italian offensive. Naval vessels were soon operating under the control of their crews.

The crumbling edifice of the Habsburg Empire tottered and fell under the hammer blows of revolution. Between 28 and 31 October, 1918, the monarchy collapsed. Its armies were scattered and broken, and new national governments were springing up in the regions. The old Austro-Hungarian state had ceased to exist.

COLLAPSE OF LUDENDORFF'S OFFENSIVE
Despite the dire state of German morale both at home and in the army, General Ludendorff launched a series of offensives in the spring of 1918 in what was to be a last desperate attempt to break the stalemate on the Western Front. Between 21 March and 4 April 1918, in the first round of these suicidal adventures, German forces suffered over 240,000 casualties. It was a futile waste of life.

By mid-June 1918, it was clear that this last gamble had failed. The Germans paid dearly for this adventure, with final losses of almost 700,000 soldiers. It is true that the losses sustained by the Allies were greater, but their numbers were boosted by the arrival of American troops. More than 200,000 fresh soldiers were arriving every month from May to October 1918. By late July 1918, more than 1 million men were part of the American Expeditionary Force on the Western Front. Germany's position was now hopeless.

The final Allied push towards the German border began on 8 August, 1918. As the British, French, and American armies advanced, the alliance between the Central Powers, already under unbearable strain, began to fall apart. Turkey signed an armistice at the end of October, Austria-Hungary followed on 3 November. Germany was left alone in the face of the renewed Allied onslaught.

By the autumn of 1918 the situation in Germany was critical. The German emperor and his military chief, Erich Ludendorff, realised that there was no alternative. Germany must beg for peace. But the situation was already spiralling out of control. Power was slipping out of their hands. After years of suffering, a war-weary and hungry country became rebellious. Discontent and hunger were rife in Germany. The whole country was a powder keg waiting for a spark to set off an explosion.

Faced with the threat of immediate revolution, Prince Max attempted to carry out reforms that would transform Germany into a constitutional monarchy. But things had already gone too far. A rumour that an order had been issued to attack the English fleet in the North Sea sparked off a revolt of the sailors in Wilhelmshaven and Kiel on 30 October. Everybody knew that the war was lost. The morale of the sailors was already at rock bottom. Such a suicidal attack, while armistice negotiations were underway, would have been yet another senseless loss of life.

The men passed a resolution stating their refusal to take the offensive. The officers replied by arresting some of the sailors, which led to a mass demonstration of the sailors on 3 November. These demonstrations were fired upon, resulting in eight deaths and twenty-nine wounded. The incident had an electrifying effect on both workers and sailors.

The Kiel workers joined the movement on 4 November, creating the first soldiers' and workers' council in Germany. From Kiel, the mutiny spread quickly to other provinces and cities, such as Lübeck and Hamburg. In Cologne, the councils were established within days. There was little resistance. The revolutionary councils demanded an end to the war, the abdication of the Kaiser, and the declaration of a republic.

The Council demanded the release of political prisoners, freedom of speech and press, abolition of censorship, better conditions for the men, and that no orders be given for the fleet to take the offensive. On 5 November, one northern newspaper wrote:

> The revolution is on the march: What happened in Kiel will spread throughout Germany. What the workers and soldiers want is not chaos, but a new order; not anarchy, but the social republic.

The German Revolution had begun.

THE GERMAN REVOLUTION
Within only a few days, the revolt spread throughout the empire with little or no resistance from the old order. Everywhere, the workers joined forces with the troops in an unstoppable mass movement against the hated monarchical regime. Throughout the empire, Workers' and Soldiers' Councils were formed and moved to take power into their hands. But which party was prepared to take power?

The Social Democratic Party had the support of most workers. It now put itself at the head of the revolution. But in 1917 it had split into the Majority Social Democratic Party of Germany (MSPD) and the Independent Social Democratic Party of Germany (USPD). On 5 October, 1918, the Independent Socialists issued a call for a socialist republic. In Berlin, a committee of revolutionary shop stewards was formed and began to collect arms.

In Bavaria, on 7 November, 1918, a mass demonstration of thousands of workers demanded peace, bread, the eight-hour day, and the overthrow of the monarchy. The next day, the Independents organised a Constituent Soldiers', Workers', and Peasants' Council, and this body proclaimed the establishment of a Bavarian Democratic and Social Republic, headed by Kurt Eisner.

Under the pressure of the masses, the socialist ministers resigned *en masse* from the cabinet of Prince Max. The Greater Berlin Trade Union Council threatened a general strike if the emperor did not abdicate. The general strike and mass demonstrations were called on the morning of 9 November. A Workers' and Soldiers' Council was formed, and the regiments and troops stationed in Berlin were won over to the side of the revolution.

In spite of these facts, and the reports from his military advisors indicating that his support, even in his entourage, was rapidly evaporating, Wilhelm continued to equivocate over abdication. Even if he was forced to give up the imperial throne, this deluded man believed he could remain as King of Prussia. Such pathetic delusions are always the last refuge of a regime facing the prospect of imminent overthrow.

A deputation of Majority Socialists, including Ebert and Scheidemann, went to see Prince Max. They informed him that the troops had joined the revolution and that a new democratic government had to be formed. Ebert was asked whether he wanted to take power on the basis of the constitution or the Soldiers' and Workers' Council. Prince Max had no choice but to announce the abdication of the Kaiser, although no word had been received from that quarter. Prince Max then handed over his office to Ebert, and the latter declared himself Reich chancellor.

THE SOCIAL DEMOCRATS IN POWER

In a state of panic, the German ruling class hastily handed power to the only people who they thought could control the working class. They transferred parliamentary leadership to the right-wing Social Democrats under Friedrich Ebert, who was working in cahoots with the army. Ebert believed that the simple transfer of power from Prince Max to himself represented the final victory of the revolution. For these gentlemen, the whole purpose of the revolution was merely to bring about a ministerial reshuffle at the top. Ebert would even have been satisfied with a constitutional monarchy as long as the new state was given a baptismal blessing by a constituent assembly.

That was the mentality of those who sat in comfortable ministerial seats. But the mood in the streets was very different. Was it for this that the workers and soldiers had fought and died? The working men and women soon delivered a resounding answer. The carefully planned scenario in the corridors of power was immediately rendered obsolete by the movement of the masses. A mass demonstration of Berlin workers surrounded the Reichstag building, forcing the Socialist leaders to react. At 2.00 pm on 9 November, the Social Democrat Philipp Scheidemann mounted the balcony and proclaimed to the crowd:

> These enemies of the people are finished forever. The Kaiser has abdicated. He and his friends have disappeared; the people have won over all of them, in every field. Prince Max von Baden has handed over the office of Reich chancellor to representative Ebert. Our friend will form a new government

consisting of workers of all socialist parties. This new government may not be interrupted in their work, to preserve peace and to care for work and bread. Workers and soldiers, be aware of the historic importance of this day: exorbitant things have happened. Great and incalculable tasks are waiting for us. Everything for the people. Everything by the people. Nothing may happen to the dishonour of the Labour Movement. Be united, faithful, and conscientious. The old and rotten, the monarchy has collapsed. The new may live. Long live the German Republic!

When Scheidemann came in from the balcony, he was met by a furious Ebert. "You have no right to proclaim the republic!" Ebert shouted. "What becomes of Germany – whether she becomes a republic or something else – a constituent assembly must decide." But the masses had compelled the Majority Socialists to proclaim a republic before the Constituent Assembly had even met. In his memoirs, Scheidemann says that he made this speech in order to frustrate Liebknecht's proclamation of a soviet republic and Ebert's secret plan to restore the monarchy.

Still living in the clouds, as doomed monarchs tend to do, Wilhelm asked the Defence Minister, Wilhelm Groener, and military chief, Paul von Hindenburg, what he should do. To his astonishment, they informed the Kaiser that the military could no longer support him. The very next day, 10 November, he boarded a train and fled to the Netherlands, where he would remain until his death in 1941. Allied demands for his extradition and trial were ignored by the Dutch monarch.

THE END OF THE WAR

The First World War was thus ended by the German Revolution. At this point it was a bloodless revolution. Only fifteen people lost their lives in Berlin on 9 November. We must compare this with the huge numbers who were slaughtered like cattle on the killing fields of Ypres, Passchendaele, and the Somme. The new German government accepted the inevitable. There was no way Germany could continue the war.

The Social Democratic leaders had the illusion that they would be treated honourably by the victors. They were sadly mistaken. Had Ebert and Scheidemann paid more attention to Roman history, they would have remembered the chilling words spoken by the chieftain of the Gauls who sacked Rome: *Vae victis!* – Woe unto the defeated! The French and British treated the German delegation with complete contempt. They were not prepared to listen to even the most modest proposals for compromise.

Not conciliation, but revenge was on the order of the day. The French imperialists were particularly vindictive. The signing of the Armistice took place not in Paris, but in the Forest of Compiègne, about 37 miles (60 km) north of the French capital. The venue, chosen by Ferdinand Foch, a French military commander, was not the marble halls of Versailles, but his own railway carriage. This nice little touch was calculated to deepen even further the humiliation of the Germans.

On 11 November, an armistice was signed that formally ended hostilities. With Foch's jackboot on their necks, the German delegation swallowed hard and signed the terms dictated by the French Marshall. The following communiqué was issued:

> Official Radio from Paris – 6.01 am, 11 Nov., 1918. Marshal Foch to the Commander-in-Chief.
>
> 1. Hostilities will be stopped on the entire front, beginning at 11 o'clock, 11 November (French hour).
> 2. The Allied troops will not go beyond the line reached at that hour on that date until further orders.
>
> [Signed]
> Marshal Foch
> 5.45 am

This was essentially a German surrender. The terms of the Armistice were severe. Germany was ordered to give up 2,500 heavy guns, 2,500 field guns, 25,000 machine guns, 1,700 aeroplanes, and all the submarines they possessed (as a matter of fact, they were asked to give up more submarines than they possessed). They were also asked to surrender several warships and disarm all of the ones that they were allowed to keep. Germany was to be rendered defenceless. If Germany broke any of the terms of the Armistice, such as not evacuating areas they were ordered to evacuate, or not handing over weapons or prisoners of war in the timescales given, fighting would recommence within forty-eight hours.

Little did the victors of World War I imagine that, just over two decades later, in 1940, another armistice would be signed in the very same railway carriage in the Forest of Compiègne. But this time it was Germany forcing France to sign an agreement to end the fighting on their terms. Adolf Hitler sat in the same seat that Marshall Foch had occupied in 1918. The carriage was taken and exhibited in Germany as a war trophy. It was finally destroyed in 1945.

THE SOCIAL DEMOCRATS BETRAY

As the deafening roar of artillery was silenced and the thick smoke of gunfire lifted, the workers and soldiers of the former belligerent nations looked up and saw their former enemies in a new light. The Russian Revolution shone like a beacon of light amidst the darkness. Had the German Revolution of 1918 followed the example of the Russian Revolution, the whole history of the world would have been transformed.

But because of the policies of the labour leaders, it was not carried out to the end, and was finally defeated. Liebknecht and Luxemburg established the new German Communist Party on 30 December, 1918. But they were still a minority, as Lenin and the Bolsheviks had been in the first months of the Russian Revolution. By an irony of history, it was right-wing German Social Democrats, the same men who had betrayed the working class by voting for the war credits in 1914, who were thrown up by the first impulsive movement of the German Revolution and stood at its head.

For Ebert and Scheidemann, like the Mensheviks in Russia, the achievement of a bourgeois republic was the end of the matter. They wanted to avoid any threat of a Bolshevik-style revolution. The Kaiser was gone, but the essential infrastructure of the old imperial state remained intact: the bureaucracy, the power of the military, the church, and the old elite remained firmly in place.

The workers' and soldiers' councils existed side by side with a bourgeois National Constitutional Assembly in January 1919. But whereas in Russia the Soviets dissolved the Constituent Assembly, in Germany it was the other way around. Behind the façade of an elected assembly, all the old political and economic institutions remained intact.

Hiding behind the Social Democracy, the reactionary forces began to build a force capable of crushing the revolutionary workers. They recruited demobilised soldiers to form the paramilitary Freikorps, armed gangs dedicated to restoring the status quo and re-establishing 'Order'. In January 1919, there was an uprising in Berlin, the Spartacist Revolt, which was brutally crushed. The Bavarian Soviet Republic was drowned in blood.

The new-born Hungarian Soviet Republic was crushed by Romanian troops in collusion with the French and British imperialists. Béla Kun's confused policies contributed to this defeat, and Soviet Russia was too weak and beleaguered to come any assistance. Power passed to the counter-revolutionaries under Miklós Horthy, former Admiral of the Austro-Hungarian Navy, who crushed the workers and peasants under the heel of a White Terror.

REVOLUTION AND COUNTER-REVOLUTION IN ITALY

A somewhat similar scenario unfolded in Italy, although it took rather longer and, as in Germany, the work of the counter-revolution was accomplished by internal forces, not a foreign invasion, as in Hungary. The social and political divisions engendered by the war effort fractured even further in the revolutionary crisis of 1919-20.

The Italian imperialist bourgeoisie had been persuaded to join the war on the Allied side by tempting offers of new territories in the Treaty of London in 1915. The treaty encouraged the illusions of the Italian imperialists, their vanity puffed up with dreams of recovering the grandeur of the Roman Empire. But these illusions were soon dashed. The British and French bandits took the lion's share of the loot and left the Italians with a few crumbs.

There was a wave of mass strikes and factory occupations in Italy. In 1919, 1 million workers were on strike, followed by another 200,000 in early 1920. In those factories that were still operating, workers elected councils (soviets). By September 1920, 500,000 workers were on strike. Italy teetered on the brink of revolution.

The bourgeoisie, terrified by the threat of revolution, resorted to duplicity, offering to negotiate wage concessions if only the workers would abandon the factories. The ruse worked. The colossal revolutionary energy displayed by the working class dissipated for the lack of a determined revolutionary leadership. The workers ended their strikes, giving time for the ruling class to mobilise the forces of counter-revolution.

The proletariat had thrown down the gauntlet to the bourgeoisie, which was unable to solve the deep contradictions of Italian society. These could only be solved by forces outside the narrow limits of bourgeois democracy: either by the victory of the proletarian revolution, or of fascism. Italian bourgeois democracy had very weak roots. During the war, parliament rarely met. Real power was concentrated in the hands of a tiny clique of politicians, industrialists, and generals.

Fascism was a movement based on the petty bourgeoisie and the lumpenproletariat: embittered army veterans, former army officers and NCOs, the sons of the rich, and assorted de-classed elements. With its peculiar mix of chauvinism, imperialism, and social demagogy, it gave a banner under which all the disparate discontented elements could unite and acquire the appearance of unity, discipline, and purposefulness.

The son of a blacksmith, Mussolini started his political life as a member of the Socialist Party. He was initially opposed to Italy's entry into World War I, but later became a rabid chauvinist. Mussolini attacked the Italian government for weakness over the Treaty of Versailles. He united several right-wing groups into a single force and, in March 1919, formed the Fascist Party. Mussolini's plebeian origins, his earlier credentials as a socialist, and his talent as a demagogue and mob orator made him the perfect leader for such a movement.

Under the pretext of fighting against the establishment, the main target of fascist violence were the revolutionary workers and peasants. The enraged petty-bourgeois nationalists provided a fertile recruiting ground for the reactionaries. Mussolini had used the fascist gangs as a battering ram to smash the labour movement and save the bourgeoisie from the threat of revolution.

Mussolini declared that only he could restore order. The bourgeoisie, terrified by the prospect of revolution, handed him the power he demanded after the theatrical March on Rome. But in return for his services, he compelled the bourgeoisie to allow him to place his jackboot on their necks. Over the next few years, he proceeded to dismantle the institutions of bourgeois democracy, taking the title 'Il Duce' ('The Leader'). The failure of the workers' leaders to take advantage of the revolutionary situation to take power led directly to the victory of fascism in Italy. In Germany, the betrayal of the Social Democratic leaders prepared the way for the rise of Hitler and another, far bloodier and destructive world war.

16. THE TREATY OF VERSAILLES: THE PEACE TO END ALL PEACE

One hundred years ago, the representatives of the triumphant imperialist powers gathered in Paris to determine the fate of the entire world. The Treaty of Versailles formally ended the state of war between Germany and the Allied Powers. It took six months of wrangling at the Paris Peace Conference to conclude the peace treaty. It was finally signed on 28 June, 1919, exactly five years after the assassination of Archduke Franz Ferdinand.

The Versailles Treaty was one of the most outrageous and predatory treaties in history. It was a blatant act of plunder perpetrated by a gang of robbers against a helpless, prostrate and bleeding Germany. Among its numerous provisions, it required Germany and its allies to accept full responsibility for causing the war and, under the terms of Articles 231-248, to disarm, make substantial territorial concessions and pay reparations to the Entente powers.

The proceedings at Versailles are highly enlightening because they reveal the inner workings of imperialist diplomacy, the crude reality of power politics and the material interests that lurk behind the flowery phrases about Liberty, Humanitarianism, Pacifism and Democracy. In the secrecy of the negotiating chamber, the leaders of the 'civilised world' haggled like merchants in a medieval fair as to how to carve up Europe and divide the entire world into spheres of interest. This prepared the basis for later conflicts that led directly to the Second World War.

THE TALKS BEGIN

The actual fighting had already ended with the armistice, signed on 11 November, 1918. Negotiations between the Allied powers started on 18 January, 1919, in the luxurious surroundings of the Salle de l'Horloge at the French Foreign Ministry, on the Quai d'Orsay in Paris. To begin with there were no fewer than seventy delegates from twenty-seven nations in the negotiations. All had their own agendas and all demanded a slice of the cake. However, there were three major absentees: the defeated powers, Germany, Austria, and Hungary. They were excluded from the negotiations.

In reality, the Conference was a sham. Most of the seventy delegates had absolutely no say in the proceedings, which were determined by a handful of Great Powers: Britain, France and the United States. The smaller nations behaved like the poor relatives who stand, cap in hand, at the door of a wealthy man, who they hope will give them something for their patience and good behaviour. Until March 1919, the real business was conducted by the so-called Council of Ten composed of the five victor nations: the United States, France, Great Britain, Italy, and Japan.

However, even this body proved to be inconvenient for the manoeuvres of the big powers. The rising Asian power of Japanese imperialism already had its eyes set on further expansion in China, which brought it into direct conflict with the ambitions of the United States and Britain. The Japanese attempted to insert a clause proscribing discrimination on the basis of race or nationality, but this was rejected, in particular by Australia. Japan and others left the main meetings, so that only the Big Four remained.

Italy, the smallest and weakest, had entered the war late and played a very minor role. Now it was making a lot of noise over its territorial claims to Fiume. As usual, when a little dog makes too much noise and annoys the big dogs, the latter snarl and show their teeth, and the former slinks away with its tail between its legs. When these claims were rejected, the Italian Prime Minister, Vittorio Orlando, indignantly walked out of the negotiations (only to return to sign in June).

The proceedings were completely dominated by the leaders of the 'Big Three' of Britain, France and the USA. David Lloyd George, Georges Clémenceau, and the American President, Woodrow Wilson, decided everything. The final conditions were determined by these men and the interests they represented. However, it was virtually impossible for them to decide on a common position because their war aims conflicted with one another. The result was a botched compromise that satisfied nobody and thus prepared the way for new explosions.

CONSEQUENCES FOR GERMANY

On 29 April, the German delegation, under the leadership of the Foreign Minister, Ulrich Graf von Brockdorff-Rantzau, arrived in Versailles. It seems that they naively expected to be invited into the Conference for some kind of negotiations. After all, following the defeat of France in the Napoleonic Wars, the Frenchman Tallyrand was invited to participate in the Congress of Vienna, where he used his considerable skills to extract concessions for France. But this was not 1815!

The German representatives were systematically humiliated before being brought into the hall, where they were confronted for the first time with the stony-faced victors. The terms of the Treaty were then read out to them. There was no discussion – not even questions were allowed. On 7 May, when faced with the conditions dictated by the victors, including the so-called 'War Guilt Clause', Foreign Minister Ulrich Graf von Brockdorff-Rantzau replied to Clémenceau, Wilson and Lloyd George: "We know the full brunt of hate that confronts us here. You demand from us to confess we were the only guilty party of war; such a confession in my mouth would be a lie."

Such protests were of no avail. The Germans were forced to drink the cup of humiliation to the last dregs. Soon afterwards, they withdrew from the proceedings of the Treaty of Versailles – a despairing and futile gesture. In vain the German government issued a protest against what it considered to be unfair demands, and a 'violation of honour'. In a theatrical act, the newly-elected Social Democratic Chancellor, Philipp Scheidemann, refused to sign the treaty and resigned. In a passionate speech before the National Assembly on 12 March 1919, he called the treaty a "murderous plan" and exclaimed: "Which hand, trying to put us in chains like these, would not wither? The treaty is unacceptable."

But this was just so much empty rhetoric. Germany was effectively disarmed. The army had dissolved and the Allies were preparing to advance. The Entente powers also kept Germany under a partial naval blockade, starving the country into submission. It was an untenable situation. The National Assembly voted in favour of signing the treaty by 237 to 138, with five abstentions. The foreign minister Hermann Müller and Johannes Bell travelled to Versailles to sign the treaty on behalf of Germany. The treaty was signed on 28 June, 1919, and ratified by the National Assembly on 9 July, 1919, by a vote of 209 to 116.

This is the origin of the black legend of the 'stab-in-the-back'. Rightwing nationalists and ex-military leaders began to blame the Weimar politicians, socialists, communists, and Jews for a supposed national betrayal of Germany. The *November Criminals* and the newly formed Weimar Republic were held to be responsible for the defeat. This was a theme that the Nazis and other right-wing nationalists harped on about continually in the next period, blaming foreigners, Jews and 'traitors' for the miseries and sufferings of the German people.

FRANCE'S WAR AIMS

The most belligerent of the Big Three was France, which had lost more than Britain and the USA: some 1.5 million military personnel and an estimated 400,000 civilians. Much of the western front had been fought on French territory. Mutinies and revolution were threatening. Now the French ruling class needed to find a scapegoat, and offload its economic problems onto someone else. The press whipped the public into a frenzy of anti-German chauvinism, and the Prime Minister Georges Clémenceau was implacable.

Clémenceau was determined to cripple Germany militarily, politically, and economically so as it would never be able to invade France again. He naturally wanted the return of the rich and industrial land of Alsace-Lorraine, which had been stripped from France by Germany in the Franco-Prussian War of 1870-71. But the French General Staff wanted to go a lot further than this: they wanted France to have the Rhineland, which they had always regarded as France's 'natural' frontier with Germany.

Britain's war aims were different because her interests were not those of France. The wily British Prime Minister, Lloyd George, supported reparations but less than the French. He wanted to bleed Germany in the interests of British capitalism, and reduce its economic and military power. But he did not want to destroy Germany utterly. He was well aware that if France got its way, it could become the most powerful force on the continent, and the balance of power in Europe could be upset. This did not suit British imperialism, which wanted to play Germany off against France to keep both in check.

Apart from these strategic considerations, there were also British economic interests. Before the war, Germany had been Britain's main competitor, but also its largest trading partner, and therefore, the French proposal for the destruction of German industry did not suit the long-term interests of British capitalism. The British imperialists were more inclined to be sympathetic to the appeals of the German government, particularly when it came to helping them defuse the revolution. In the end, however, the prospect of plundering a defeated Germany was too tempting to resist. So, Lloyd George managed to increase Britain's share of German reparations by demanding compensation for the huge number of widows, orphans, and men left unable to work through injury, due to the war.

Always the supreme political opportunist, Lloyd George supported the slogan 'Hang the Kaiser' in order to make his people happy and gain votes at home. Lloyd George was irritated by Woodrow Wilson's so-called idealism. The French and British supported secret treaties and naval blockades, which Wilson opposed. In particular, the American President's proposal for 'self-determination' did not please Lloyd George. The British imperialists, like the French, wanted to preserve their empire. If the idea of self-determination was applicable in Europe

(Czechoslovakia, Yugoslavia), why should it not be applicable to British and French colonies?

The leaders of Europe were not to be fooled by the likes of Wilson. They were sufficiently experienced to read between the lines and distinguish between fact and fiction. They could see that, behind the gaseous screen of idealism, there lay very solid interests. They knew that the rising power of America was flexing its muscles and would one day have to test its strength against theirs. The worldwide struggle for markets would bring them into conflict, just as it had with Germany.

Behind the fine words about self-determination lay a threat to break up the old European empires to the benefit of the United States. Now it was interfering for the first time in the internal affairs of Europe and was taking the side of Germany against Britain and France. But what did these Americans know about war? They had come in at the last minute and tipped the balance against Germany. But they had not sacrificed as the British and French had done. Their lands had not been invaded. Their cities had not been shelled and bombed. And they lecture us on justice and humanity! It is intolerable!

UNITED STATES' WAR AIMS

The USA was becoming the most powerful nation on earth. It had already embarked on its career of imperialist expansion in its wars with Mexico, but the process experienced a qualitative leap with the war with Spain and the seizure of Cuba and the Philippines at the end of the nineteenth century. However, being a vast country with a huge internal market, one section of the American bourgeoisie, and a big section of the petty bourgeoisie, remained inclined to isolationism.

There was a powerful non-interventionist sentiment before and after the United States entered the war in April 1917. When the war ended, many Americans felt eager to extricate themselves from European affairs as rapidly as possible. The United States took a more conciliatory view toward the issue of German reparations, which brought them into collision with the British and particularly the French imperialists.

Amidst the bloody wreckage of Europe, many people looked to the transatlantic giant for some signs of hope. Woodrow Wilson's woolly

16. THE TREATY OF VERSAILLES: THE PEACE TO END ALL PEACE

pacifist and democratic rhetoric struck a chord in the hearts and minds of millions of war-weary people in Europe, particularly in the defeated countries and in small nations struggling to assert themselves. So, in the beginning, Wilson was regarded as a hero – much the same as Barack Obama was.

The similarity between their speeches is striking: a combination of high-sounding phrases, idealism and populism that sounds very good and is completely empty of any real content. When he first arrived in Europe, Wilson was greeted by huge crowds of cheering people. But this enthusiasm did not last long. Behind the wonderful phrases the same old great power interests and sordid diplomatic wheeling and dealing continued as usual.

Even before the end of the war, Woodrow Wilson put forward his Fourteen Points, which he now presented in a speech at the Paris Peace Conference. It is interesting to speculate to what extent Wilson believed in his own rhetoric. He seems to have been nothing more than a provincial academic with a narrow and formalistic mentality coloured with a large dose of sentimentality and Christian moralising. His manner of speaking, which resembled that of a small-town preacher, must have had the same effect on the ears of the hard-bitten Clémenceau and the smiling cynic Lloyd George as the sound of a dentist's drill.

At first, they listened in silence as he lectured them on the need for morality in world affairs, justice and humanity for defeated enemies and the right of self-determination for small nations. They did not know who Wilson was, but they knew that America was the country that held the fate of Europe in the palm of its hand, and therefore they swallowed their pride and contained their indignation, confining themselves to ironic comments in the corridors.

America wanted peace and stability in Europe in order to secure the success of future trading opportunities and hopefully collect some of the huge debts owed to it by the Europeans. Much of the money paid to Britain and France by the Germans would wind up in American banks. However, America could afford to be more magnanimous and did not have revolution knocking at the door.

In the United States, disillusionment with the war caused a backlash against Wilson. The isolationists, led by Henry Cabot Lodge, launched an offensive against the treaty in the Senate, which voted against ratifying. An old, sick and embittered man, Wilson refused to support the treaty with any of the reservations imposed by the Senate. He died shortly afterwards. Wilson's successor, Warren G. Harding, continued American opposition to the League of Nations. His administration later collapsed in the midst of an unprecedented corruption scandal.

REPARATIONS

The terms of the Treaty were draconian indeed. Much of the rest of the Treaty set out the reparations that Germany would pay to the Allies. The total amount of war reparations demanded from Germany amounted to a staggering 226 billion Reichsmarks in gold. This was an impossible amount for Germany to pay, a fact that was later tacitly accepted by an Inter-Allied Reparations Commission. In 1921, it was reduced to 132 billion Reichsmarks (£4.99 billion). But even that figure was ruinous for Germany. Reparations were paid in a variety of forms, including coal, steel, agricultural products, and even intellectual property (for example, the patent for aspirin).

The young John Maynard Keynes had been the principal representative of the British Treasury at the Paris Peace Conference. Angry that his suggestions about reparations had been ignored, he published a damning account of the Conference, *The Economic Consequences of the Peace* (1919). In this famous book he referred to the Treaty of Versailles as a "Carthaginian peace". His argument was that the burden of reparations would ruin Germany, drag down the rest of Europe, and lead to revolution:

> If the distribution of the European coal supplies is to be a scramble in which France is satisfied first, Italy next, and every one else takes their chance, the industrial future of Europe is black and the prospects of revolution very good. It is a case where particular interests and particular claims, however well founded in sentiment or in justice, must yield to sovereign expediency.

16. THE TREATY OF VERSAILLES: THE PEACE TO END ALL PEACE

He was attempting to focus the minds of the victorious powers on the bigger picture:

> A victory of Spartacism in Germany might well be the prelude to Revolution everywhere: it would renew the forces of Bolshevism in Russia, and precipitate the dreaded union of Germany and Russia; it would certainly put an end to any expectations which have been built on the financial and economic clauses of the Treaty of Peace.

From a capitalist point of view, he was quite right. The war had put the international socialist revolution firmly on the agenda. The conditions of the treaty were so vicious that it was seen unanimously as *unacceptable* by all political parties. The main victims, as always, were the working people. The shattered German economy was so weak that only a small percentage of reparations were paid in hard currency. Even the payment of a small percentage of the original reparations still placed an intolerable burden on the German economy, and was the cause of the hyperinflation that subsequently plunged it into a bottomless pit.

'GERMANY'S GUILT'

An attempt was made to shift all responsibility for the sufferings of the war onto the shoulders of the former German Emperor, Wilhelm II. The British and French ranted and raged. He was to be tried as a war criminal. However, in the end, nothing was done and the former Kaiser lived out his days in comfortable exile in Holland. But if Wilhelm escaped unscathed, the German people were not to be let off so lightly. Article 231 (the 'War Guilt Clause') laid all responsibility for the war on Germany, which would be accountable for all the damage done to civilian population of the allies.

There were military restrictions. The preamble Part V of the treaty states:

> In order to render possible the initiation of a general limitation of the armaments of all nations, Germany undertakes strictly to observe the military, naval and air clauses which follow.

German armed forces were to number no more than 100,000 troops, and conscription was to be abolished. Enlisted men were to be retained for at least twelve years; officers to be retained for at least twenty-five years. German naval forces would be limited to 15,000 men, six battleships (no more than 10,000 tons displacement each), six cruisers (no more than 6,000 tons displacement each), six destroyers (no more than 800 tons displacement each) and twelve torpedo boats (no more than 200 tons displacement each). No submarines were to be included.

The manufacture, import, and export of weapons and poison gas was prohibited. Armed aircraft, tanks and armoured cars were prohibited. These decisions would render Germany defenceless against external attack. Its territories were placed at the mercy of a vengeful France in the West and a thrusting, newly independent Second Polish Republic in the East.

However, in view of the growing threat of revolution in Germany, the Allies decided to allow the Reichswehr to retain 100,000 machine guns for use against the German working class. These weapons were used by the Freikorps to suppress the revolutionary movement in Germany.

Then there were the territorial claims, mainly aimed at weakening Germany and strengthening France. In order to do this, an independent Poland was necessary. Clémenceau was convinced that Germany had "20 million people too much". So West Prussia was ceded to the Poles, thus giving Poland access to the Baltic Sea via the 'Polish Corridor'. East Prussia was separated from mainland Germany. In addition, Germany was compelled to hand over all its colonies. Germany was also forbidden to unite with Austria to form a larger nation to make up for the lost land.

Northern Schleswig was returned to Denmark following a plebiscite on 14 February, 1920, while Central Schleswig opted to remain German in a separate referendum on 14 March, 1920. Alsace-Lorraine was restored to French sovereignty without a plebiscite as from the date of the Armistice of 11 November, 1918. But, on the question of the Rhineland, Clémenceau suffered a defeat. The French General Staff made it clear that they expected the Rhineland to be handed over to France. But Lloyd George would have none of it. The Rhineland was to become a demilitarised zone administered by Great Britain and France jointly.

Most of the Prussian province of Posen (now Poznan) and of West Prussia, which Prussia had annexed in partitions of Poland (1772-1795), were ceded to Poland. The Hlučínsko (Hultschin) area of Upper Silesia went to Czechoslovakia (333 km², 49,000 inhabitants) without a plebiscite. The eastern part of Upper Silesia also went to Poland. The area of the cities Eupen and Malmedy were given to Belgium, which also received the track bed of the Vennbahn railway.

The area of Soldau in East Prussia was given to Poland. The northern part of East Prussia, known as Memel Territory, was placed under the control of France, and later occupied by Lithuania. The province of Saarland was placed under the control of the League of Nations for fifteen years. After that, a plebiscite between France and Germany was to decide to which country it would belong. During this time, the coal produced in that region would be sent to France.

The port of Danzig, with the delta of the Vistula River at the Baltic Sea, was made the Free City of Danzig under the permanent governance of the League of Nations, without a plebiscite. The German and Austrian governments had to acknowledge and strictly respect the independence of Austria. The unification of both countries was strictly forbidden, although a big majority of both populations were known to be in favour of it. There were other smaller 'adjustments' at the expense of Germany and its allies.

THE BOLSHEVIKS AND VERSAILLES

Soviet Russia was naturally excluded from the Paris peace talks. The formal reason was because it had already negotiated a separate peace with Germany. In the Treaty of Brest-Litovsk (March 1918) Germany had taken away a third of Russia's population, one half of Russia's industrial undertakings and nine-tenths of Russia's coal mines, coupled with an indemnity of six billion marks. But although physically absent, Russia's presence made itself felt in all the deliberations at the Peace Conference.

Lenin and the Bolsheviks based themselves on the perspective of world revolution that would move westward, across Central Europe to Germany, France and the whole of Europe. Nowadays it is fashionable to portray this as a utopian idea, but the victors at Versailles took it very seriously. The Russian Revolution had a powerful effect on the German working class, which rose in revolution exactly twelve months after October. We have already described the German Revolution of November 1918. This was followed by a revolutionary wave that swept over Europe.

The real reason for the exclusion of Russia was that all the imperialist powers were the sworn enemies of Bolshevism, which they correctly saw as the most dangerous threat to their interests. Even while the Great Powers sat around the negotiating table, fighting over the map of the world like dogs fighting over a bone, the flames of revolution were spreading to Germany, a soviet republic had been declared in Hungary and also Bavaria, and Trotsky's Red Army was beating back the counter-revolutionary White forces. British, American, Japanese and French forces were intervening actively on the side of the Whites in an anti-Bolshevik crusade.

This explains the haste with which the German ruling class capitulated to the Allies. However, they hoped that a reasonable deal could be reached. After all, the Kaiser was gone and Germany now had a democratic government. Moreover, the Germans, and especially the Social Democratic leaders had high hopes for the American President Woodrow Wilson and his Fourteen Points.

In 1919, Lenin was still hoping that Soviet Revolution in Vienna would support Soviet Hungary. All his hopes were placed on a revolution in Germany. In *'Left Wing' Communism* Lenin wrote:

> The Soviet revolution in Germany will strengthen the international Soviet movement, which is the strongest bulwark (and the only reliable, invincible and world-wide bulwark) against the Treaty of Versailles and against international imperialism in general.

But he sharply castigated the German Left Communists for their idea of 'No Compromise' – including the rejection of the Versailles Treaty and a so-called German People's War against the Entente. Lenin placed his hopes firmly on revolution in Germany:

> To give absolute, categorical and immediate precedence to liberation from the Treaty of Versailles and to give it *precedence over the question* of liberating *other* countries oppressed by imperialism, from the yoke of imperialism, is philistine nationalism (worthy of the Kautskys, the Hilferdings, the Otto Bauers and Co.), not revolutionary internationalism. The overthrow of the bourgeoisie in any of the large European countries, including Germany, would be such a gain for the international revolution that, for its sake, one can, and if necessary, should, tolerate a *more prolonged existence of the Treaty of Versailles*. If Russia, standing alone, could endure the Treaty of Brest-Litovsk for several months, to the advantage of the revolution, there is nothing impossible in a Soviet Germany, allied with Soviet Russia, enduring the existence of the Treaty of Versailles for a longer period, to the advantage of the revolution.
>
> The imperialists of France, Britain, etc., are trying to provoke and ensnare the German Communists: 'Say that you will not sign the Treaty of Versailles!' they urge. Like babes, the Left Communists fall into the trap laid for them, instead of skilfully manoeuvring against the crafty and, *at present*, stronger enemy, and instead of telling him, 'We shall sign the Treaty of Versailles now.' It is folly, not revolutionism, to deprive ourselves in advance of any freedom of action, openly to inform an enemy who is at present better armed than we are whether we shall fight him, and when. To accept battle at a time when it is obviously advantageous to the enemy, but not to us, is criminal; political leaders of the revolutionary class are absolutely useless if they are incapable of "changing tack, or offering conciliation and compromise" in order to take evasive action in a patently disadvantageous battle.

It goes without saying that the Bolsheviks regarded it as an act of imperialist plunder, like the even-more-vicious Treaty of Brest-Litovsk.

But they understood that the imperialists (especially the French) were looking for an excuse to invade Germany, which would have been a setback for the revolution. By flirting with German nationalism, the German Left Communists were abandoning the policies of revolutionary proletarian internationalism in favour of 'national Bolshevism', which Lenin considered an abomination.

Whereas the right-wing Social Democrats like Noske, Scheidemann and Ebert placed themselves on the side of the German ruling class and imperialism, and the Left Social Democrats (the Independents) took up a vacillating and ambiguous position, Lenin and Trotsky approached all questions from the standpoint of the international revolution. For Lenin, the question was not for or against the Treaty of Versailles, but how to prepare the most favourable conditions for the German workers to come to power.

Lenin's perspectives for Germany were confirmed in 1923, when Germany stopped paying the reparations 'agreed' upon in the Treaty of Versailles. As a result, French and Belgium forces occupied the Ruhr, the heartland of German industry. German workers launched a campaign of passive resistance, refusing to work the factories while they remained in French hands.

The German currency was now useless: a wheelbarrow full of notes was necessary to buy a box of matches. The middle class was in a revolutionary mood and the Social Democrats were discredited. The Communist Party was growing by leaps and bounds and the question of power was posed. Even the fascists were saying: let the Communists take power first, then it will be our turn.

Unfortunately, the leaders of the German Communist Party vacillated and failed to take decisive action. They looked to Moscow for advice, but Lenin was incapacitated by his final illness and Trotsky was also ill. The German leaders instead saw Stalin and Zinoviev, who advised them not to try to take power. And so, an exceptionally favourable opportunity was lost. The masses were disappointed and turned away from the Communist Party.

The crisis was over and German capitalism began to recover, benefiting from the economic revival in Europe and aid from the USA.

16. THE TREATY OF VERSAILLES: THE PEACE TO END ALL PEACE   221

But fundamental contradictions were gnawing at the entrails of the Weimar Republic. The German bourgeoisie, alarmed at the growing strength of the Socialists and Communists, began to prepare for the final showdown with the working class. The end result was the rise of Hitler, the destruction of the mighty German labour movement and the Second World War.

THE EFFECTS ON FRANCE

The Treaty of Versailles was at the expense of the German people, but the people of Britain and France derived no benefit from it. At that time, in the 'Resolution on the Versailles Treaty', which he wrote for the Fourth Congress of the Comintern, November-December 1922, Trotsky made the following prophetic analysis:

> The appearance is that France, of all the countries, has grown most in power. But in reality, the economic basis of France, with her small and steadily diminishing population, her enormous domestic and foreign debt, and her dependence on England, does not provide an adequate foundation for her greed for imperialist expansion. So far as her political power is concerned, she is thwarted by England's mastery of all the important naval bases, and by the oil monopoly held by England and the United States. In the domain of economy, the enrichment of France with the iron mines given her by the Treaty of Versailles, loses its value inasmuch as the supplementary and indispensable coal mines of the Ruhr Basin remain in German hands. The hopes of restoring shattered French finances by means of German reparations have proved illusory. When the impracticability of the Treaty of Versailles becomes apparent, certain sections of French heavy industry will consciously bring on the depreciation of the franc in order to unload the costs of the war on the shoulders of the French proletariat.

Despite all his stubbornness, Clémenceau had failed to achieve what he had promised. Field Marshal Foch did not hide his bitterness about the failure to get the Rhineland. He complained that Germany had been let off too lightly (!!) and declared, "This is not Peace. It is an Armistice for twenty years." The French press stoked the feelings of resentfulness and disappointment and Clémenceau was voted out of office in the elections of January 1920.

Even at the Peace Conference, differences emerged between Britain and France. As we have seen, it was not in Britain's interests to bleed Germany white. The ruin of Germany had negative effects on the British economy, which experienced a slump, with mass unemployment and a sharpening of the class struggle. The same was true of France.

It is now a banal statement to say that the strangling of Germany prepared the way for the rise of Hitler. In fact, a new world war could have been prevented by revolution. But the leaders of the mass organisations, by preventing revolution, made avoiding a new war impossible. The policies pursued by both the Social Democrats and the Stalinists rendered the powerful German labour movement impotent and allowed Hitler to come to power in 1933.

From that point onwards, a new war was inevitable. The worst fears of the French ruling class were confirmed as Hitler launched a programme designed to rebuild Germany's economic and military might. In 1934, five years before the outbreak of the Second World War, Trotsky declared in the theses, 'War and the Fourth International':

> The collapse of the League of Nations is indissolubly bound up with the beginning of the collapse of French hegemony on the European continent. The demographic and economic power of France proved to be, as was to be expected, too narrow a base for the Versailles system.

THE NATIONAL QUESTION

It is a matter of speculation to what extent Woodrow Wilson actually believed in his idealistic plans. What is certain is that his demagogic appeals for self-determination were aimed at breaking up the old European empires, and that this was in the interests of American imperialism.

Every time the imperialists proclaim self-determination, the result is new injustices, new contradictions, new oppressions and new wars. This is a classical case. The Versailles Treaty signified the dismemberment of the Austro-Hungarian Empire and the creation of new states like Yugoslavia, Poland and Czechoslovakia. But the national question has always been used by imperialism for its own selfish ends. In the hands of the Great Powers, the right of self-determination is just so much small change, to be bartered away.

The creation of new states in Europe was accompanied by new injustices, cruelty and national oppression. Millions of Germans in the Sudetenland and in Posen-West Prussia were placed under foreign rule in a hostile environment, where harassment and violation of rights by authorities are documented. Out of 1,058,000 Germans in Posen-West Prussia in 1921, 758,867 fled their homelands within five years due to Polish harassment. This harassment of German minorities later served as a pretext for Hitler's annexations of Czechoslovakia and parts of Poland.

Although the main sphere of operations was in Europe, this was indeed the First *World* War, and was fought on a global scale. There were serious repercussions in Asia. Article 156 of the treaty transferred German concessions in Shandong (which was part of China) to Japan instead of returning it to China. This outrage led to demonstrations and a cultural movement known as the May Fourth Movement, which was the starting point for an upsurge of the revolutionary movement in China.

Since Turkey had been an ally of Germany, it also suffered the loss of many of its old possessions. The former Ottoman Empire was divided among the victors, who had been watching its decay for a long time, like hungry vultures waiting for a wounded animal to die.

THE THIEVES' KITCHEN

The Treaty of Versailles led to the creation of the League of Nations, an organisation intended to arbitrate international disputes and thereby avoid future wars. This was mainly agreed to by Britain and France in order to placate President Wilson and pander to his pacifist prejudices. It also had the advantage of casting the victors of Versailles in a most favourable light before world public opinion. These predatory imperialists were presented to the world as 'men of peace', at the very time that they were plundering Germany and engaging in a bloody intervention against Soviet Russia.

The Covenant of the League of Nations was designed to produce the impression that this organisation's aim was to combat aggression, reduce armaments, and consolidate peace and security. The League's goals included upholding the new-found Rights of Man, disarmament, preventing war through collective security, settling disputes between countries through negotiation, diplomacy and improving global quality of life. Wilson claimed that he could "predict with absolute certainty that within another generation there will be another world war if the nations of the world do not concert the method by which to prevent it." To begin with, as a result of the growing mood of isolationism, the United States did not join the League of Nations.

In practice, however, its leaders shielded the aggressors and fostered the arms race and preparations for the Second World War. Lenin denounced the League of Nations as a "thieves' kitchen." The subsequent history of the League of Nations showed that Lenin was right. It did not prevent Franco's war against his own people. Nor did it do anything to halt Japanese aggression against China or Hitler's expansionist plans in Europe.

The League of Nations accepted Mussolini's bullying of Greece and failed to stop him invading Abyssinia. The Italian fascist army used chemical weapons like mustard gas against undefended villages, poisoning water supplies and bombing Red Cross tents. When the League complained, Mussolini replied that, since the Ethiopians are not fully human, the human-rights laws did not apply. The Italian dictator stated that, "The League is very well when sparrows shout, but no good at all when eagles fall out." These words admirably expressed the real situation.

Naturally, the existence of the League of Nations did nothing to stop the Second World War. In March 1935, Adolf Hitler introduced compulsory military conscription and rebuilt the armed forces in direct violation of the Treaty of Versailles. In March 1936, he again violated the treaty by reoccupying the demilitarised zone in the Rhineland. He

16. THE TREATY OF VERSAILLES: THE PEACE TO END ALL PEACE

followed this by annexing Austria in the Anschluss in March 1938. These steps paved the way for the annexing of the Sudetenland and the occupation of Czechoslovakia, which led to the invasion of Poland and World War II.

The League of Nations could serve as a forum for discussion as long as the interests of the major powers were not involved. But when serious matters were involved, it was utterly useless. The same is true of the UN today. The Soviet Union was not a member of the League, and for good reasons. To the question "Why does not the Soviet Union participate in the League of Nations?" Stalin replied in 1927:

> The Soviet Union is not a member of the League of Nations and does not participate in its work, because the Soviet Union is not prepared to share the responsibility for the imperialist policy of the League of Nations, for the 'mandates' which are distributed by the League for the exploitation and oppression of the colonial countries, for the war preparations and military alliances which are covered and sanctified by the League, preparations which must inevitably lead to imperialist war. The Soviet Union does not participate in the work of the League because the Soviet Union is fighting with all its energy against all preparations for imperialist war. The Soviet Union is not prepared to become a part of that camouflage for imperialist machinations represented by the League of Nations. The League is the rendezvous of the imperialist leaders who settle their business there behind the scenes. The subjects about which the League speaks officially, are nothing but empty phrases intended to deceive the workers. The business carried on by the imperialist ring-leaders behind the scenes, that is the actual work of imperialism which the eloquent speakers of the League of Nations hypocritically cloak. ('Questions and Answers, A Discussion with Foreign Delegates' by Stalin, J., Moscow. 13 November, 1927.)

This answer is more-or-less correct and reflects the attitude of Lenin to the League. However, later on, Stalin changed his mind. After the victory of Hitler, he tried to get the support of the so-called European democracies and joined the League. It did him no good. Weak and indulgent in the face of German and Italian fascism and Japanese militarism, the League was brave enough to expel the Soviet Union in December 1939 after it invaded Finland. This was its last significant action. The Second World War signified the ignominious collapse of the League of Nations – and the even more ignominious dissolution of the Communist International.

Imperialist wars are fought over very concrete questions: the control of markets, colonies, raw materials and spheres of influence. Over the past century there have been many such wars, and two of them were world wars. The second one resulted in the deaths of 55 million people, the big majority of them civilians. Of course, the imperialists can never openly admit the true causes that motivate them. They possess a vast propaganda machine designed to convince public opinion that all their wars are just wars, for the defence of peace, civilisation, democracy and culture. It is sufficient to remind ourselves that the First World War was presented as 'the War to end all Wars'!

EPILOGUE: REVOLUTIONARY OPTIMISM

About 17 million soldiers and civilians were killed during the First World War. One of those who survived was my grandfather. As I write these lines, I have before me the big old family bible I remember from my childhood. Inside there is an entire page headed with the title Roll of Honour. It is decorated in colour with the flags of our gallant allies: the French, Americans, Belgians, Serbs – and the double headed eagle of tsarist Russia. And here we can read the same infamous slogan that is inscribed on every war memorial in the land: *Dulce et decorum est pro patria mori* (It is sweet and seemly to die for the fatherland).

George Woods entered the war on 1 September, 1914, a young enthusiastic volunteer. He is listed as private number 13793 of the Welsh Regiment, and served nine spells of action in France in a period of five years. He was demobilised on 24 March, 1919. He left the army a changed man. Inspired by the example of the Russian Revolution, he joined the Communist Party and remained a committed Communist until he died. I learned about the ideas of Marx and Lenin, about the class struggle and the Russian Revolution from him, and I am eternally grateful to him for that and so many other things.

My grandfather, a Welsh tinplate worker, was not alone. The South Wales Miners' Federation voted to affiliate to the Communist International. In Scotland, the Clydeside shop stewards did the same.

Out of the blood-soaked ruins of the Great Slaughter, a new spirit of revolt was born. In all the belligerent countries – in Paris and Berlin, in Vienna and Budapest, in Sofia and Prague – millions of workers were on their feet fighting for change, for a better world, for bread and justice: for socialism.

It is easy to draw pessimistic conclusions from human history in general, and wars in particular. There are always those who draw pessimistic conclusions from the objective situation. Scepticism and cynicism are merely hypocritical expressions of moral and intellectual cowardice. Such people blame the working class for their own impotence and apostasy. Lenin never showed the slightest sign of pessimism when the nightmare of war and reaction seemed never-ending. He showed utter contempt for the pacifists, who moaned about the evils of war but avoided drawing revolutionary conclusions.

During the dark days of the First World War the situation of the revolutionary forces must have seemed hopeless. Lenin once more found himself isolated in Swiss exile. He was only able to maintain contact with a very small group. But he was not afraid to fight against the stream, convinced that the tide would turn. He dedicated all his strength to educating and training the cadres on the basis of the genuine ideas of Marxism.

Answering a pacifist who said that war is terrible, Lenin said, "Yes, terribly profitable." And in the end, he was proved right. Contradicting all the pessimistic predictions of the sceptical Cassandras, the imperialist war ended in revolution. The Russian Revolution offered humanity a way out of the nightmare of wars, poverty, and suffering. But the absence of a revolutionary leadership on an international scale meant that this possibility was aborted in one country after another. The result was a new crisis and a new and even-more-terrible imperialist war.

The great wheel of human history turns continuously. It knows great sorrows and great joys. It is a never-ending story of victories and defeats. And it teaches us that any situation, however hopeless it may seem, will sooner or later turn into its opposite, and we must prepare for this. This was expressed most strikingly by Shakespeare when he wrote:

> There is a tide in the affairs of men,
> Which taken at the flood, leads on to fortune.
> Omitted, all the voyage of their life is bound in shallows and in miseries.
> On such a full sea are we now afloat.
> And we must take the current when it serves,
> Or lose our ventures.

Lenin said that capitalism is horror without end. The bloody convulsions that are spreading throughout the world right now show that he was right. All these horrors are the expression of a socio-economic system that has exhausted itself and is ripe for overthrow. Middle-class moralists weep and wail about these horrors, but they have no idea what the causes are, still less the solution. Pacifists and moralists point to the symptoms but not the underlying cause, which lies in a diseased social system that has outlived its historical role.

Now, as then, the conditions are being prepared for an explosive upsurge of the class struggle on a world scale. In the convulsive period that lies ahead, the working class will have many opportunities to transform society. The power of the working class has never been greater than now. But this power must be organised, mobilised, and provided with adequate leadership. This is the main task on the order of the day.

We stand firmly on the basis of Lenin's ideas, which have withstood the test of time. Together with the ideas of Marx, Engels, and Trotsky, they alone provide the guarantee of future victory. Not world war, but an unprecedented upsurge in the class war is the perspective for the period into which we have entered. The horrors we see before us are only the outward symptoms of the death agony of capitalism. But they are also the birth pangs of a new society that is fighting to be born. It is our task to cut short this pain and hasten the birth of a new and genuinely human society.

INDEX

A

Alexander II, Tsar 57
Algeciras Conference 68, 70
Ali, Hussein bin 197–198, 201
Asquith, Herbert 152, 199
Atatürk, Mustafa Kemal 123, 124, 155

B

Baden, Max von 206–208
Bak, Per 67
Balfour, Arthur 201
Balkan League, The 18–19
Barbusse, Henri 163–164, 166, 168, 174–176
Bell, Johannes 218
Bethmann-Hollweg, Theobald von 26, 46–47, 49–50
Black Hand, The 24
Bolsheviks, The 81–82, 105, 182, 184–185, 202, 203–205, 211–212, 225–227
Brockdorff-Rantzau, Ulrich Graf von 217
Brusilov, Aleksei 104–105, 109, 180
Bülow, Bernhard von 37

C

Cadorna, Luigi 127–128, 183
Carol I of Romania 158
Central Powers, The 19, 64–65, 109, 114–116, 125, 129, 131–132, 151, 158–160, 182, 191, 197, 205
Churchill, Winston 120–122, 124, 151, 192
Clémenceau, Georges 217, 218, 221, 224, 229
Constantine I of Greece, King 132, 151, 153–154
Cox, Sir Percy 193
Crowe, Eyre Sir 29–30, 41, 71
Czernin, Ottokar 158, 183, 188, 189

D

Dartiguenave, Philippe Sudré 146
Debs, Eugene 141

E

Ebert, Friedrich 208–209, 211, 228
Eisner, Kurt 207
Engels, Friedrich 34
Entente, The 25, 39, 53, 55, 64, 65, 69, 70–71, 103, 125–126, 131, 148, 151, 154–155, 157, 189, 192, 215
Esterhazy, Moritz 185

F

Falkenhayn, Erich von 179–180
Feodorovna, Alexandra 53, 105, 111
Ferdinand, Franz 15, 20, 21, 57, 131–132, 158, 210, 215
Ferdinand I of Bulgaria, King 131–132
Ferdinand I of Romania, King 158–159
Fisher, Admiral John 121
Foch, Marshal Ferdinand 83–84, 210–211, 229
Ford, Henry 139
Freikorps 212, 224

G

Georges-Picot, François 191, 199
Gompers, Samuel 141
Grey, Sir Edward 29–30, 40–41, 42–43, 47, 69, 72, 82, 137
Groener, Wilhelm 209

H

Habsburg Monarchy 16, 31, 57, 154, 205
Haig, General Douglas 180
Harding, Warren G. 222
Hegel, Georg Wilhelm Friedrich 15, 67, 136
Heraclitus 31, 201
Hindenburg, Paul von 180, 183, 209
Hitler, Adolf 211, 214, 229, 230, 231, 232–234
Hoffmann, Max 204
Hogarth, David 198–199
Horthy, Miklós 212

J

Joffre, Marshal Joseph 83–84, 182–183
Josef I, Franz 16, 22, 25, 185

K

Karl I of Austria 185, 188–190
Keynes, John Maynard 222–223
Kluck, General Alexander von 83–84
Kun, Béla 212
Kuropatkin, Alexei 112

L

La Follette, Robert M. 139
Lawrence, Thomas Edward 196–198
League of Nations, The 149, 222, 225, 230, 231–233
Lenin, Vladimir 103, 135, 148, 184, 185, 202, 211, 226–229, 232, 233, 236–237

INDEX

Liebknecht, Karl 171, 209, 211
Lloyd George, David 155–156, 189, 201, 217, 219, 221, 225
Lodge, Henry Cabot 221
Ludendorff, Erich 107, 180, 205
Luxemburg, Rosa 211

M

Mackensen, August von 108
Marx, Karl 36, 90
Mehmet V, Sultan 115
Moltke, Helmuth von 45
Morganthau Sr., Henry 120
Müller, Hermann 218
Mussolini, Benito 65–66, 213, 232

N

Nicholas II, Tsar 28, 31, 36, 53–55, 56–63, 81, 111, 117, 180
Nikolayevich, Nicholas 111
Nivelle, Robert 182–183
Nixon, Sir John 193–194
Noske, Gustav 228

O

Orlando, Vittorio 217
Ottoman Empire 16–17, 18–20, 113, 114–118, 120, 122, 124, 152, 154–155, 178, 191, 199, 200–202, 231
Owen, Wilfred 90–101

P

Pasha, Enver 113–114, 115, 117–118, 196
Pasha, Talaat 114
Pétain, Philippe 183

Poincaré, Raymond 27, 73, 81, 188–189
Princip, Gavrilo 15, 21–24, 30–31

R

Radoslavov, Vasil 131
Rennenkampf, Paul von 107–108
Roosevelt, Theodore 139–140, 144
Ruszky, Nikolai 110

S

Salandra, Antonio 126–127
Sam, Jean Vilbrun Guillaume 145
Samsonov, Aleksandr 107–108
Sassoon, Siegfried 96–99
Saud, Abdel Aziz bin 198
Sazonov, Sergei 28–29, 51–53, 191
Scheidemann, Philipp 208–209, 211, 218, 228
Schlieffen Plan, The 45–46, 82
Second International, The 81
Serge, Victor 174
Stalin, Joseph 105, 174, 228, 233–234
Sukhomlinov, Vladimir 104
Sykes, Sir Mark 191, 199–200, 201

T

Taft, William Howard 139, 145
Tirpitz, Admiral Alfred von 71, 142
Tisza, Count István 24–26, 185–186
Tocqueville, Alexis de 185
Townshend, Sir Charles Vere Ferrers 194–196
Treaty of London (1915) 65, 126, 189, 212

Treaty of Versailles (1919) 39, 155,
    160, 213, 215, 217, 222,
    226–228, 229, 231–232
Triple Alliance, The 64, 125, 127,
    158
Trotsky, Leon 44, 110, 141, 147,
    149, 174, 185, 202, 204,
    226, 228, 229–230, 237
Tukhachevsky, Mikhail 105

V

Venizelos, Eleftherios 132–133,
    151, 153–154, 155, 157

W

Wilhelm, Kaiser 25–26, 29, 31,
    34–37, 38, 39, 40, 43,
    47–48, 49, 53–64, 68, 115,
    190, 206, 207, 208–209,
    223, 226
Wilson, Woodrow 136, 138–139,
    140–141, 142, 143–144,
    145–146, 148–149, 217,
    219–220, 220–221, 226,
    230, 231
Witte, Count Sergei Yulyevich
    54–55

Z

Zinoviev, Grigory 228

LIST OF TITLES BY WELLRED BOOKS

Wellred Books is a UK-based international publishing house and bookshop, specialising in works of Marxist theory. A sister publisher and bookseller is based in the USA.
Among the titles published by Wellred Books are:

Anti-Dühring, Friedrich Engels
Bolshevism: The Road to Revolution, Alan Woods
China: From Permanent Revolution to Counter-Revolution, John Roberts
Dialectics of Nature, Frederick Engels
Germany: From Revolution to Counter-Revolution, Rob Sewell
Germany 1918-1933: Socialism or Barbarism, Rob Sewell
History of British Trotskyism, Ted Grant
Imperialism: The Highest Stage of Capitalism, V.I. Lenin
In Defence of Marxism, Leon Trotsky
In the Cause of Labour, Rob Sewell
Lenin and Trotsky: What They Really Stood For, Alan Woods and Ted Grant
Lenin, Trotsky and the Theory of the Permanent Revolution, John Roberts
Marxism and Anarchism, Various authors
Marxism and the USA, Alan Woods
My Life, Leon Trotsky

Not Guilty, Dewey Commission Report
Permanent Revolution in Latin America, John Roberts and Jorge Martin
Reason in Revolt, Alan Woods and Ted Grant
Reformism or Revolution, Alan Woods
Revolution and Counter-Revolution in Spain, Felix Morrow
Russia: From Revolution to Counter-Revolution, Ted Grant
Stalin, Leon Trotsky
Ted Grant: The Permanent Revolutionary, Alan Woods
Ted Grant Writings: Volumes One and Two, Ted Grant
Thawra hatta'l nasr! - Revolution until Victory! Alan Woods and others
The Classics of Marxism: Volume One and Two, by various authors
The History of the Russian Revolution: Volumes One to Three, Leon Trotsky
The History of the Russian Revolution to Brest-Litovsk, Leon Trotsky
The Ideas of Karl Marx, Alan Woods
The Permanent Revolution and Results & Prospects, Leon Trotsky
The Revolution Betrayed, Leon Trotsky
The Revolutionary Philosophy of Marxism, John Peterson [Ed.]
The State and Revolution, V.I. Lenin
What Is Marxism?, Rob Sewell and Alan Woods
What is to be done?, Vladimir Lenin

To order any of these titles or for more information about Wellred Books, visit wellredbooks.net, email books@wellredbooks.net or write to Wellred Books, PO Box 50525, London E14 6WG, United Kingdom.